D1601621

The Secret Constitution and the Need for Constitutional Change

The Secret Constitution
and the Need for
Constitutional Change

ARTHUR S. MILLER

Contributions in American Studies, Number 90

Greenwood Press

NEW YORK • WESTPORT, CONNECTICUT • LONDON

Library of Congress Cataloging-in-Publication Data

Miller, Arthur Selwyn, 1917–
  The secret constitution and the need for
constitutional change.

  (Contributions in American studies, ISSN 0084-9227 ;
no. 90)
  Bibliography: p.
  Includes index.
  1. United States—Constitutional law. 2. Reason of
state. I. Title. II. Series.
KF4550.M47   1987   342.73'029   87-235
                         347.30229

ISBN 0-313-25745-0   (lib. bdg. : alk. paper)

British Library Cataloguing in Publication Data is available.

Library of Congress Catalog Card Number: 87-235
ISBN: 0-313-25745-0
ISSN: 0084-9227

First published in 1987

Greenwood Press, Inc.
88 Post Road West, Westport, Connecticut 06881

Printed in the United States of America

The paper used in this book complies with the
Permanent Paper Standard issued by the National
Information Standards Organization (Z39.48-1984).

10 9 8 7 6 5 4 3 2 1

Hell is truth seen too late.

—John Locke

Time is running out on the very American creed of utopian prag-
matism, i.e., the religious conviction that all problems can be
solved in the middle of the road by a process of bumbling along.
The ills that afflict our society...are systemic....

America—Western capitalism, the world—desperately needs
not a legislative shopping list but a vision. Not a religion, not a
secular salvation, but a new sense of purpose.

—Michael Harrington

CONTENTS

PREFACE

This book has had a long gestation period. It was begun in the fall of 1981 when I had the honor of being a scholar in residence at the Villa Serbelloni, the Rockefeller Foundation's study center at Bellagio on Lake Como in Italy. Anticipating the ceremonies in 1987 on the 200th anniversary of the constitutional convention, I became convinced that major alterations were necessary in the constitution that emerged on September 17, 1787, from the conclave in Philadelphia. My basic thesis is that the time has come to think seriously about promulgating a "constitution of human needs."

The book has gone through several drafts. Although it is documented in proper scholarly fashion, it was written as much for the so-called educated layman as for the specialist. As so often happens, the final product differs substantially from my original conception. I found it necessary to think in terms of constitutional dualism, with the document drafted in 1787 being labeled the *formal* constitution, and the second, parallel constitution given the title of the *secret* constitution.

I deeply believe that Americans are experiencing a crisis in constitutionalism. Little recognized in the literature, it has become all too evident that the governmental structure promulgated by the framers is not up to the tasks confronting the nation today and the emergent problems of the future. Two previous books—*Democratic Dictatorship* and *Toward Increased Judicial Activism*—were preliminary disquisitions of the subject matter of the present volume. To quote what I said in the preface to the latter book, American "constitutional theory, including the theory of judicial review, has come to a dead end." A new beginning is necessary, one that defines a new sense of purpose for the United States. We can no longer muddle along, hoping for the best and expecting that sooner or later something will turn up to resolve the pressing problems that confront the nation.

This book is in two main parts. The first sets forth an outline of the reasons why a new constitution is necessary; the second deals with the nature of a "sustainable society" and constitutional changes that have to be made to attain it. The long prologue explains our system of constitutional dualism; and the brief epilogue is an effort to tie the stands of argument together. The polemical tone that is readily identifiable, particularly in Part I, is unavoidable. It is far too late in the movement of American and human history to use anything other than strong language. The endnotes and the bibliographic essay amply document all that is said in this volume.

I should like to thank the Rockefeller Foundation for its generosity in allowing me to spend an idyllic month on the shores of Lake Como, and also Bob Celli, the director of the center at the Villa Serbelloni. Thanks are due also to the School of Law at Washington and Lee University, where in 1984 I was honored to be invited to give the thirty-sixth annual John Randolph Tucker Lecture; many of the ideas in the present volume were first aired in that lecture.

No one who writes about constitutionalism today does so on a *tabula rasa*. The books and periodicals cited in the endnotes and the bibliographic essay will serve to show some, but not all, of the writers who offered relevant and fruitful analyses and discussions. My thanks are extended to all of them.

I should like to express my gratitude to my friend and former colleague Robert Walker, for his incisive criticism of the first draft of this volume. Thanks are due also to Jeffrey Bowman and Bart Cox for their comments on portions of the manuscript.

Finally, I think it necessary to explain that I have used the masculine "he" in a generic sense. No one has yet produced a satisfactory word for designating both genders; and I feel that the oft-used substitute of "he and she" or "he/she" is too cumbersome.

PROLOGUE:
CONSTITUTIONAL DUALISM

Of all great subjects, much remains to be said.

—John Stuart Mill[1]

This is an essay in constitutional politics. The central thesis is that our constitutional system has a particular moral theory at its core—that people have certain moral rights against the state—and that highest among those rights is the obligation of the state to satisfy human needs and fulfill human deserts within environmental constraints. For the state to do so would, of course, necessitate major revisions in the American constitutional system as it has evolved since 1787.

To explore the reasons for such alterations in our fundamental law is the burden of Part I of this book, which sets forth the social and political context in which any constitution must operate. As the third century of the republic is approached (and duly celebrated with extensive and even fulsome ceremonies), a number of thoughtful observers are growing less confident that the governmental structure created in 1787 is up to the mark of handling an increasing number of difficult, perhaps intractable, problems. There is confusion and debate about what government should do, how it should accomplish its duties, and how those who wield power can be held accountable for their actions. This is the very stuff of what constitutions are all about. An irony of the constitutional bicentennial celebrations presided over by former Chief Justice Warren Burger is that none of the many participants has perceived the need for taking a hard look, a comprehensive look, at what the framers wrought that hot summer in Philadelphia in 1787.

Part II of this book details recommendations for substantial constitutional revision. It begins with the proposition that the only valid purpose of government—and thus of a constitution—is to achieve, so far as possible, a "sustainable" society. That society is one in which human needs and deserts are maximized. This goal will require a basic change in the idea of the obligations of the state—of government, of society—to the individuals that make up the body politic. Certain structural constitutional changes also are recommended. The essential point is that the collectivity (the nation-state, however defined) owes obligations to the people beyond those traditionally recognized and undertaken. Duty is a two-way constitutional street—from the person to the collectivity *and* from the collectivity to the individuals. Finally, because this is an age of rapid, continuous social change and because law and constitutions tend to reflect rather than to guide social affairs, it will be recommended that a means of periodic constitutional revision be adopted.

A brief epilogue focuses on the point that the American constitution—rather, as this prologue will demonstrate, constitutions—will change in the future, whatever is done to plan an update. It could be no other way, for the United States is confronted with unprecedented problems and exists in a social milieu far different from that of 1787. Social change means legal change, constitutional change, unavoidably. The American constitutions have always been relative to circumstances; the future will not differ.

Governments, wherever located and of whatever ideology, have but two basic functions: providing internal order and ensuring external security. Their constitutions, whether written or unwritten, deal exclusively with those broad categories. The United States is said to have a written constitution—indeed, the oldest one extant—which is believed to make it different from, for example, Great Britain, with its unwritten fundamental law. This belief, however, is only partially correct: Americans are governed by two, not one, constitutions—the *formal* and the *secret* (or *parallel*). This prologue outlines the system of constitutional dualism in America.

I shall begin with an assumption (which requires no proof because it is beyond argument) that all human groups up to and including the nation-state itself are oligarchically ruled. Although the rhetoric of course differs, this assumption includes the political entity called the United States of America. The people do not rule, either directly or through their elected "representatives." There is, therefore, no valid reason for calling the United States a "democracy"; it is not now, was not in the past, and shows no likelihood of becoming, a true democratic polity—however one defines democracy (more than 200 definitions exist). To call any government democratic is always a confusing piece of propaganda. It mistakes doctrine for theory; we may and perhaps should wish the democratic element in government to be increased, but it is still only one element when it is government at all. Of course, there are numerous writers in and out of government who are simply naive democrats. It should always be remembered, however, that democracy, "in its clearest historical and sociological sense, is simply a characteristic of modern governments both free and unfree."[2] In the last analysis, all governments must be based on consent.

As for the United States, it seems clear beyond doubt that we have always had an elitist form of actual government, however much the popular wisdom is to the contrary. As Professor Robert Dahl observed in 1964, "the key political, economic, and social decisions" are made by "tiny minorities." Indeed, Dahl continued, it is difficult and perhaps impossible to perceive how it could be otherwise "in large political systems."[3] The most that the citizenry can do in the United States is to elect some, but not all, of those who rule under the formal constitution—members of Congress and the president, in the federal government, and their counterparts in state and local governments. Federal judges are not elected, although some state judges are, and the millions of men and women who work in the public bureaucracies are appointed rather than elected. Citizens have no role at all in the selection of those who rule in the institutions of the secret constitution. The moneyed and the propertied exercise a disproportionate amount of power in both constitutional orders.

"Great family wealth, as well as corporate wealth," a careful study by Professor Philip Burch concludes, "has long exercised more influence in American government than has been generally realized. In fact, if anything, this is an understatement. . . . It would be more accurate to say that, regardless of its changing form, America has almost always been dominated by some kind of wealth."[4] In other words, those who formally rule take their signals and commands, not from the electorate as a body, but from a small group of men (plus a few women). This group will be called the Establishment. It exists, even though that existence is stoutly denied; it is one of the secrets of the American social order. A second secret is the fact that the existence of the Establishment—the ruling class—is not supposed to be discussed. A third secret is implicit in what has been said—that there is really only one political party of any consequence in the United States, one that has been called the "Property Party."[5] The Republicans and the Democrats are in fact two branches of the same (secret) party.

There is, accordingly, a large chasm between the pretenses of American constitutionalism and the reality of minority power. The pretense bespeaks government of the people, *by* the people. Reality differs: at the very best, Americans have a system whereby they can elect the elites that formally govern them. Those elites usually accord little attention to what often is called public opinion. This has created an intellectual requirement—thus far, unfulfilled—to fashion a theory of American "democracy" that will recognize the fact that minorities—*tiny* minorities—count for much, and lead, whereas majorities who do not count for much are seemingly forever fated to follow. This is not to say that America is a closed, authoritarian society. Under the norms of the formal constitution, it is far from that. But it is to say that the institutions of the secret constitution have marked anti-democratic, authoritarian characteristics.]

Constitutional dualism has long been known, here and elsewhere. In 1867, Walter Bagehot in his classic *The English Constitution*[6] invited attention to the division of all constitutions into two parts—the *dignified*, which "excite and preserve the reverence of the population," and the "*efficient*, by which government in fact works and rules." Woodrow Wilson echoed that theme in 1885 when he observed that the constitution of the books was a quite different thing from the constitution in operation.[7] America's formal constitution—the Document of 1787 and its amendments—is the dignified part of our system of constitutional dualism (in Wilson's terminology, the constitution of the books); the secret constitution is Bagehot's "efficient" part or Wilson's constitution in operation. It is worth special mention that although this dualism has long been known, it is not studied as such, in either undergraduate or law school classes on the constitution. Nor is it acknowledged by politicians or the professoriate (generally); it thus becomes a part of the secret, noted above, of the existence of a ruling class.

Public life in the United States, therefore, has two parts. First is a ceremonial pattern of things that are laid out for the purpose of placating the people; second, there is an unofficial pattern of influence that operates behind the scenes and controls the ways that things public are actually done. This is not the work of criminals; nor is it aberrational. It is the Establishment that wants government to operate in this way. The mass of the population usually goes along. (The people can even be persuaded to vote against their own interests.) Any ruler, particularly any president, is always in the position of persuading through use of one of the formulas or procedures of the formal constitution an acceptance of decisions that have already been reached behind the scenes. As Walter Karp has demonstrated in *The Politics of War*, one of the techniques of persuasion is outright mendacity.[8] When persuasion fails, those who in fact rule resort to other techniques to attain their goals.

But if the secret constitution's institutions and practices are not the work of criminals, then surely there is much mythology attendant to the ceremonial role of the formal constitution. We shall see that the pretense that Americans are governed by the norms of the Document of 1787 belies a different and much harsher reality. In Chapter 1, some of the myths that envelop the formal constitution are discussed.

The formal constitution is the familiar one—the Document of 1787, its twenty-six amendments, and exegesis of its lean language, principally but not exclusively by the Supreme Court. This fundamental law sets forth in general terms—with some large silences admittedly present—what is supposed to occur in the American constitutional (social) order. Professor Michael Reisman has given it the fancy title of our *jurisprudence publique*.[9]

It is called *jurisprudence* because American constitutionalism has from the beginnings been viewed as constitutional *law*—the highest law—rather than the exposition of principles of political economy that it really is. This makes constitutionalism the province of lawyers, although not entirely, because political scientists and economists have ventured to tread upon the legal turf.

[The secret constitution is not engrossed on parchment, nor is it recognized as such in statutes or judicial opinions. It is what Reisman has called the operational code, or the *jurisprudence confidentielle* of America; it consists of the informal understandings and conventions governing what occurs in fact in societal and governmental affairs. As our second constitution, it is by any criterion save that of mythology far more important than the formal constitution.

The secret constitution is not to be confused with what at times is called the "living" constitution, which in essence is a label to describe the ways in which the formal constitution has been updated since 1789 as different exigencies confronted succeeding generations of Americans. The secret constitution, rather, is similar to what Dean Don K. Price recently called (in his book of the same title) America's "unwritten" constitution.[10] Price's book is a preliminary probe into a segment of the secret constitution, the actual decision-making processes within the executive and legislative branches of the federal government. Professor Reisman explains:

> *Jurisprudence confidentielle* is never expressed openly. High government lawyers and private practitioners who may advise the elite will be privy to secret agreements that they interpret; pleadings and arbitrations, sometimes rendered by judges of public courts in their private capacity, will be suppressed by agreement of the parties; opinions rendered for corporations will be kept confidential; and vast amounts of legal material in the public sector will be classified. None of this *jurisprudence confidentielle* will be expressed by these same practitioners in the *jurisprudence publique*.... The *jurisprudence publique* is not a sham, for it may apply to some events and to certain groups; given the curious and almost sacramental role of generative logic in legal scholarship, *jurisprudence publique* can always be presented as a complete system of thought. But since it represents only part of what is going on, it is inadequate as an explanatory or predictive tool.[11]

Reisman's description of the *jurisprudence confidentielle* does not go far enough. He does not mention the set of invisible but nonetheless existent rules by which Americans are actually governed. The important question to ask of any constitution and any political order is this: Who gets what, when, how, and in what circumstances? No one should believe that the question can be answered by sole reference to the norms of the formal constitution. There is a lot of what Professor Hans Vaihinger called the "as if " in the popular understanding of the constitution; the as if, to him, meant that "appearance, the consciously false, plays an enormous part in science, in world-philosophies and in life."[12]

I have adverted above to the idea that all groups, including the nation-state, are oligarchically ruled. It is time now to spell out the meaning of this notion. Robert Michels's "iron law of oligarchy" is accepted as an accurate shorthand label for the American constitutional order.[13] The iron law is this: "Who says organization says oligarchy." Save perhaps in pre-civilized times, about which little persuasive evidence exists, there is no real reason to think that any nation or any group has been ruled other than oligarchically. "Representative democracy" in the United States, if the term means anything, at best signifies that the people are able to choose a few of their formal rulers. The people have no role at all in the selection of those who rule in the institutions and practices of the secret constitution—for example, as will be demonstrated below, corporate managers. The further meaning is obvious: the United States has always been a society of class, even caste, despite the myth to the contrary. The moneyed and the propertied have always been on top of the social and political pecking order, and there has always been an underclass.

Implicit in such an analysis is one relevant fact and one distinction, both crucial to the present discussion. The fact: No society has ever been able to exist without power being exercised by someone or some group. It is the irreducible core of any group's behavior or system of governance. The key concept of constitutionalism is power, which can be defined as the ability or capacity to make decisions affecting the values of others, the ability or capacity to impose deprivations and bestow rewards so as to control the behavior of others. Franz Neumann explained:

> No society in recorded history has ever been able to dispense with political power. This is as true of liberalism as of absolutism, as true of laissez-faire as of an inter-ventionist state. No greater disservice has been rendered to political science than the statement that the liberal state was a "weak" state. It was precisely as strong as it needed to be in the circumstances. It acquired substantial colonial empires, waged wars, held down internal disorders, and stabilized itself over long periods of time.[14]

The relevant distinction is between those who wield formal authority and those who exercise effective control over societal decisions. The former refers to those vested with the trappings of officiality—national, state, and local. They are the officers of the state—legislative, executive, administrative, and judicial. Their decisions are widely but erroneously accepted as the true nature of our governmental system. Effective control is another matter: those who wield it operate in the institutions of the secret constitution. They are the "officials" of our second constitution, which Price defines as "the fixed political customs that have developed without formal constitutional amendment but that have been authorized by statute or frozen, at least temporarily, in tradition."[15] Consider, for example, the notorious "iron triangles" or "issue networks" that exist in Washington, D.C. and provide the means by which much public policy is made. An iron triangle consists of the industry or other group being regulated or affected by legislation, the relevant administrative agency, and the congressional committee(s) having jurisdiction over the agency and thus the industry. No doubt the most prominent triangle is the military-industrial complex, but many others exist. The principal function of the corporate body called Congress is to approve the decisions of the iron triangles, which are reached by a complicated system of bargaining among the three principal participants. Effective control, accordingly, resides in those who influence or direct the flow of triangle decisions.[16]

No sharp line necessarily always exists between formal authority and effective control. At times, the two classes of decision-makers meet and merge, although it remains true that those who exercise effective control prefer to operate through surrogates. This gives the appearance of political democracy—the surrogates are elected officials or their appointees—but not the substance. When the two classes do merge, their decisions are from time to time constitutionalized by the Supreme Court. The landmark historical example is the Court's 1905 decision in *Lochner v. New York*,[17] in which the justices invalidated a New York statute regulating labor conditions in bakeries as improperly interfering with the liberty of contract of both management and workers. The Court blithely ignored the crucial fact that the workers themselves desired that legislation; the justices, nonetheless, ordered them to be "free," forgetting what even Alexander Hamilton knew—that "a power over a man's subsistence amounts to a power over his will."[18] The implication is that those who wield effective control in America—in this instance, the corporate oligarchy—were able to get their wishes validated by the Supreme Court. (This is not to say that federal judges speak in terms of the merger of formal authority and effective control. Quite the contrary—a fact, it is appropriate to note, that led Justice Richard Neely of the West Virginia Supreme Court to assert that "most of what appears in legal opinions on constitutional law cannot be given or received with a straight face.")[19]

Americans, therefore, are governed by two constitutions, and no constitutional analysis is complete without acknowledgment of that fact. When, furthermore, any official action is taken, one basic question must always be asked: *cui bono?* Who benefits from it? In the American system of constitutional dualism, there are often two types of beneficiaries—the manifest (or obvious) and the latent (or hidden). This dualism will be shown in outline form in the remainder of this prologue. The pretense may be—likely is—to the contrary, but it will not stand rigorous analysis.

To lend specificity to the nature of the secret constitution, I shall focus mainly upon the giant business corporation as the principal exemplar of that constitution, and draw upon Professor Charles E. Lindblom's classic *Politics and Markets* to illustrate how the secret constitution operates. Lindblom concludes:

> It has been a curious feature of democratic thought that it has not faced up to the private corporation as a peculiar organization in an ostensible democracy. Enormously large, rich in resources, the big corporations...command more resources than do most government units. They can also, over a broad range, insist that government meet their demands, even if these demands run counter to those of citizens.... Moreover, they do not disqualify themselves from playing the partisan role of a citizen—for the corporation is legally a person. And they exercise unusual veto powers. They are on all these counts disproportionately powerful.... The large private corporation fits oddly into democratic theory and vision. Indeed, it does not fit.[20]

Corporations, in sum, are "private" governments.

Large corporations—the supercorporations—are the most important institutions of the secret constitution. Created by the laws of the formal constitution, they confront individual persons with abuses of power, actual and potential, of the peculiar type of private sovereignty that results when several individuals bind together in a combination or collectivity. Save for a few, whose voices have largely been unheeded, constitutionalists in America have throughout history failed to confront the brute fact of economic power. The framers in 1787 completely neglected the dimension of private governments. They assumed that political and economic equilibria could be achieved by independent natural persons, each acting for his individual interest, guided by an invisible hand to serve the common welfare. The assumption was faulty—then and certainly now. It has led to the tacit delegation of substantial governing power from government to the managers of the supercorporations. That this transfer of power runs contrary to the command of the formal constitution does not deter the practice. In 1935 the Supreme Court unanimously ruled that the federal government could not delegate its power to a trade guild consisting of the very businesses purportedly being affected by the National Industrial Recovery Act of 1933.[21] But what was outlawed under the formal constitution has become a central principle of the secret constitution: the supercorporations have been tacitly delegated the power to rule over large segments of American society: "No individual or corporate body can engage in activities of rule except as an organ, agent, or delegate of the state; and the state alone assigns and determines the extent of those activities according to its own rules, backed by its own sanctions."[22] (That this implied delegation of governing power to the supercorporations poses serious problems of legitimacy under the formal constitution will be discussed later.)

How, then, do the supercorporations rule? Several basic principles are illustrative (although not necessarily exhaustive).

The *first principle* is that corporate managers rule within the corporate community. As Lindblom observes, "Corporate executives in all private enterprise systems . . . decide a nations's industrial technology, market structure, resource allocation, and, of course, executive compensation and status."[23] This decision making sets the tone for the national economy, for the supercorporations dominate that economy; they are more than a mere interest group. Corporations are themselves political orders, ruled by and large in an authoritarian manner.

As political systems, corporations thus are ruled *vertically*. Employees are subject, for example, to the *diktat* of management, a condition alleviated only by the countervailing power of trade unions (if they exist in the corporation) and certain federal statutes (such as those proscribing racial or sex discrimination). The *second principle* is that corporations, through the operations of iron triangles among other devices, are able to control or at least greatly influence the decisions that public government makes. Much of government in the United States has come under the domination, in one way or another, of narrowly based and large autonomous elite groups. Government and business have entered—long ago—into a type of partnership, one that permits the businessman to wield an enormous influence over public policies. Corporations thus govern *horizontally*. It is not a two-way street. Government can regulate (at least, ostensibly so) to a degree, and it can prohibit certain kinds of activity. But the formal constitution, which sees supercorporations as private property not subject to constitutional duties, does not permit government to command business to perform. Businessmen must, in general, be induced rather than commanded.

The *third principle* follows: government supports business. Subsidies, tariffs, patents, "fair trade" laws, use of military force to protect business in Latin America, a compliant judiciary that places protection of property highest in the hierarchy of values—all these, and more, are ways in which government actively aids business enterprise. The United States has always been a welfare state for the moneyed and propertied. Alexander Hamilton's *Report on Manufactures* (1791) is one of the great state documents of American constitutional history, but little recognized as such.[24] It set the tone for what has followed in the ensuing two centuries. The implication, as Lindblom points out, is that government officials tend to see businessmen (those who control the supercorporations) as people performing functions considered to be indispensable. The welfare of business is equated with the welfare of all of society. Harold Brayman, a former Du Pont executive, makes the point as follows: "The strength of the position of business and the weakness of the position of government is that government needs a strong economy just as much as business does, and the people need it and demand it even more."[25]

The secret constitution, thus, is an economic constitution. And it is also a corporatist constitution. This is the *fourth principle*. The nineteenth century was the heyday of liberalism (in the John Stuart Mill sense); the twentieth is the century of corporatism, the fusion of political and economic power. Corporatism is more than a system of interest representation; it is a shorthand label for an emerging system of governance. In such a system, "public" and "private" have for all practial purposes become indistinguishable. This is not to say that the links between government and corporations are formally announced, as in statutes; the only time this was done was in the National Industrial Recovery Act of 1933. But it is to say that there are definite links, often by contract, between the two entities (as in the arms industry) and that the underlying postulates of the American constitutional order tend toward what Professor Phillippe Schmitter has called "societal" corporatism—as distinguished from "state" corporatism.[26] (Mussolini's Italy provides the classic example of the latter.)

Societal corporatism is essentially a product of government's need to avoid operating with the appearance of authoritarianism—in accordance, that is, with the spirit and letter of the formal constitution—and thus it is a diffusion of state power rather than centralized control. Corporatism is the manner in which the formal and secret constitutions meet and merge. The modern state and modern interest groups—corporations, unions, farmers' leagues, veterans' legions, and the like (although corporations are more than a mere interest group)—seek each other out. The state seeks to foster maximum employment, promote economic growth, curb inflation, smooth out business cycles, help alleviate economic and social risks, and resolve labor disputes. This cooperation Andrew Shonfield in his magisterial *Modern Capitalism* calls corporatist: "The major interest groups are brought together and encouraged to conclude a series of bargains about their future behavior, which will have the effect of moving economic events along the desired path."[27] The point, for present purposes, is that the "desired path" is one reached by agreements, formal or tacit, between public officers and the managers of the supercorporations. Modern constitutionalism, in sum, increasingly exemplifies the reality of the third great "-ism"—not capitalism and not socialism, but corporatism.[28]

Of course, the supercorporations do not rule across the board. Other groups exercise similar powers within narrowly defined areas. For example, the National Rifle Association and the American Medical Association are able either to stop legislation considered adverse to their respective interests or to water down any proposal to limits acceptable to them. This is the *fifth principle* of the secret constitution.

The *sixth principle* is this: a pervasive system of thought control exists within the United States, the basic purpose of which is to legitimize that privileged position of business in American society. The citizenry is indoctrinated by employment of the mass media and by the system of public education. The people are not always told what to think but, as Michael Parenti has demonstrated, they are told what to think *about*.[29] The agenda for public discourse and thus for what passes for public opinion is set by those who control the levers of power in the secret constitution—often in concert with those in power in the institutions of the formal constitution.

The *seventh principle* is this: When indoctrination and propaganda fail to achieve desired objectives, those who control the institutions of the secret constitution use other techniques to attain their goals. These can be relatively benign, as will be shown, or extremely harsh.

In net, pursuant to a central principle of the secret constitution, there is a conscious concealment from the mass of the people of how American government really works. Elitism in America is covered up, first of all, together with the authoritarianism implicit in the operation of the secret constitution, by the very notion of constitutionalism, which is said to be a set of limitations on governmental power, and by ostensible adherence to the norms of the formal constitution.

Americans also adhere to a bit of nonsense—that sovereignty rests in the people, who delegate it to politicians, who hold it in trust for them. This is said to make the United States a nation with a government of laws, not of men. The bare-bones truth is contrary. Rather than being trustees, those who wield effective political and economic power are unseen manipulators of the body politic. The formal trappings of "democracy"—the Constitution of 1787—hide rather than adorn the realities within the polity.

We are accustomed to hearing the formal constitution described, even reverently described, as a mechanism subtly and cleverly constructed by a group of wise men to enable the will of the people to be transmitted through elected representatives to executive agencies that administer the affairs of government, with the help of a benevolent civil service and under the guidance of a neutral and independent judiciary. This description is given not only to schoolchildren but may also be found in the curricula of institutions of higher learning (including the law schools). All of this, we are solemnly told, is epitomized by the "Rule of Law," a sacred and untouchable concept, but one which in fact most benefits those who wish to preserve the status quo. The putative Rule of Law, celebrated each May 1st, is a profoundly conservative concept. But it does have at least some validity. If it means that adequate machinery should exist for dealing with crimes and civil wrongs (what lawyers call torts) and for ensuring that public officers do not exceed their lawful powers, no thoughtful person would object. If, however, it is extended much beyond that, so as to preserve and protect certain legal and political institutions that governing elites want protected, it becomes a fantasy. Law then becomes politics under another name.

A government of laws and not of men is an unattainable ideal. Law cannot be—it never has been—a substitute for politics.[30] Written constitutions do not achieve the rule of law. This may be a hard and even unpleasant truth, but it is truth nonetheless. Even the minimal meaning of the rule of law is not an accurate description of what transpires in fact. The appeal to law is an appeal to human reason, which is notoriously faulty. Behind the resort to reason is the omnipresent power of the state to enforce decisions desired by those who exercise effective control in the nation. Under the liberal theory of the rule of law, the disputes of private individuals are governed by a neutral body of rules that are impartially administered. This is the unstated theory of the formal constitution. But the secret constitution differs. In fact, laws governing private transactions are far from neutral. Judges and the laws they enforce are class-oriented—in favor of the moneyed and the propertied.

This has long been known, but it has been systematically concealed. For example, Oliver Wendell Holmes, later to become a justice of the Supreme Court, knew it more than a century ago. He wrote in 1873 that the notion that the law was neutral, impartially imposed by judges, "presupposes an identity of interests between the different parts of the community which does not exist in fact."[31] Holmes maintained that not only was there no unity in law as a whole, but that a lack of unity at the social level was eventually translated into law. He saw that the decisions of courts represented the interests of the strongest in society (an idea, it bears mention, that can be traced as far back as Plato's Thrasymachus): "Whatever body may possess the supreme power for the moment is certain to have interests inconsistent with others which have competed unsuccessfully. The more powerful interests must be more or less reflected in legislation; which, like every other device of man or beast, must tend in the long run to aid the survival of the fittest."[32]

Holmes had a bleak and despairing jurisprudential universe. He was a Social Darwinist, pure and simple. Without using the term, he was in fact describing the secret constitution as it operated in 1873. He saw things true and saw them whole; and in so doing, presented an as yet unresolved and unanswered question about the nature of constitutions: Can they be altered away from Social Darwinism, so as to achieve a constitution of human needs? This volume is an effort to address that question and to provide the beginnings of an answer.

[Americans, Professor Lindblom remarks, are "torn between two control systems"—between, that is, the inconsistencies between the formal and the secret constitutions.[33] But that is not all. *Neither* constitution implies a commitment to social justice in so many words. In this volume, social justice will be equated with a sustainable society and with the satisfaction of human needs and deserts within environmental limitations.]

Social justice, moreover, will be considered to be a form of distributive justice, concerned with the ways in which benefits are distributed in society through its major institutions—how wealth is allocated, personal rights protected, and other positive benefits divided among the people. It is normative: "The just state of affairs is that in which each individual has exactly those benefits and burdens which are due to him by virtue of his personal characteristics and circumstances."[34] And it is "prosthetic": it aims at modification of the status quo.[35] A person's "due" may be perceived in one of two ways: either as protection of his present rights ("vested" rather than "civil") or as furtherance of the ideal of prosthetic justice.

The term *rights* requires some explanation. As generally used, rights "derive from publicly acknowledged rules, established practices, or past transactions; they do not depend upon a person's current behavior or other individual qualities." For this reason, it is appropriate to describe this conception of justice as "conservative." "It [justice] is concerned with the continuity of a social order over time, and with ensuring that men's expectations of one another are not disappointed."[36] Social justice, in this conception of rights, thus requires judges and others to protect the "is" in society—precisely what the Supreme Court and other courts have done throughout American history. I shall, however, modify this meaning of rights in Part II of this volume so as to include the satisfaction of human needs as a right that inheres in every person. This, to be sure, is an ideal construct, but its meaning is clear: the attainment of social justice, as defined above, is the only valid purpose for which constitutions are developed and governments are formed.

America's constitutions, formal and secret, have been and are a means by which social control is effected within society. In the remainder of this prologue, principal attention will be accorded to how social control operates within the United States. Again, this overview is more illustrative than exhaustive.

Social control refers to those processes, whether planned or unplanned, by which individuals are persuaded or compelled to conform to the values of others. In broadest perspective, it operates on three levels: group over group, a group over its members, and individuals over other persons. Our interest here lies in outlining some of the ways that the American people have been controlled. Social control can be coercive, as in the sanctions of the criminal law, but usually it takes more subtle forms, such as the socializing functions of public education and the mass media. The purpose is to "bring about conformity, solidarity, and continuity of a particular group or society."[37] Finally, social control can be either formal, as in the application of the written (positive) law, or informal, as in the insidious pressures of the invisible but nonetheless existent conventions of society.

The purpose of internal order (the ultimate goal of social control) is to suppress defection and divert discontent into innocuous channels. The ruling or governing class (the elites) of any societal entity must perforce have several techniques available by which its privileged position can be protected and solidified. One technique is to pretend that everyone benefits, or can benefit, from the operations of the American political economy. This pretense is accomplished, as will be shown, by providing cosmetic gains in the formal constitution, accompanied by a tacit commitment to continuing economic growth and a rhetoric that extols popular sovereignty. Another elitist technique is repression (of which more is said below). Still another has been described by Professor B. F. Skinner:

> A government may prevent defection by making life more interesting—by providing bread and circuses and by encouraging sports, gambling, the use of alcohol and other drugs, and various kinds of sexual behavior, where the effect is to keep people within the range of aversive sanctions. The Goncourt brothers noted the rise of pornography in the France of their day: "Pornographic literature," they wrote, "serves as a Bas-Empire.... One tames a people as one tames lions, by masturbation."[38]

Skinner's point was anticipated by Aldous Huxley in his anti-utopian novel, *Brave New World*, in which he spoke of the future uses of "soma pills" to keep the "proles" quiescent (in 532 A.F., by which he meant "After Ford"). Huxley, writing in 1932, projected his fantasy far into the future; but in 1958 he took another look at things present and those to come and concluded that he had been too optimistic.[39] Some of his long-range dire projections had already occurred, and others were imminent. For present purposes, the point is that what is often called the permissive society arose in America in the post-World War II period for definite reasons and specific aims: in many respects it was and still is a means of mass mental maturbation by many of the people.

Our interest now lies less in Skinnerian behavior modification, although surely it is relevant, than in its alternatives—principally in what will be called the Principle of Minimal Satisfaction of Human Needs, and in the calculated use of violence and the legal system to suppress what is considered to be excessive discontent and even defection. The Principle is this: *Those who wield effective control in the United States make, when considered necessary, that amount of social adjustments that will help siphon off sufficient discontent among the disadavantaged to enable the societal status quo—the balance of power in America's class system—to be maintained.* Stated another way, token or cosmetic gains are extended under the formal constitution, while under the secret fundamental law no real redistribution of wealth, prestige, or social power takes place. The "system" abides, but under two constitutions.

Where to begin? At the beginning, of course, and the beginning was the early seventeenth century, when what was to become America experienced its first "West"—Jamestown, Virginia, in 1607 and ensuing decades. There, the moneyed planters controlled politics through a combination of domination of the legal system and violence: "What remains so impressive and alarming about the Jamestown story is its proven record of violence and its abuse of people—red, white, and black—and of the law."[40] Nonetheless, in order to prevail and to keep the peace, the gentry were forced to give other whites the right to own property; in so doing, they also gave them the privilege to vote. This combination of violent repression and the subtle "bribery" of extending minimal gains to the populace characterizes American history to the present day.

Jump ahead to the constitutional convention of 1787, the political "immaculate conception" that gave birth two years later to the United States of America. When the fifty-five men (out of the eighty-four who had been named to attend) straggled into Philadelphia to the conclave whose assigned purpose was merely revising the Articles of Confederation, it was an era characterized by Professor Michael Kammen as one "when values were unclearly defined, when instability often seemed beyond control, when public rancor and private vituperation were rampant, and institutions frail and unformed."[41] Small wonder, therefore, that the delegates exceeded their mission: they were determined to establish a stronger national government, with an executive separate from the national legislature, and with certain designated powers couched in such ambiguous language that subsequent interpretation, and consequent rewriting, were unavoidable. Although the preamble of the document they produced (signed by only thirty-nine of the delegates) spoke in terms of "We, the people . . . "—a putative acknowledgment of popular sovereignty—neither the people as such were represented at the convention nor were their wishes determined and followed. There can be little question that the framers feared what some called a "democratical despotism." Alexander Hamilton, by all odds the most important of the framers because his politico-economic views have largely guided the course of American constitutional history, struck the note that dominated the convention when he stated:

All communities divide themselves into the few and the many. The first are the rich and well-born, the other the mass of the people. The voice of the people has been said to be the voice of God; and however generally this maxim has been quoted and believed, it is not true in fact. The people are turbulent and changing; they seldom judge or determine right. Give therefore to the first class a distinct, permanent share in the government.[42]

This "share" then was to permit only white, male property owners to vote, to insulate both the presidency and the Senate from direct election, and (implicitly) to establish the predominance of the Supreme Court in disputes over constitutional interpretation. Today this share is to control the institutions and practices of the secret constitution and thus of the formal constitution.

The sops thrown to Hamilton's "mass of the people" and a classic example of the operation of the Principle of Minimal Satisfaction of Human Needs were the House of Representatives, which was to be elected biennially by the people, and the principle of federalism, which supposedly established dual sovereignties. These were the means by which popular discontent was diluted and the constitution promulgated. Not without opposition, to be sure: only by cavalierly ignoring the provision in the Articles of Confederation that called for unanimity in order to make any change was the formal constitution ratified in time for the new government to be assembled in 1789. Not until May 29, 1790, did the thirteenth state, Rhode Island, ratify the constitution; the twelfth, North Carolina, did so on November 21, 1790—well after the new government had begun to operate.

Even then, the absence of a bill of rights was a major obstacle. State legislators and others were simply not deluded by Hamilton's specious argument in *Federalist No. 84* that the formal constitution was itself a bill of rights. In the first Congress, therefore, James Madison introduced the amendments now called the Bill of Rights (the first ten), the ratification of which was completed in December, 1791, in another example of the operation of the Principle of Minimal Satisfaction. In other words, part of the price paid for ratification of the formal constitution was insertion of a bill of rights that promised that reasons of freedom and liberty would, at least in the letter, prevail over reasons of state.

That the propertied elite were the chief beneficiaries of the system established in 1789 cannot be seriously doubted. There was, however, enough flexibility in the governmental order, plus the far more important fact of the untapped wealth of the new nation, to convince small property owners and middle-class mechanics and farmers to support the new government. These people provided a base of support for the elite. They were (and still are) "buffers against the blacks, the Indians, the very poor whites."[43] This support enabled the elite "to keep control with a minimum of coercion, a maximum of law—all made palatable by the fanfare of patriotism and unity."[44] Not that all was calm and peaceful, as witness the Shays' Rebellion in Massachusetts in 1786 and the Whiskey Rebellion in Pennsylvania in 1794, both of which terrified the propertied elite and both of which were quickly smashed by use of violence. The formal constitution, as drafted, was, in sum, a counterrevolution to principles enunciated in the Declaration of Independence. As such, it was a means of social control in the interests of the moneyed and propertied. This control is evidenced, for example, by the Supreme Court's 1810 decision in *Fletcher v. Peck*,[45] which legitimized the gigantic Yazoo land fraud (concerning most of what is now Alabama and Mississippi), and in the way that a government with unparalleled generosity gave away the "commons"—the riches of the nation—to a favored few.[46] *Fletcher* is the first judicial example of a core principle of the secret constitution: *the many shall not be allowed to do to the few what the few do to the many.*

The many were placated, as noted, by direct election of the House of

Representatives—although it should be remembered that a numerical majority of the people could not vote—and by their ability to direct some of the flow of events in state and local governments. Local people could not, however, stem the tide toward centralization of power in the national government. When they tried to do so, they were neatly checked by a Supreme Court that issued a series of "nationalizing" decisions early in the nineteenth century. The decisions are significant in providing the legal basis for a strong general government. Four are worth mention:

- *Martin v. Hunter's Lessee* (1816), holding that state courts are subject to Supreme Court review in civil actions involving "federal questions," so as to provide uniform interpretation and application of federal law.[47]
- *McCulloch v. Maryland* (1819), sustaining Congress's power to incorporate a national bank and proscribing state taxation of it, thus reading an "implied" powers authority into the express grants of power to Congress in the formal constitution.[48]
- *Cohens v. Virginia* (1821), establishing the Supreme Court's authority to review state criminal decisions.[49]
- *Gibbons v. Ogden* (1824), sustaining an act of Congress granting authority to navigate in United States waters, and superseding a New York licensing requirement.[50]

To these decisions should be added *Marbury v. Madison* (1803) and *Dartmouth College v. Woodward* (1819),[51] which, respectively, established the Supreme Court's supremacy in constitutional interpretation and invalidated a New Hampshire statute attempting to regulate the college. As a group, this clutch of rulings made it utterly clear that the United States was to become, insofar as law could influence it, a united state. What began in 1789 as a paper promise of "heterarchy"[52]—a commitment to maximize local autonomy—was soon supplanted by hierarchy: actual governing power began to flow toward the new capital in Washington, D.C. The process began early and has continued to the present day.

By no means was the constitution, as drafted, or the Marshall Court's decisions mere fortuities. We have come to realize, as the text of the Pentagon Papers clearly revealed, that those who wield power usually—perhaps always—know what they are doing, at least in the short run, and in fact want to do it. They may not be able to forecast all or even most of the long-term consequences of their actions, and they likely will not be able fully to control the flow of events. Nevertheless, they do proceed with certain philosophies and have rather clear objectives in mind. The policies they make are not promulgated with an absentminded lack of concern; they know what they want and strive to get it. The framers of the formal constitution based their conclusions on John Locke's principles of the protection of property as the *ne plus ultra* of governmental action. As Charles Beard put it, "The Constitution was . . . based upon the concept that the fundamental private rights of property are anterior to government and morally beyond the reach of popular majorities."[53] John Marshall's Supreme Court made that concept a living principle of governance, alive to this day.

The pretense, of course, was and is otherwise. We—at least, many of us— pretend that the men of 1787 were altruists vested with a special wisdom and that they created a document rather like "the ark of the covenant, too sacred to be touched,"[54] a document that established a democracy. As such, the formal constitution was and is the chief artifact of America's civil religion. This pretense was one way of allaying popular discontent. It was accompanied by a uniquely significant environmental factor: the frontier gave room for maneuvering and breathing space for some of the poor and huddled masses, as well as providing an immense store of natural resources. As will be shown, the wealth and strength of the United States derived not so much from the formal constitution but in spite of it.

When the frontier began to close in the post-Civil War period, the political economy—the constitutional order—started to be a zero-sum game. The riches of the expanding nation had been seized or given away, fully exploited by new owners. The business class, following Hamiltonian principles enunciated in, for example, his *Report on Manufactures* (1791), had been in effective control of politics since the beginnings. In the latter part of the nineteenth century, however, new groups began to emerge and exercise social and political power. Prior to that time, the "manufacturing aristocracy," as Alexis de Tocqueville called it, was "one of the harshest" the world had seen.[55] Before the impact of technology greatly increased industrial productivity, and thus enlarged the supply of consumer goods available to an expanding population, newly emergent groups, feeling the closure of the frontier, began to vie with the business class for larger shares of material goods. An expanding populace, believing the rhetoric of American democracy, demanded more. But the economic pie was basically static.

The reaction of those who wielded effective control in the nation was immediate—and brutal. Another form of social control was employed by the elite. Dissent was savagely suppressed. Indians were killed or consigned to reservations in barren lands. Newly freed blacks found that they had merely exchanged the legal bonds of slavery for the de facto bonds of peonage. The labor of the blacks was needed, but their freedom was denied under the secret constitution. The South, defeated in the Civil War, became an economic colony of the industrial North. Douglas F. Dowd has aptly described the situation:

The profits of southern industry were dependent upon cheap and abundant labor. The self-respect of the mass of southern whites was dependent, to a critical degree, upon the existence and oppressed position of the Negro. The power of southern business and political leaders rested on the creation and maintenance of the one-party system, a post-bellum development in the South. The maintenance of the South as an economic preserve of the North was dependent to an important degree on the continued political sterility of the South in national affairs. All these, of course, were interconnected.[56]

Black Americans, during the First Reconstruction, got neither the consolations of actual equality nor the practice of equal protection under the laws. The elite saw no need for bettering the condition of the freed slaves, nor, it should be noted, of the poor whites. When in *Hall v. DeCuir* (1878) Justice Nathan Clifford intoned that "equality does not mean identity," he provided a justifying maxim for the de facto caste system.[57] Professor J. R. Pole explains: "White racial prejudice was profound and resilient, as the history of Reconstruction shows. The [Supreme] Court chose to settle [the problem of racial antagonism] not in accordance with its authority under the Fourteenth Amendment... but in accordance with the actual distribution of social and economic power in southern states."[58] And so it was for class antagonism: The justices in effect legitimized violence and in fact legitimized the use of the legal system against the "have-nots" of the nation. They thus were major contributors to what eventually became a boiling volcano of social discontent, which erupted in the mid-twentieth century.

The first major, and still the most important, use of violence as social control came in the sanguinary Civil War, which was fought, as President Lincoln candidly admitted, to preserve the Union rather than to free the slaves. Said Lincoln in 1862: "My paramount object in this struggle *is* to save the Union, and is *not* either to save or to destroy slavery. If I could save the Union without freeing *any* slave, I would do it."[59] Many, perhaps most, of Lincoln's actions taken at the beginning of the war were obviously contrary to the letter and spirit of the formal constitution. They were promulgated under the then secret constitution of the Union, but they merged with the formal constitution when the Supreme Court decided *The Prize Cases* (1863)—sustaining a presidential blockade of southern ports.[60] The war settled in blood what the Supreme Court and Congress could not do in law—that the United States was truly a united state, "one nation, indivisible." Localism, already reeling under the blows of the Marshall Court and the unifying forces of such new technologies as the railroad and the telegraph, began to become a dead issue; federalism as originally visualized declined. Only in theory and myth did the formal constitution remain intact.

Hegemonic control over politico-economic matters was solidified in the industrial North after the war. Simultaneously, two important developments occurred. First, the technological revolution culminated in the creation of giant corporations (then often called "trusts"), which the Supreme Court dutifully—without hearing oral argument on the question—designated as constitutional persons in 1886.[61] What was born was corporate capitalism, a lusty infant that would then, and still does, dominate the American political economy. Second, the American frontier closed about 1890, which meant that corporate enterprise would have to look overseas and become multi-national. The question soon became not, as is often said, whether the constitution followed the flag, but whether the flag followed the corporations. The answer is obvious: American foreign policy was largely involved in protecting American business abroad—first in the Spanish-American War, then in the savage repression of Filipinos who had the temerity to seek their freedom, and then with the use of military force to ensure that corporate enterprise prevailed in other lands. Major General Smedley D. Butler, former commandant of the Marine Corps, summarized this type of external control through violence:

I spent thirty-three years and four months in active service as a member of our country's most agile military force—the Marine Corps. . . . And during that period I spent most of my time being a high-class muscle man for Big Business, for Wall Street, and for the bankers. In short, I was a racketeer for capitalism. . . . Thus I helped make Mexico and especially Tampico safe for American oil interests in 1914. I helped make Haiti and Cuba a decent place for the National City Bank boys to collect revenues in. . . . I helped purify Nicaragua for the international banking house of Brown Brothers in 1909–1912. I brought light to the Dominican Republic for American sugar interests in 1916. I helped make Honduras "right" for American fruit companies in 1903. In China in 1927 I helped see to it that Standard Oil went its way unmolested.[62]

Internal instances of social control through violence typified the latter part of the nineteenth and early twentieth centuries. The Army was often used to quell civil disorders, usually at the behest of American businesses involved in labor disputes. Illustrative was the Pullman strike of 1894, led by Eugene V. Debs, which resulted in the use of troops by President Grover Cleveland to suppress it—extralegally, it should be noted, although the Supreme Court dutifully sustained Cleveland's act. Corporate officers also used private armies, often the Pinkerton guards, to repress labor unrest. With the economy essentially a zero-sum game, those in effective control turned first to violence, as Barbara Tuchman, among others, has shown:

When the Pullman strike in the United States in 1894 stopped trains and the mail, Judge William Howard Taft, far from a ferocious man, wrote to his wife, "It will be necessary for the military to kill some of the mob before the trouble can be stayed. They have only killed six . . . as yet. This is hardly enough to make an impression." Here was class war in operation.[63]

Indeed, it was class war. But brutal repression has only a limited utility. It cannot be sustained indefinitely, particularly in a nation that trumpets itself as a democracy and has a rhetoric extolling human freedom.

What, then, to do? became the question for those who wielded effective control in the nation. The answer, when it came, was in bending what is now called the Progressive movement to their ends. The philosopher for the takeover was Woodrow Wilson, who plumped for the need to adjust legal institutions to the new political economy. Wrote Wilson in 1914:

If you do not adjust your laws to the facts, so much the worse for the laws, not for the facts.... We must [adjust the laws to the facts]; there is no choice ... because the law, unless I have studied it amiss, is the expression of the facts in legal relationships. Laws have never altered the facts; laws have always necessarily expressed the facts; adjusted interests as they have arisen and have changed toward one another.[64]

The facts to Wilson were economic in nature. He "out-Coolidged" Silent Cal, who was later to utter the oft-quoted aphorism, "The business of America is business." The central fact was the emergence of the giant corporation that had replaced the individual entrepreneur as the dominant exemplar of capitalism. The task, therefore, was not to try to resurrect the past of entrepreneurial competition or to dissolve the corporate behemoths, but to adjust law to the new economic reality. "Our laws," said Wilson, "are still meant for business done by *individuals*; they have not been satisfactorily adjusted to business done by great *combinations*, and we have got to adjust them.... There is no choice."[65] That, in effect, was a plea to merge the ancient principles of the formal constitution with the emergent principles of a secret constitution dominated by giant business combines.

What should be done? The farmer-labor-populist movements were becoming ever more aggressive. Adjustments thus would have to be made not only to the new economic facts of large-scale corporate enterprises, but also to the social facts of the Progressive movement. Repression continued to be employed, buttressed by a complaisant Supreme Court that was a de facto arm of the capital-owning class. Acting as an ultimate faculty of political economy, the Court stood as a bulwark against what was considered to be the advancing mob. After intuiting that a corporation was a person and thus entitled to constitutional protections, the justices invented, through a flash of revelation peculiar to them, the notion that due process of law protected in the formal constitution had a substantive dimension (in addition to its historical procedural aspect); this notion enabled the Court to protect corporations against social legislation, such as minimum wages and maximum hours in industry. Stoutly refusing to concede that necessitous men cannot be free men, they in effect ordered the workers who wanted such legislation to be "free" and to bargain on allegedly equal terms with a collectivity called a corporation. That could only have been willful judicial blindness to the facts of life. That this is an accurate conclusion is evidenced also by the fact that the Supreme Court in 1911 neatly eviscerated the Sherman antitrust law, thus making it possible for corporations to grow as large as they desired (and could).[66]

But that was not enough. Something more was needed, something that would at once satisfy the public's clamor for reining in business excesses and permit the businessman to carry on as before. Those who ruled under the secret constitution neatly co-opted the Progressive movement. The technique employed was the regulatory system, under which some businesses were supposedly regulated in the public interest, but in fact were not. Regulation got its genesis in the Interstate Commerce Act of 1887 (establishing the Interstate Commerce Commission), and had the Sherman Act, the Federal Trade Commission Act, and the Federal Reserve Act as principal exemplars.

Wilson, again, set the intellectual tone. In a 1912 speech to leading businessmen, he remarked:

> You have heard the rising tide of socialism.... Socialism is not growing in influence in this country as a programme. It is merely that the ranks of the protestants are being recruited.... If it becomes a programme, then we shall have to be very careful how we propose a competing programme.... The programme of socialism will not work; but there is no use saying what will not work unless you can say what would work.... If you want to oust socialism you have got to propose something better. It is a case, if you will allow me to fall into the language of the gutter, of "put up or shut up."... It is by constructive purpose that *you are going to govern and save the United States*.... Very well, then, let us get together and form a constructive programme.... [Posterity will say that after America had passed through] a simple age ... when the forces of society had come into hot contact ... there were men of serene enough intelligence, ... of will and purpose to stand up once again ... [and who found out] how to translate power into freedom, how to make men glad that they were rich, how to take envy out of men's hearts that others were rich and they for a little while poor, by opening the gates of opportunity to every man.[67]

That was woolly language, to be sure, but its theme was translated into public policy programs that gave the appearance of regulation without the substance. The pattern of ostensible, but not actual, regulation was early set. After Congress, in a burst of unprecedented energy, had established the Interstate Commerce Commission (ICC) to regulate the railroads—then the most important members of the corporate community—the question arose as to what the railroad executives should do about it. Should they try to get the ICC declared unconstitutional as an impermissible exercise of Congress's commerce power? That the corporate managers wanted to do exactly that cannot be doubted. After all, they had in the Supreme Court a tribunal that was all too willing to invalidate socioeconomic legislation. Nevertheless, they listened to the sage advice of Richard Olney, who was to become attorney general in the Cleveland administration. Counseled Olney: Do not try to get the ICC abolished. Rather, control it. In that way, the public's desire for business regulation would be satisfied without undue harm to the companies.[68]

And that is precisely what happened. The manifest beneficiaries of the ICC were members of the general public, but the latent and more important beneficiaries were the railroads. Once more dutiful to the wishes of the corporate community, the Supreme Court helped. In 1898, the Court's decision in *Smyth v. Ames* in effect guaranteed that railroads and other businesses "affected with a public interest" would make profits.[69] (Only such businesses could be regulated—those that would today generally fall into the category of public utilities. Others were beyond the reach of governmental power.) Principles of Social Darwinism and laissez-faire economics were read into the formal constitution, which meant that in economic matters the formal and secret constitutions met and merged. Justice Samuel Miller knew what was happening; he wailed in an off-bench speech: "It is vain to contend with judges who have been at the bar the advocates for forty years of railroad companies, and all the forms of associated capital, when they are called upon to decide cases where such interests are in contest. All their training, all their feelings are from the start in favor of those who need no such influence."[70]

The statutes that marked the Progressive movement in effect "amended" the formal constitution. But in large part they were little more than mere pretense. They gave the appearance of regulation "in the public interest," but in fact the new agencies, and Congress, were surrogates of the regulatees. The businessmen who controlled the levers of power in the secret constitution's institutions knew what they were doing. They wanted to allay the working class's discontent. This goal was so neatly accomplished that orthodox thinking to the present day views Progressivism as a serious and substantial governmental intervention into, and control of, corporate affairs. Less purblind historians, however, have demonstrated that the movement was really a conservative achievement in liberal guise. It was a classic illustration of the operation of the Principle of Minimal Satisfaction of Human Needs.

What, therefore, had been implicit in the American constitutional order during the nineteenth century—a close, interlocking connection between government and business—became explicit with the advent of Progressivism. A new form of rule emerged, at least in the rhetoric, whose purported aim was the overall national interest and the common good of all the citizenry. World War I fructified the syzygetic nature of the government-business interface: The corporate state,[71] American style, came into being, the logical outgrowth of the Progressive movement. The state was not labeled as such, to be sure, and still is not; the term, a "mixed economy," was the euphemism coined.

The Progressive movement was a sea change in formal constitutional development, marked neither by amendment nor even by judicial decisions, but by a series of statutes and a subtle but definite alteration in the relationship between business and government. Collectivism during World War

I lent a major impetus to the new posture. And the enactment of a national income tax, following passage of the sixteenth amendment, changed the nature of both the constitutional order, mainly in federal-state relations, and the national government itself. This change became clear with the coming of the Great Depression and subsequent New Deal legislation. The economy had broken down. Mass public despair, accompanied by huge ranks of unemployed, swept the nation. Something had to be done by government, for the business community had become morally and intellectually bankrupt. The ruling elites—the moneyed and propertied—were like ths storied Bourbons: they had learned nothing and forgotten nothing. Or, as George Orwell said about Great Britain, "Whether the British ruling class are wicked or merely stupid is one of the most difficult questions of our time, and at certain moments a very important question."[72] That comment applied to the United States after the great crash.

In other words, those who wielded effective control under the secret constitution were too stupid to realize that President Franklin Roosevelt's measures, which began in 1933 in the depths of the depression, were actually probusiness. The enemies of the New Deal were mistaken. They should have been its friends. Corporate capitalism was protected, beginning with the National Recovery Act of 1933, which surrendered actual governing power to business guilds. This protection was a form of corporatism, declared unconstitutional, as we have seen, on other grounds. The New Deal framed institutions to protect against major business cycles and started the *overt* process of trying to ensure continuous economic growth. In this sense, it merely made explicit what had been implicit throughout American history. Security was the primary goal, and the New Deal "underwrote a vast apparatus of security." The tiny benefits of Social Security for the individual person were insignificant as compared with the security that government provided for large businesses. But on the whole, as Professor Barton Bernstein has observed, the New Deal was far from a success insofar as the general public was concerned:

> The New Deal failed to solve the problem of depression, it failed to raise the impoverished, it failed to redistribute income, it failed to extend equality and generally countenanced racial discrimination and segregation. It failed generally to make business more responsible to the social welfare or to threaten business's pre-eminent political power. In this sense, the New Deal, despite the shifts in tone from the earlier decade, was profoundly conservative and continuous with the 1920s.[73]

FDR, thus, may be said to have tried to help save the businessman from his own stupidity and shortsightedness. New Deal programs also helped to dilute public discontent over the manifest shortcomings of an economy that had rendered so many ill-fed, ill-clothed, and ill-housed. The confusion of the business elite was matched by a similar confusion among members of the lower classes, who saw in Roosevelt a savior and in the New Deal a way out of the morass into which the country had sunk.

But if the New Deal, when finally validated by the Supreme Court, was far from revolutionary in that it did not alter basic configurations of social power, it nonetheless marked another sea change in America's constitutional history. The New Deal did move in new directions, even though the old order was left intact. The net total was a classic example of the Principle of Minimal Satisfaction. Property, wealth, and privilege were still highest among protected constitutional rights, but seemed to give way to the advancement of human rights. Reality belied the appearance. New Deal programs, as Professor Bernstein and others have observed, did not solve festering economic problems, such as unemployment. There were still at least six million unemployed as late as 1941.[74] What got the nation out of the depression was precisely what has kept it from truly serious economic distress since: a war economy, shooting in World War II and "cold" since then. This is pure Keynesian economics written into public policy—but with a military face. The manifest beneficiaries of the New Deal were those in the working classes who had suffered most in past economic reverses; but the latent and more lasting beneficiaries were members of the capital-owning class, Hamilton's rich and well-born, who had always benefited most from the constitutional system.

In all of this, it bears emphasis, the Supreme Court was a willing ally, a part of the governing coalition of the nation with views in consonance with that coalition. After erecting seemingly insurmountable barriers to the New Deal—a heritage of the days of laissez-faire—the justices suddenly discovered in 1937 that their holdings in economic policy matters no longer accorded with the formal constitution. In a remarkable intellectual flip-flop, they found a basis in the fundamental law for socioeconomic legislation.[75] The formal constitution has not been the same since. (This is not to suggest that the nation deals generously with the less fortunate members of the population. To the contrary: just enough material support is accorded to help siphon off most of the discontent.)

Enough has been shown to validate the proposition that violence is one of a number of techniques that governing elites employ to keep the "lower" classes "in their place" and that the more lasting and socially more significant technique is the operation of the Principle of Minimal Satisfaction of Human Needs. The principle can operate, however, only during periods of sustained economic growth. The same may be said with the final example of the principle—the contemporaneous one of the civil rights/civil liberties decisions of the Supreme Court during the tenure of Chief Justice Earl Warren (1953–1969).

After 1945, most of the industrialized world outside of the United States was prostrate from the damage and casualties inflicted during the Second World War. The United States stood tall in the saddle, and a time of what many called *Pax Americana* emerged. The dollar was king among world currencies; American military might was supreme; the United Nations was an arm of American foreign policy; and economic growth and low inflation were taken for granted. Our true "golden age" was the consequence. But at about the time that President Richard Nixon cut the dollar loose from the gold standard and the Arabs began to play the capitalistic game with their hoarding of oil, the American empire began to crumble. The golden age came to an abrupt halt, and the political economy again became a zero-sum game.

The Warren Court's decisions spanned almost exactly the years of the golden age. No one knows—not least because few have asked and no one has definitively answered—whether a causal connection existed between the times of relative economic plenty and the civil rights/civil liberties decisions of the court.[76] What is known is that for the first time in American history serious attention was accorded to enforcing all of the limitations of the formal constitution, not just those that favored the business class. This "revolution" occurred in formal constitutional law, it seems to me, because it became possible for the first time in history to satisfy some of the pent-up material demands of the underclasses. The pattern is best seen in two parallel developments—first, the spate of decisions that altered the formal constitution to aid black Americans, and second, in the growing number of "entitlements" that Congress saw fit to bestow upon the people. Both may be taken to illustrate the operation of the Principle of Minimal Satisfaction.

It is enough now to focus on the judicial rulings, of which *Brown v. Board of Education*,[77] offering the promise of decent treatment to blacks, is the key decision. Judicial decisions are political epiphenomena. The justices of the Warren Court knew what they were doing. They knew, in sum, that by helping blacks—the manifest beneficiaries of their decisions—they were also, and principally, helping to preserve the existing social order. The justices thereby aided the latent beneficiaries, those who have always been highest in the social pecking order and thus would have most to lose from widespread unrest among black Americans.[78] The justices were elitists whose philosophies and interests coincided, in the last analysis, with those of the governing class whence they came or for whom, as lawyers, they had been surrogates or minions. With rare exceptions, their rulings came solely within the ambit of the formal constitution; they erected a standard toward which they hoped the American people would aspire. But they did not unduly disturb those who sat at, and wielded, the levers of actual power within the nation. Contrary, therefore, to the popular belief that the Warren Court was principally interested in furthering human rights and that egalitarianism was the drummer to which it marched, when all is said and done, it was the protection of corporate capitalism that mainly motivated the justices on the Warren Court.

This is not to say that the court did not try to further human rights. It did, but only within the confines of the formal constitution. Black Americans and other manifest beneficiaries were aided. In addition to attacking racial segregation, which was an effort to pronounce principles of social justice for blacks, the "rotten boroughs" of malapportioned legislatures, state and federal, were eliminated, and criminal suspects were recognized as constitutional persons entitled to a measure of decency from officials.[79] The list is not long, but it is significant. The indisputable residue, however, is that those changes were not accompanied by like alterations in the secret constitution.

Those who control the levers of actual power in the American constitutional order have other techniques to stifle or dilute discontent among the have-nots. High among them is the use of the mass media to help socialize the people to the norms of corporate capitalism. All governments, as Jacques Ellul has observed, employ propaganda systematically (both externally and internally).[80] In this sense, the major media of communication are best perceived as arms of government, there being a myth of a true adversarial press. The mass media have three main functions: to make a profit; to help market the output of consumer goods; and to help imbue the populace with loyalty to the ideas and views of the politico-economic system. The first amendment's protection of freedom of the press, rather than buttressing popular sovereignty, has become a means by which popular opinion is canalized into what are considered to be proper channels. As a consequence, no serious public debate takes place over many areas of great concern to the citizenry. Television has become a modern version of Aldous Huxley's vision of a world in which people come to love technologies that take away their capacity to think, that destroy their critical faculties, and that deprive them of their autonomy, maturity, and history. "In the age of advanced technology," Professor Neil Postman comments, "spiritual devastation is more likely to come from an enemy with a smiling face than from one whose countenance exudes suspicion and hate."[81] Technology is not normatively neutral—certainly that is true for television. It is true also for the major print media. The question that should be asked is: Who benefits from the system? The answer is that those who own the media are the immediate beneficiaries and those who control the politico-economic institutions of corporate capitalism are the ultimate beneficiaries. (This is *not* to say that most of what appears in the mass media is untrue. The point is different: Much that should be news is not published, and the commentary in the major media is almost entirely one-sided.)

This prologue has been an adumbration of the American system of constitutional dualism. No one can understand what constitutions are all about unless serious attention is paid to the fact that, as Bagehot and others wrote more than a century ago, the United States operates with parallel sets of constitutional institutions—the formal and the secret. The existence of a second (secret) constitution poses difficult problems to anyone who would think meaningfully about the constitutional order. One of these problems is *legitimacy*. Where do those who exercise effective control in the polity, who are at the levers of power of the secret constitution, get their right or title to rule? This question cuts to the very core of constitutionalism as the concept has been received and understood in the United States. From time to time in the ensuing pages, the question will be addressed. The principal conclusion can, however, be stated now: The power of those in control is illegitimate under the letter and spirit of the formal constitution.

PART I

CONSTITUTIONAL INADEQUACY

The extraordinary affluence of the United States has been produced by a set of fortuitous, nonreplicable, and nonsustainable factors.
—Rufus E. Miles, Jr.

The plight of modern democracies is serious. They have suffered great disasters in this century and the consequences of these disasters are compounding themselves. The end is not yet clear.
—Walter Lippmann

CHAPTER 1

CONSTITUTIONAL MYTHOLOGY

In our present political situation, the usual American myths no longer give us meaning and comfort; they ring as hollow and false as a replay of a high school commencement address at the brink of the Great Depression.

—Rollo May[1]

Americans are incurable romantics.

They have a national myth of creativity and progress and believe that both individuals and the country as a whole are steadily proceeding upward toward power and prosperity. And they romanticize the past, which is viewed through the haze of history as one long golden age. This is particularly true of 200 years ago, when men thought to be larger than life— those now called the Founding Fathers (the initial capital letters are significant, for those men are believed to have had divine guidance)—strode the earth and produced what is now the oldest written constitution. These men, all white, Anglo-Saxon property owners, are largely unknown today—save for a few, such as Washington and Franklin, Madison and Hamilton. (One man, Thomas Jefferson, is often considered to be a Founding Father, but he did not attend the 1787 constitutional convention.) They are the principal saints in America's pantheon, the subject of a vast secular hagiology. The formal constitution they hammered out during the hot summer of 1787 has a special significance for Americans: it is a symbol of our national life, fulfilling a function similar to that of the Queen (or King) of England.

As the United States commemorates the 200th anniversary of its only constitutional convention, most Americans view the formal constitution with awe and reverence. They unthinkingly take part in the eulogies of 1987, which resemble the celebrations in 1976 when the Declaration of Independence had its 200th anniversary. To the extent that people believe—as many say they do—that what was written in 1787 has an enduring significance and that the views of the men who drafted the formal constitution should be determined for present-day constitutional interpretations—again, as many believe—the United States may be said to be a hagiocracy, ruled (if those views are accurate—which they emphatically are not) by a gaggle of men long dead.

Are uncritical awe, praise, and eulogy of the formal constitution enough? Has not the time come to reexamine the ancient document to determine whether it is adequate for present and future needs? These questions, more felt or sensed than seen or thought through, float like dark clouds behind today's interminable political debates; they cast shadows over the preparations, led by former Chief Justice Warren Burger, to extol the formal constitution. (It is noteworthy that Burger and others are making no inquiry whatsoever into the existence and operation of the secret constitution.)

Although few are willing to voice what is certain to be called constitutional heresy, the questions must be asked and adequately answered, simply because what the framers produced is beginning to show some worrisome cracks. In the past, questioning the perfection of the formal constitution was ignored or derided as the feverish working of an overwrought mind. But not now. Rexford Tugwell and Robert Hutchins had no success a few years ago when they came forth with a new constitution;[2] their efforts were little noted and quickly forgotten. Today is different: a growing number of thoughtful Americans, as well as people in other nations, are pointing out shortcomings in the Document of 1787. Chief among the critics is the Committee on the Constitutional System, a group of several dozen leaders of opinion headed by Lloyd Cutler, Douglas Dillon, and Nancy Kassebaum.[3]

The present volume goes far beyond most current analyses, such as those of Professor James Burns,[4] to ask these basic questions: Were the formal constitution to be rewritten today, what should be in it? How can changes be made? How can the institutions of the secret constitution be altered? Must political (constitutional) change be preceded by or at least accompanied by a simultaneous change in human values? To answer these and similar questions, which is the burden of this book, requires an open mind about the constitution, an ability to see it whole and see it truly, and a capacity to rethink the popular wisdom about it.

The central argument is that the formal constitution, as written and as interpreted, requires substantial revision. So, too, does the secret constitution, the institutions of which should be formally melded with those of the formal. (Since both constitutions are so closely intertwined, I shall speak of them in the singular. Only when it is necessary to make specific mention of aspects of the secret constitution will mention be made of it.)

The constitution requires a complete reevaluation both of its express provisions and of the political and economic institutions that have grown up under its aegis. Are they adequate for the present and the emergent future? This question is asked in full recognition of the fact that to doubt the continuing usefulness of the ancient document is controversial, for Americans rally around the constitution as well as the flag as symbols of our national purpose. No one quite knows what is symbolized by the constitution and there is no consensus on its purpose, but the fact remains that the few thousand words written in 1787 do have a mystical significance for Americans.

This reaction is understandable. The United States has waxed strong and prosperous in the two centuries of its independent existence. There should be little wonder, therefore, that the American people tend to attribute our position of dominance to the constitution and to think of the framers as "supermen." This attribution, however, is fallacious—a prime example of *post hoc* reasoning. We have become wealthy and powerful less because of the constitution than, quite often at least, in spite of it. Our wealth and strength derive mainly from a set of unique environmental conditions that will not, because they cannot, be repeated.

Constitutional mysticism or mythology comes in many guises. The foundation, or basic, myth has four features. First, the myth sees the United States as being born by a political immaculate conception, pure and untrammeled. This is the creation myth. Nothing constitutionally significant is considered to have occurred prior to 1787—not even the Declaration of Independence or the Articles of Confederation. In significant respects, the formal constitution as written is a counterrevolution to the principles of the Declaration. Second, the myth views the constitution as a set of immutable truths revealed—some think by divine inspiration—to the framers. Among other things, this means that the constitution is—or as Attorney General Edwin Meese would have it, should be—the same today as it was in 1789, when the new government began operations. Third, those "truths" serve to limit government on behalf of individual liberty and also allow the people to rule. This is the idea of popular sovereignty. Finally, the foundation myth stoutly rejects any suggestion that the constitution is inadequate and needs change. Some view it as a perfect instrument, good for all times and all circumstances.

These myths have little relationship to reality. We are, to be sure, not accustomed to thinking about the United States as having myths. But all nations, all peoples, have myths; they are part of the accepted belief-system of any political order. "Depend upon it," Max Muller wrote in 1873, "there is mythology now as there was in the time of Homer, only we do not perceive it, because we ourselves live in the very shadow of it, and because we all shrink from the full meridian light of truth."[5] So it is today, as any careful and dispassionate analysis will reveal. Myths can even be called necessary, for they serve several functions: they provide an understanding of creation, they structure community and political experience, they establish a framework that gives people a sense of identity, and they are often a basis for personal morality. The formal constitution as myth and as symbol serves all four functions.

According to the foundation myth, the framers established a nation out of what the power structure then thought was a growing chaos imperiling property rights. The powerful thought the government under the Articles of Confederation was inadequate to their needs. Whether America was in fact so badly governed under the Articles is by no means clear today.[6] Be that as it may, a nation stepped into the shoes of a prince, the English king, for the constitution was a counterrevolutionary document contrary to the spirit and some of the letter of the Declaration of Independence—particularly in the dropping of any mention of human equality. But the popular wisdom today is that the fifty-five men who attended the constitutional convention had a special and perhaps even a unique wisdom—although, as mentioned, most Americans would be hard put to name more than a few of the delegates.

When in September 1787 the conclave ended its secret sessions, only thirty-nine men were willing to sign the product—less than half of the eighty-four who were supposed to have attended (but about two-thirds of those who did take part). As white, male property owners, the delegates were the Establishment of the day, those who were mainly interested in protection of their property and of their privileged position in society. Slavery was discussed, was denounced, and was retained, thus making the formal constitution one that institutionalized (until the Civil war) a caste system that made some Americans mere chattels.

Four groups were not represented at Philadelphia: women, slaves, indentured servants, and men without property; these groups made up the bulk of the population numerically, particularly so when the native Americans, the Indians, are added to the unrepresented. The fifty-five men not only dropped the Declaration of Independence's claim that all *men* (note: not all *people*) were created equal with certain "unalienable" rights, they also failed to list "life, liberty, and the pursuit of happiness" as governmental goals. Only in 1791, in the fifth amendment, did life and liberty become protected by "due process of law"; the pursuit of happiness was permanently jettisoned. In an intellectual and political tour de force and after some fierce politicking, enough people with votes were convinced that the Articles of Confederation should be dropped and the new constitution should be the fundamental law. Then and now, economic interest is to be seen behind the political clauses of the constitution. The document, therefore, is not so much the work of a gaggle of wise men trying to establish a decent and orderly society as the creation of a propertied elite determined to retain its privileges.

The elite conceded just enough to the great unrepresented majority to ensure popular support.

So the new nation came into being, catapulted on the world scene, a puny and weak infant at the mercy of the then superpowers—France and England (as the War of 1812 evidenced). For many Americans, history begins not earlier than 1787 or perhaps 1789, when George Washington was inaugurated as the first president and the first Congress convened. The United States is considered to be like Athena emerging fully formed from the head of Zeus. Athena was the goddess of wisdom, skills, and warfare. Under the myth, the constitution is the repository of wisdom and skills of governance without parallel. This aspect of the myth does not refer to the secret constitution. To be sure, the third feature of the foundation myth—that the constitution is a set of limitations on government—was not included in the original document. But that is of minor significance today: after promulgation of the Bill of Rights (the first ten amendments) in 1791, the original document and the Bill of Rights became merged in the public (and legal) mind as one instrument.

There is, finally, the tacit belief that ours is a perfect constitution, with only minor flaws, and that tinkering with it verges on blasphemy. Any suggestion for major revision cuts against the grain of the American civil religion of Americanism, a tenet of which is that, in English Prime Minister William Gladstone's effusive praise, the constitution is "the most wonderful work ever struck off at a given time by the brain and purpose of man."[7] Or, as Supreme Court Justice William Johnson wrote in 1823, "In the Constitution of the United States—the most wonderful instrument ever drawn by the hand of man—there is a comprehension and precision that is unparalleled; and I can truly say after spending my life in studying it, I still daily find in it some new excellence."[8] Those statements are sheer balderdash; such hyperbole serves no useful purpose.

The foundation myth has several corollaries, each also a myth, and each worthy of extended discussion. These, however, can only be listed here. If one wishes to think seriously about the constitution, he should begin by understanding that the foundation myth has little basis in reality, and then should probe deeper and learn about other constitutional myths. The following listing of ten myths is more illustrative than exhaustive, but it serves to make the point of constitutional mythology.

Forget, for example, the idea that the United States has only a written constitution. As has been shown, that, too, is a myth. The constitution is mostly unwritten—in two ways. First, many of the original clauses have been updated by succeeding generations of Americans, mainly by Supreme Court decisions but also by some presidential and congressional actions. Constitutional interpretation is distinctly *not* a judicial monopoly. As for Congress, the War Powers Resolution of 1973 is a clear instance of a change in the balance of power between the two avowedly political branches of government. It is countered, however, by the fact that the president exercises de facto control over the war-making power, as every use of military violence in this century attests. The words of the formal constitution remain the same but their content changes through time. The appropriate label for this process is the "living" constitution. Second, government operates in large part by unofficial, extraconstitutional means. The secret constitution that exists parallel to, and often overlapping, the written instrument, and is as important as the explicit provisions of the Document of 1787, requires acknowledgment and understanding. Both constitutions must, however, be understood if one is to have a full comprehension of what American constitutionalism is all about.

Forget, also, the notion that the formal constitution established a democracy. It did no such thing. The framers feared what some called a "democratical despotism" and made every effort to forestall any serious movement toward a true democracy. They created a republic, something quite different, with the reins of power firmly in the hands of those that Hamilton called the rich and wellborn. Two centuries after the Philadelphia conclave, only two things can be said with certainty about representative democracy in the United States. First, effective power does not reside in Congress (which really does not want to rule). Secondly, there is little that is democratic about the exercise of that power. Walter Karp's account of how the United States was manipulated into the First World War by President Woodrow Wilson provides a classic illustration of the point.[9]

Forget the belief that the Bill of Rights, through judicial action, actually fully protects human rights and liberties. Those seeming limitations on government are not true binding commitments; in reality, they are mere hortatory admonitions for government officers to act decently in the circumstances. It is the circumstances that control. Here, as elsewhere, when important societal matters are at stake, important as seen through the eyes of those who wield effective control in the nation, the government *always* wins in the Supreme Court. The Court thus becomes a part of the governing coalition and in fact an arm of the political branches—the presidency and the Congress.[10] Seen correctly, the Court is a part of the political process, seldom if ever out of phase with those who control the institutions of both constitutions.

Forget, too, the idea that the constitution actually separates the powers of the national government. It does not. The operations of the secret constitution see to that. Moreover, under even the formal constitution, the norm is that of separated institutions sharing powers, with more cooperation than conflict. This has led Don Price to recommend that we should "quit talking about separation of powers."[11] This does not mean that conflicts do not occur and that the president can have his way without negotiating with Congress; but it does mean, as Woodrow Wilson observed in 1908, that cooperation is the norm between the branches.[12]

And *forget* about the United States having a true federal system. Whatever the men of 1787 may have intended, since 1789 the nation has developed in the direction of hierarchy—a stronger and stronger central government—with the states increasingly being mere administrative districts for centrally established policies. The fifty states today are more a source of senators than repositories of sovereignty, a condition not at all likely to change. Economically and technologically the United States really is a single entity; this means it is politically one as well. No doubt the state lines will remain, for they will be uncommonly hard to erase, but there is little or no likelihood of a serious attempt at devolution.

Forget, furthermore, the view that the United States is governed only by public government. It is not. The "private" governments of the nation, principally the supercorporations, have as much and probably more control over the lives of Americans as does public government. These companies are economically, and thus politically, more important than all except two or three states (California, Texas, and perhaps New York). They are the units of "functional" federalism, entities that cooperatively (with public government) govern major segments of given industries; they thus are local governments.[13] And as we have seen, they also control or greatly influence the making of public policies at all levels of government. As private governments, the supercorporations are the principal institutions of the secret constitution.

Forget the pious propaganda that the formal constitution guarantees true representative government. It never has and does not now. The people as such are not represented, and never have been. Groups, however, are represented through the operations of the secret constitution. Recall, in this instance, the so-called Iron Triangles, or issue networks, that operate throughout the federal government. As a *body*, Congress has lost the will to govern (if, indeed, it ever had it). Individual members differ, especially those who chair the standing committees and subcommittees; they govern by participating in Iron Triangle negotiations.

Forget the fervid assertions that the natural person in the basic unit of society. He (she) is not. In economics and in politics, the individual as such counts for little. Groups are the fundamental units of American society. This is the age of collective and thus of bureaucratic action, a time when the natural person attains significance principally as a member of a group (or perhaps of groups). The myth still bespeaks the individualism of autonomous personalities, but the operational fact reflects the role of individuals as members of groups. As long ago as the turn of this century, John D. Rockefeller remarked that large-scale organization had "revolutionized the way of doing business" and that individualism was gone, never to return.[14]

The normal way for a person to express himself is through his group. Other than the rare hermit or the person who has "dropped out," everyone must belong to one or more groups.

[Forget the popular wisdom that the Supreme Court is all-powerful. That tribunal—all courts, for that matter—are seldom out of phase wiith the wishes of the ruling elites of America. Judges of course have law-making power, but they employ it with full cognizance of political constraints. This means that judicial independence, speaking generally, is also mythical. Judges, always chosen from that invisible but nonetheless existent group called the Establishment, only rarely announce decisions contrary to that group.]

Forget, in sum, most of the received wisdom about the constitution, simply because reality differs so widely. Learn, rather, to see things true and see them whole, with full knowledge of the mythology of American constitutionalism.

That such views are controversial does not invalidate them. [As written and as interpreted, the formal constitution's political and economic institutions are unable to satisfactorily resolve many of today's problems. In the nuclear age, national survival cannot be guaranteed. And in this age of information, there is a growing population redundancy. Many people have become surplus to the needs of the economy. They cannot find work because increasingly there is no work to be had. More and more live below the poverty line. Environmental degradation continues. There are few signs of alleviation. This is something new under the constitutional sun. In the past, Americans were able to ride out the crises that speckled their history. But now there are serious doubts that this survival can be achieved.]

The United States emerged from World War II certain that the miracles of science and technology could and would solve any human problem. In much the same way that the long-hidden secrets of the atom were unlocked, technological "fixes" were to be able to handle all social problems. Americans had a blind, unthinking faith in the capacity of scientists and technicians. People were convinced that unleashed atomic power had settled the need, for all time, of energy supply. Today, however, there are increasing doubts about nuclear power. The mishaps at Three Mile Island and Chernobyl highlighted a dismal picture of failure. And we thought that the American politico-economic systems were up to any task, however large or complex. That confidence has dwindled.

On reflection, it is strange that people can believe that the fifty-five men who drafted the formal constitution were intellectual and moral giants, who in a burst of altruism and idealism brought forth, in Lincoln's famous (but erroneous) words a nation "conceived in liberty and dedicated to the proposition that all men are created equal."[15] Instead of being conceived in liberty, the United States emerged out of conflict, at a time when public values were hotly disputed, when instability seemed to reign, when rancor and vituperation were the order of the day, and when our governmental institutions were frail and unformed. The previously quoted excessive praise of Gladstone and Johnson of the perfection of the formal constitution is an interesting but scarcely accurate sentiment. Virginia's Judge Spencer Roane was much closer to the mark when he observed in 1819 that "the great fault of the present times is in considering the constitution as perfect."[16] The same fault is evident today, particularly among those like Warren Burger who simply do not understand the true nature of American constitutionalism.

Contrary to popular belief, the United States was born on the second of July, 1776 (not the fourth), when the Second Continental Congress voted that the thirteen colonies were "and of right, ought to be, free and independent States." The central principle was not only independence from Great Britain but local self-government. The Congress thus created less a nation than thirteen supposedly sovereign states. Our first constitution, the Articles of Confederation, went into effect in 1777. It spoke of a confederacy that was styled "The United States of America," but immediately went on to ensure that "Each state retains its sovereignty, freedom, and independence."

The self-determination principle was to last only a few years, although its death did not come until General Robert E. Lee surrendered his sword at Appomattox. Its decline began in the 1787 convention.

After the fifty-five delegates straggled into Philadelphia to their conclave, they neatly subverted the Articles by exceeding their mission to create a superstate that in time would become a political juggernaut capable of overriding the wishes of any one state (or even a combination of states). The original revolutionary right of local autonomy was shelved—not without considerable difficulty, to be sure, which lasted for decades and still surfaces when politicians and pundits, who should know better, speak of a "new federalism." "States' rights" has become a mere meaningless shibboleth. A national economic system sits astride a decentralized political order, and has largely made state lines insignificant. Speaking sententiously, a nation with a central income tax, supercorporations, large external concerns, and technological ties, cannot be truly federal. Few, indeed, want it to be; people's loyalties run to the nation, not to the several states. A person is an American before he is a New Yorker, a Californian, or even a Texan.

Although conditions then and now are superficially quite different, there is more than a faint resemblance between the United States in the 1780s (under the Articles of Confederation) and in the 1980s. Some large differences may of course be discerned. The nation is far greater in size; sophisticated transportation and communication networks bind the country together; citizenship is more national than state; our military might is awesome; and we are urbanized and industrialized. Consider, however, the following, the net effect of which shows a remarkable parallelism between the 1780s and the 1980s.

Then there were thirteen supposedly sovereign states, each competing with the others for trade and commerce in what had been wilderness not long before; *now* the United States is one, albeit the most important one, of some 160 nation-states, each competing for the resources and bounty of a finite planet.

Then the businessman, the man of property, the *white* man of property, was dominant in social and political affairs; *now* his successors still ride tall in the saddle.

Then rancor and divisiveness pervaded the nation; *now* the body politic is fraught with mutual antipathies and clashing interests.

Then Congress was inept; *now* the United Nations is a political nonstarter, and Congress is still inept.

Then and now, no center of political gravity existed in the relevant political arena (*then*, it was the thirteen former colonies, *now* it's the entire globe).

Then existed an urge for equality, expressly stated in the Declaration of Independence; *now* exists a growing drive for equality, both of opportunity and of condition. But it was denied then and is being denied today.

Then economic conflict continued among the states; *now* a similar conflict continues not only among the fifty states but among the 160-plus nation-states.

Then there was growing friction among social classes, mainly between creditors and debtors; *now* similar frictions trouble the world over, between debtor and creditor nations and between nations with opposing ideologies.

Then there was a legal system that in fact, though not in theory, favored the rich and privileged; *now* precisely the same is true.

Then people knew slavery and indentured labor; *now* there is a growing underclass that is beginning to exist in a state of de facto peonage.

Then existed a pervasive selfishness among the "haves," both domestically and globally; *now* exists a socially cruel polity, national and planetary, that consigns growing numbers of the "have-nots" to permanent poverty.

Then a generally low moral fiber was true of the people and their leaders; *now* there is also a deteriorating moral fiber, accompanied by a growing contempt for all centers of authority.

Then consumerism and materialism reigned; *now* we have even greater consumerism and materialism, generated by technological inventions.

Then people felt disregard for the future; *now* people sardonically ask, "What has posterity done for me?", and act accordingly.

Then protection of property was considered the highest human right; *now* exactly the same is true.

Then exploitation of national riches by the powerful and the well-to-do was the rule; *now* much the same holds true, although power is corporate power rather than the power of discrete individuals, and the riches are of the globe rather than of the nation.

Then existed a formal and a secret constitution; *now* precisely the same exists.

And yet, out of the partial anarchy of the 1780s came a strong and prosperous United States of America, but only, it merits iteration for emphasis, because a unique set of environmental conditions favored that development. Two centuries later, Americans are confronted by the end of both the domestic and the world frontiers. Future expansion can therefore occur only within severely constricted bounds, as viewed historically, and then only through expanded use of science and technology. But, again it must be emphasized, there is no ultimate technological fix that will serve as a replacement for the frontiers.

This hard truth, for truth it is, has significant implications for the constitutional order. Niccolò Machiavelli, the most maligned (wrongfully) political theorist in western history, saw history as constant change, to which forms of government must adapt, and as uncertainty, to which any form of government must be adaptable. "All human affairs are ever in a state of flux, and cannot stand still."[17] Therefore, he remarked, there must be either an improvement or a decline. Social equilibrium has not been the human lot, although the formal constitution as written was based on Newtonian principles of balance. Isaac Newton likened the universe to a great clock, with interacting parts, each reacting to others in a harmonious whole. By their very nature, however, constitutions, whether written or unwritten, are Darwinian in scope and operation. Charles Darwin is the philosopher of American consitutional *development*, just as Newton was the philosopher of its *creation*. Constitutions develop in a continuing process rather than remaining in a fixed state. They are evolutionary, not static, and are always being updated as new exigencies emerge.

For one to advocate that major constitutional revision is now necessary is, therefore, merely to invite attention to what is sure to occur in any event. The American constitutions, formal and secret, will change, as they have for two centuries, and the only questions are whether the alterations will come willy-nilly, by *ad hoc* reactions to new circumstances, or in a planned way; and whether changes will be effected for the benefit of all rather than merely for the favored few. Given those choices, should there be any doubt as to the avenues to be followed? To the extent that humans can guide and determine the future—itself an unanswered question—surely there should be concerted efforts aimed at creating a political and cultural environment that furthers everyone's needs.

That goal may be called utopian, but so be it. There is value in utopian thought. Ideas have consequences. That of major constitutional revision may not have fully come, but surely it is on the horizon. It will come, in one way or another, given the state of the world. New and unique demands are being leveled against the American constitutional order, which will change, as it has in the past, to reflect changing circumstances. It should always be kept in mind that throughout American history necessity has been the mother of constitutional law. High on the list of today's necessities is the satisfaction of human needs and the fulfillment of human deserts within environmental limits.

Utopian thinking can be helpful in several ways. First, it helps to justify why better communities should be built, or at least striven for. Second, it helps to guide our deliberations, once an idea is broached and accepted for serious dialogue. Third, such thinking justifies our actions: the constitution is often considered to be an ideal to which Americans should aspire. (A new constitution of human needs would erect a standard toward which the citizenry should aim.) Fourth, it provides a basis for evaluating existing institutions and practices. Do these ways measure up to what they should? The answer set forth in this volume is that they do not.

It should be remembered that the framers were themselves engaged in a form of utopian thought when they violated their charge and produced the formal constitution, and when they asserted that it would become effective when ratified by nine states rather than the vote of all thirteen. (It is appropriate to mention that one state, Rhode Island, was not even represented at the convention). Many of the framers had a vision of a strong and powerful nation; believing that the mass of men are neither wise nor good, they constructed a document that at once enabled the moneyed and the propertied to control government and the bulk of the population to think that they had both an important role in government and a chance to rise toward wealth and power.

The framers also cannily separated church and state, but at the same time plumped for the civil religion of Americanism and patriotism—for what was to be called the American Dream.[18] They created a government suitable to their fancy and interests and developed a cultural milieu that propped up their privileged positions. They pretended that the formal constitution created a government hemmed in by laws, rather than a government of men, all the while knowing full well that the contrary was closer to the mark. It was an extraordinary event, unique in human history. The framers managed to stave off popular discontent by funneling it into innocuous avenues and by extending token gains to the disadvantaged. Deep down, they knew that societies are in their nature authoritarian and governments even more so. They spoke about popular sovereignty and wrote it into the preamble of the constitution, but only as a means of placating the people. Two centuries later, their successors and their academic *apparatchiks* speak woefully about how "democracy" has become "ungovernable"[19]—precisely what worried the men of 1787.

As discussed in the prologue, the United States has never really been a democracy—assuming that a definitive meaning can be given to that ambiguous term. Whether the United States *should* be and whether it *can* be are other, far more difficult questions. If elitism, as has been argued, characterizes all groups (and all nations), can there be any escape from it? I think not, particularly in a large nation such as the United States that has interests not only planet-wide but extending far into outer space. This may be a harsh and even unpleasant belief, but it is one that much of American history confirms and that any clear-sighted analysis of contemporary America corroborates. If, then, Americans wish to have a constitution that furthers human dignity in its broadest sense, thought will have to turn to something other than democracy. And if this means the continuation of an elitist government, no one should be shocked. Our constitutional mythology is to the contrary, of course, but it is just that: mythology. Stripped to its essentials, the core problem is to find ways of altering the beneficiaries that have always been present so as to include the entire population, not just the few. In the past, as in the present, elitism favored the few over the many. This should not—indeed, cannot—long continue. To the argument that an elitist government is certain to benefit the elite only, or at least disproportionately, the answer is easy: either the group of beneficiaries will be substantially enlarged or social turmoil will erupt, sooner or later. There is no middle ground; America cannot continue on its present path.

[The framers, ideologues to a man, knew what they wanted, and by one means or another—some far from morally pure—got it. But of course the framers had an opportunity unparalleled in human history. Never before, and certainly not since, were environmental conditions so favorable. The framers could, accordingly, easily afford to be utopians. Today the insistent question has become: Can Americans afford *not* to be utopians? The answer, quite obviously, is no.]

Despite the preamble (to the formal constitution) which states that it was written for "ourselves and our posterity," it was mainly drafted by the framers for themselves and themselves alone. It is not cynical to maintain that the document was not designed to endure for the ages to come, as Chief Justice Marshall stated in 1819,[20] but to start the nation on its way. By no means did the framers foresee what the United States was to become. Some may have dreamed about a continent-sized superpower, but if so, those ideas did not creep into the formal constitution. Thomas Jefferson, among others, well knew that it could well be a sometime thing, a mere temporary expedient. Toward the end of his life, he wrote:

Some men look at constitutions with sanctimonious reverence, and deem them like the ark of the covenant, too sacred to be touched. They ascribe to the men of the preceding age a wisdom more than human, and suppose that what they did to be beyond amendment. I knew this age well; I belonged to it, and labored with it. It deserved well of its country. It was very like the present, but without the experience of the present; and forty years of experience in government is worth a century of book-reading; and this they would say themselves, were they to rise from the dead.[21]

That statement has a modern ring; Jefferson could have been writing today. He knew that the United States cannot be, and indeed is not, ruled from the grave. To think otherwise is to engage in fantasy. A major reason for this conclusion is the subject of the next chapter.

CHAPTER 2

AN EPOCH ENDS

The frontier phenomenon ... appears as a remarkable but transitory wound, arising as a result of a demographic and cultural catastrophe to the normal equilibrium of the human ecosystem. Signs that the regimen of the past five hundred years is at an end are not wanting. For the process through which Europeans created the Great Frontier and occupied so many lands wound down very fast after 1914.
　　　　　　　　　　　　　　　　　　　—William H. McNeill[1]

To suggest that American world dominance has ended and that limits to economic growth exist is to invite quick dismissal as a doomsayer. Americans seem to have a sublime faith in the nation's destiny and a blind, even mindless, belief in technology and the capacity of technicians to create fixes that will satisfactorily solve any human problem.

This belief may have been partly true during the past 200 years—for a large number of people, at least—but, if so, it is no longer true. We now live on an overloaded planet, whose carrying capacity is reaching its outermost limits. Present-day political and economic institutions are increasingly unable to cope. Whether basic institutional alteration can help to alleviate what should be an obviously perilous condition is the central question of this book.

The United States has come to the end of a unique (to itself) epoch and is fast approaching the limits of several hundred thousand years of human evolution. *Homo sapiens* has been a spectacular biological success. But for reasons far from fully understood, that very success has been carried to excess. Disastrous consequences loom ever closer. We have entered "the age of triage," Professor Richard Rubenstein warns: "The revolution of rationality, the glorious and terrible revolution which brought forth the modern world, has reached its limits."[2] The ideas of progress and of the perfectability of man are now seen as puerile dreams of the age of the Enlightenment. We will do well if we can hold our own, let alone improve the condition of billions of humans the world over.

For two million years, humans have exploited Earth's life-supporting capacity, often at the expense of other species and even of other humans. Population has grown exponentially in the past 300 years. For a relatively brief time, technology helped to ameliorate age-old problems of human existence. That time is rapidly coming to an end. We have overshot the number of people that the planet can support in any reasonable degree of creature comfort. This is true even though had humans the wit and the will to satisfy those material demands, the demands could be met. How, then, to generate the required impetus toward that end?

Social bankruptcy is the consequence, throughout much of the world. Any thinking person knows, or should know, that humans have come to a great turning point in their journey from an unknown past to an unfathomable future.[3] Although the future, short- or long-term, cannot be forecast with certainty, one thing is sure: it will not—it cannot—be a mere extension of the recent past. We are daily confronted with new problems and have only yesterday's inadequate tools to cope with them.

There is a hard lesson here. Far too many still believe in the limitlessness of Earth's bounty and in the capacity of humans to reason through and solve their problems. This is the arrogance of humanism, a belief that has come hard up to the specter of too much technology in the hands of too many people on a planet that definitely has a limited carrying capacity. However much such supreme Micawberists as Julian Simon and Ben Wattenberg protest to the contrary,[4] the world *under its present institutions and values* is fast becoming—perhaps, has become—a zero-sum game. For everyone who gains in the game of life, there will be a loser somewhere. The material pie is not infinitely expansible. Only a born-again optimist who keeps his head firmly buried in the sand can believe that the economic pie will increase in size both to parallel population growth and to assist the 800-plus millions who today live in absolute poverty. A zero-sum game may be likened to a poker game: the sum of the winners and losers adds up to zero. In the game of life, only inherent docility and apathy and numbing despair, coupled with repression, keep people from breaking free from the confines of the planetary zero-sum game.

The problem this zero-sum game poses for anyone who wishes to think seriously about improving the lot of the have-nots is that of how to develop ways in which Earth, with its nation-state system, can become a positive-sum game. This is a game in which the game itself helps to expand the store of material plenty; theoretically, everyone gains or can gain. There are no losers, but only winners in some degree. Although Robert Kuttner has argued, convincingly in my judgment, that there is no incompatibility between a society committed to social justice and a dynamic economy,[5] whether the world can become a positive-sum game is an intellectual task of staggering complexity. Is there a contradiction between a just society and a dynamic economy? Are liberty and equality congruent goals? Must the poor and the impoverished always be with us? Is social justice really bad for economic growth? On another plane, is personal liberty threatened as much by market forces as by the state?

These and similar questions require answers, and soon. The time is growing short, yet few are concerned with the problems. In modern America three basic routes can be taken. One is to continue to drift along, in the time-honored way of making incremental adjustments as the political economy continues to stutter. Another is to restructure society, both domestically and globally, in ways designed to reasonably satisfy human needs. The third route, and the one that seems to be emerging, is to move toward a socially cruel but economically functional future.

The path that the United States takes will depend upon three factors. First, there must be a willingness, thus far not visible, to reexamine institutions that, in the myth at least, have been effective in the past. Second, cultural values, those characteristics of an acquisitive society that exalts materialism and hedonism, must be altered. Again, there is little evidence of such a change. Third, whatever the United States does must be done in cooperation with other nations. Some halting beginnings, far from sufficient to the need, have been made in this direction. If any of the three factors is missing or fails in achievement, then Arnold Toynbee's doleful forecast would, almost certainly, come true: "In all developed countries, a new way of life—a severely regimented way—will have to be imposed by ruthless, authoritarian governments."[6] Only an unthinking and willful cheerfulness, with little regard for the essential facts of the modern age, will permit one to take a roseate view of the future.

Humans have short memories. And they know little history. What they believe about the past often tilts toward mythology, if for no other reason than that each generation writes its own history. Napoleon likely was correct when he said that history was merely a "convenient lie." What is believed about the past reflects present needs and values more than it accurately portrays what actually took place.

Americans seem to believe that their familiar political and economic institutions—their constitutional order—are the natural scheme of things. This simply is not correct. If anything, these institutions are aberrational. The United States is not a microcosm of the world, with people from the planet over coming together and living peacefully. The storied melting pot is a myth; the truth about it, as Daniel Patrick Moynihan and Nathan Glazer have demonstrated,[7] is that it did not melt—except for those of African descent who are all lumped together as blacks, whatever their original derivation.

"We have it in our power to begin the world again," Thomas Paine asserted in 1776 in an early example of America's "special mission" (which has always been central to our national ideology).[8] There are reasons for this. Americans did have a uniquely favorable environment for their political and economic systems to flourish. Small wonder, therefore, that an unquestioning faith in our own omnipotence, not to say omniscience, became pervasive. Our forebears had an unequaled opportunity to create something new and lasting—and good. Said John Winthrop in 1630: "Men shall say of succeeding plantacions: the Lord make it like that of New England: for wee must consider that wee should be as a City upon a Hill, the eies of all people upon us."[9] A new and socially just society could have been created, but the chance was blown. Why that is so is one of the great unanswered questions of American history. A partial answer is set forth in this chapter: We Americans, it will be argued, have come to the end of an epoch unique in human history.

Instsitutions characteristic of that epoch, which began with the Great Discoveries that followed Columbus, now require reexamination and restructuring, simply because of the wholly new environmental milieu of the modern age. Representative democracy (whatever that term means), the private enterprise economic system, and individualistic philosophy cannot be considered to be immutable truths, both permanent and easily transferrable to other lands. To believe that they are is odd and even visionary, explainable mainly by a deeply felt religious belief in America's special mission.

Most Americans do not realize that their "system"—the label is given hesitatingly, for it is less a system than a cobbled-up set of practices and attitudes—is of recent origin as time is counted and is unique to the American experience. To believe, therefore, that our ways of politics and economics can be readily transplanted elsewhere is fantasy. They are not based on innate human chracteristics. To the contrary: our ways are limited in time and in space, in time to the past two or three centuries and in space to the Western world and some of its former colonies. They are, accordingly, a mere pip on the historical graph of human experience, not at all likely to be reproduced here or elsewhere. It is worth emphasis that not one of the more than 100 nations created since 1945 has adopted the American constitutional model.

The familiar institutions are now in decline, slowly but apparently inexorably. When constitutions decay, as they do, form often outlasts substance. Age-old rituals continue and may even be intensified, but the chasm between pretense and reality grows ever wider and deeper. So it is in the United States. We continue to celebrate the formal constitution even though it is

linked to how government actually works only in metaphorical or symbolic 48- 9
ways. Speaking sententiously, the idea of a constitution as limited government, with democratic institutions, was in large part a consequence of the
Great Discoveries that began in the sixteenth century (after Columbus). Not
long after the Italian navigator lucked upon a new world, others began to
explore the globe. The results were truly remarkable—in sum, Western
hegemony over the land and treasure of the remainder of the planet.

Wealth in untold amounts poured into Western Europe, and seemingly
endless land became available. A "400-year boom" got under way. Nothing
like it was seen before—or has been seen since. The boom enabled people
to escape after a time from an ecological trap, with its rigid authoritarian
institutions, that had confined them in strict caste systems since the dawn
of civilization. Thomas Hobbes remarked in a famous sentence that life for
mankind "in a state of nature" was "poor, nasty, brutish, and short"[10]—
a view which may or may not have been accurate. No one today knows
what a state of nature really was or what type of life humans led then,
although some, such as Andrew Bard Schmookler, have asserted that people
in pre-civilizational times worked fewer hours and generally enjoyed a better
quality of life than do many people today.[11] Be that as it may, surely Europe
in pre-Columbian times was Hobbesian, as Barbara Tuchman demonstrated
in *A Distant Mirror*.[12] At that time, even the favored few lived nasty and
brutish lives, as compared today with most people in the United States and
Europe. A principal reason for the change, I am suggesting, is the impact
of the Great Discoveries.

The discoverers found treasure beyond the dreams of avarice and land
almost beyond measure that had lain fallow for eons. Small wonder, therefore, that a static society began to change, slowly at first, to become one of
permanent revolution. At about the same time, the human mind expanded,
catching glimpses of a universe theretofore unknown and even unthinkable.
Before the Discoveries and the Copernican intellectual revolution, the ancient and medieval worlds were closed. Space, rather than being infinite,
was seen as a solid sphere on which the stars were embedded. Time, too,
was finite: to medieval man the world was only 4,000 years old and would
end in a short time (after Armageddon). Learning was limited. The literate
few believed that the final truth on all subjects had been written, if not in
the Bible then by Aristotle and Plato and other ancients. The Bible was Holy
Writ, the ultimate truth for religion and for cosmology, and not to be
questioned.

With the rare exception of a Copernicus or a Galileo, those who thought
and wrote did so within a closed body of knowledge. They were confined
to refining the accepted wisdom of the day. The universe was Earth-centered,
and man was the special creature of an all-knowing and all-wise God (who
had been created in man's image). Overtly authoritarian, even totalitarian,
the age saw economics and politics and religion as all of a piece. Most

people lived lives of desperate penury and want. They were mere objects or things, rather than individuals, and were little better than slaves—and often slaves in fact.

Then came the Discoveries and the Copernican Revolution, which opened the mind of man. Copernicus smashed for all time the dominant belief-system—the worldview—of an Earth- and human-centered universe. Considering the change, John Donne wailed:

... the new philosophy calls all in doubt,
The Element of fire is quite put out;
The Sun is lost, and th' earth, and no mans wit
Can well direct him where to looke for it.
'Tis all in peeces, all cohaerance gone;
All just supply, and all Relation.

(Even today, the human mind has not fully assimilated the Copernican Revolution.)[13]

The immense wealth of the New World eventually influenced the formation of novel social institutions: liberal democracy and its counterpart, private enterprise capitalism, and the belief after the French Revolution that the individual human being was the basic unit of society. These changes did not come abruptly, but developed slowly over decades and centuries. Nothing quite like them had ever been known before, not even in the so-called cradle of democracy, ancient Greece.

In many respects, the Industrial Revolution of the eighteenth and nineteenth centuries marked a major turning point in Western history. Why it came when and where it did is an unsolved mystery. The principle of steam power, central to the Industrial Revolution, was, after all, known but not used by both the ancient Greeks and the Chinese. Max Weber, the great German lawyer-sociologist, was the first to suggest that the Protestant Reformation, particularly Calvinism, was a major factor in the development of industrial capitalism.[14] Weber's hypothesis is still debated in academic circles, but is only of secondary interest here. The relationship between capitalism and Protestantism is of course an important question, even though it is one in which Weber failed to consider the impact of the Discoveries on the established order in Europe, especially England. The wealth of the Discoveries made it possible for the rise of the capitalistic spirit, which would otherwise have fallen on barren ground. This rise in turn led to the political forms given the name of liberal democracy and to the rise of the ideology of individualism. It became possible, for one brief historical moment and in one corner of the world, to think that the attainment of material riches could be the highest goal of human activity and the ultimate criterion of human success. This belief could only have been based upon knowledge that people would have access to sufficient material goods. The 400-year boom following the Discoveries opened new vistas for human endeavor.

Within two or three centuries after Columbus sailed west through un-
charted seas from the friendly shores of Spain, the intellectual framework
of European thought and action was completely altered. So, too, were the
underlying assumptions, the metaphysic, of society. Human life on Earth
became an end in itself, not a mere prelude to heaven or hell. People began
to think of the conquest of the world in human interest and of providing
for the good life on this planet, now, without reference to any hereafter.
The ideas of progress and of the perfectability of man flowered. Rather than
living in the final days before Armageddon, people began to see themselves
as taking part in a process of the progressive movement—the *improvement*—
of the human lot. They became optimistic, rather than having a somber
melancholy. No problem was considered to be insoluble; it was the humanistic vision that through applied reason people could know and solve
all difficulties. To be sure, not everyone so believed; the bulk of mankind
was still oppressed in one way or another. Consider, in this connection,
R. H. Tawney's comment: "Few who consider dispassionately the facts of
social history will be disposed to deny that the exploitation of the weak by
the powerful, organized for the purpose of economic gain, buttressed by
imposing systems of law, and screened by decorous draperies of virtuous
sentiment and resounding rhetoric, has been a permanent feature in the life
of most communities that the world has yet seen."[15] That comment applies
to the United States, yesterday and today.

The new intellectual climate spawned by the Discoveries was limited to
the people in positions of power and their *apparatchiks* in academia and
the churches. What is quite remarkable was the ability of those rulers to
convince the bulk of the people, through their opinions, that the system
was of general benefit. Those in effective control of the constitutional order
have long been able to generate a broad base of popular support. They want
it that way. As Max Weber remarked, privileged groups have the ability
and the need to have "their social and economic positions 'legitimized'."
They wish to see their positions transformed from a purely factual power
relation into a cosmos of acquired rights, and to know that they are thus
sanctified." The person of position and wealth is seldom satisfied with merely
being fortunate. He realizes that if his property is to be secure it must have
legitimacy in society. The man of fortune, therefore, needs to know that he
"has a *right* to his good fortune. He wants to be convinced that he 'deserves'
it, and above all, that he deserves it in comparison with others. He wishes
to be allowed the belief that the less fortunate also merely experience their
due."[16] That the moneyed and propertied have been successful in this desire
is quite evident.

What the elite and their intellectual peers believe is transmitted to the
populace by several means. Each is important: the public school system,
which not only provides a pool of trained labor for the industrial system
but also indoctrinates the students in the values of corporate capitalism and

Americanism; the mass media of communication—the television networks, the major newspapers and news magazines—have as their principal social function that of convincing the populace to accept those same values; and, of greatest importance, the civil or secular religion of Americanism, which breeds a nationalistic fervor and, among other things, views the formal constitution as a sacred icon.

These are powerful instruments of propaganda and thus of mind control. It matters little whether they are employed deliberately, with full knowledge of the consequences, or whether they just happened—the result is the same. What does matter is that each vehicle, plus a fourth, repression, furthers the goals of America's elite. It should, however, be emphasized that very little "just happens" in the social order. When one asks the essential question—who benefits from social institutions?—and then determines the actual or hidden beneficiaries, as well as the manifest or obvious ones, of those programs, surely it is accurate to conclude that the techniques of bending the populace to elitist values is not happenstance.

The principal point, however, is that the worldview of Westerners changed from faith in a human-like God to faith in scientists and technicians, who were (and are) assumed to be wise and known to be powerful, that is, capable of producing technological fixes to ameliorate social problems. Thus far at least, those new objects of worship have had enormous success. Inventions have so transformed the environment that the planet bears little resemblance to that which existed only a little more than a hundred years ago. Today, humanity lives in a largely synthetic ecosystem created by science and technology. There should be small wonder, accordingly, that, to some, science has become an endless frontier, fully capable of replacing the world frontier that opened for the West after the Great Discoveries. But the price is becoming too high, and thus hard thought is required to develop ways and means of alleviating the pernicious effects of some scientific-technological changes (for example, the unleashed atom).

A new worldview has become dominant. Newtonian principles of balance have replaced the Ptolemaic Earth- and man-centered (the anthropocentric) universe. Newton's influence may be seen in the checks and balances of the formal constitution, reliance on the market and Adam Smith's "invisible hand" in economics, and the emergence of pluralism as the principal political theory. Pluralism is Adam Smith economics writ large and transferred to politics. Decentralized groups compete within the United States; their competition is believed (by many) in some magical way to redound to the general welfare. It was, and still is, a mechanistic conception of social reality. Today, much of the thinking in politics and economics still accepts the Newtonian belief-system, particularly as it was put into philosophical discourse by René Descartes; that is so even though it has been largely supplanted by Darwinian ideas of process and Einsteinian ideas of relativity. Even though for a time it served a useful purpose, and still does, save in politics and economics, and is not erroneous so far as it goes in the physical world, Newtonianism has been outmoded, perhaps dangerously so, insofar as constitutionalism is concerned. During the period of the greatest social impact of the Discoveries, Newton and Descartes seemed to be eminently sensible. They still are to some degree, but now they should be perceived as not so much wrong as disastrously incomplete.

To summarize: what are considered to be natural institutions today—"democracy" and corporate capitalism—were in fact derivative from the Great Discoveries and the principles of Newtonian celestial mechanics. Such a statement cannot, of course, be empirically proved, for no data exist to do so. And it would be far too simplistic to assign a unilinear cause-and-effect relationship to any present-day social phenomenon. Nonetheless, it is certain that prior to the Discoveries the so-called natural political and economic institutions did not exist; and further, after the domestic and world frontiers closed some time this century, those institutions seem to have run their course.

If the wealth and land of the Discoveries did precipitate a boom in European societies, and altered social institutions that had existed for millenia, the boom lasted for not more than 400 years. Frederick Jackson Turner first noted the importance of the American frontier and its closure in an influential essay published in 1920.[17] He was updated by Walter Prescott Webb in 1952, who expanded Turner's insight to the world frontier that followed the Discoveries.[18] Both frontiers, and especially their end, have had and are having important consequences for the American political and economic orders. When their ends came, not later than 1890 for the United States and some time in this century for the world, it was a slow decline, not a bang, that saw the movement of politico-economic institutions into new patterns. The old forms have remained the same, outwardly at least, but their content has been greatly altered. Henry George once observed that it was "an axiom of statesmanship" that "great changes can be brought about under old forms."[19] He should have written that great changes *are* brought about under old forms, for that is exactly what occurred in the American constitutional system. We are now able to see that the normality of nineteenth-century constitutional history was in fact an abnormality, an aberration, a brief moment in historical time when the values of liberal democracy and its economic twin, private enterprise capitalism, were able to obtain at least a partial hearing.

Reality is fast changing. We are witnessing a reversion to a variation on the theme of pre-Columbian Europe. We are entering an age of neofeudalism, with the feudal units being giant corporations rather than the patches of land over which the original feudal lords reigned.[20] The boom is over. The ecological trap is once again closing. Only the impact of new technologies has kept it from snapping shut. Although some disagree, those technologies seem to have about reached the end of the technically possible.

There will be new gadgets, to be sure, but technicians will increasingly be confined to refining what they now have or what is on the drawing boards. (In this sense, genetic engineering is the ultimate technological fix.) It is worth emphasis, however, that technicians have barely begun to function with regard to the planned application of social technologies that have the common good as a primary goal. Some primitive types of social technologies are being employed, as was noted above, but only for the strictly limited purpose of socializing the populace to the norms of corporate capitalism. This is far from enough, either as technique or as goal.

Giant forces are loose in the world today. An immense literature chronicles the slowing of economic growth, an explosion in population, and the decline of Western global dominance. Empires have crumbled. Attempts to create new ones are stoutly and even violently resisted. No new empires are likely. Imperialism as it was known is dead, replaced by the economic imperialism of multinational corporations that have spread worldwide to develop a global economy. (Much of American foreign policy in this century was aimed at protecting the interests of those companies, which are identified with the American national interest.) The planet has splintered politically. United Nations membership today is more than 300 percent higher than in 1945 when the UN was created. Powerful nations, however, really do not want colonies as such, for colonization implies at least a measure of responsibility and duty as well as of rights. The nations strive instead for spheres of influence and the economic imperialism of the supercorporations. That is so even though many corporations no longer identify with nation-states— thus creating a growing constitutional problem.

A global economy, dominated by corporate behemoths, now sits astride an almost completely decentralized political system. This is both bad and good—bad in the sense that corporate managers are able to manipulate one country against others in their never-ceasing search for maximum profits; good in the sense that, just as happened in the United States during the past century, a social basis for political multinationalism and perhaps even of globalism is being created. A cardinal question of American constitutionalism today is how to evaluate the relationship of the United States to the other nations and how to effect webs of community with them. The supercorporations make up one such "private" web.

One large fact must be added: "The natives are restless."[21] They are on the march the world over, no longer being willing to settle for only the crumbs that fall from the groaning tables of opulence of the "rich-man's club" of Western Europe and the United States. Long-submerged peoples demand more *now*. They want a fair share of the world's bounty. If that be materialistic, who can blame them? They have done without for millenia, and they have had good teachers in materialism in the affluent West. By any criterion of rudimentary justice, they have a valid claim to a more equitable share.

But their efforts are resisted, often brutally. (Witness Central America today). This resistance, as Tawney wrote, has been true throughout known human history. One basic difference, however, may exist today: the poor may not be so easily suppressed. Instant communication brings to them awareness of the material plenty of the rich-man's club. The poor are increasingly unwilling to settle for less because they believe that they should— they can, with effort and struggle—get more. Domestic and global economies may have become zero-sum games, but the demands for equality of condition as well as of opportunity grow ever more insistent. As they should: it is absurd for anyone, anywhere, to go hungry today or not to have his basic needs met. But more than 800 million humans are now in that status.

"Slaveship Earth" is replacing Spaceship Earth. The Reverend Thomas Malthus was correct: population does outrun food supply—but under *existing institutions only*. Institutional alteration would help to rectify this dreary situation. A finite world, with finite resources and employing present methods of operation, does not seem to have enough to go around. That is not really true: the appearance beclouds a starker reality—a massive institutional breakdown.[22] If humans had the wit and will to do the necessary, the needs of people everywhere could be satisfied. The know-how is available, the technology feasible. There *is* enough to go around, but the will is lacking. To locate enough and trigger it would require major institutional and value changes.

Recall, in this connection, George Orwell's biting comment about the British ruling class being wicked or merely stupid. Alter Orwell to read: "Whether the ruling elites of the rich-man's club ...," and one gets the picture today. Whether today's rulers are wicked or stupid is difficult to determine, but surely it is important to know. Greed and selfishness characterize corporate capitalism, evidencing that the ideals of the formal constitution are not being followed. This may well be a fatal human flaw. Something quite fundamental is out of kilter: Reality does not comport with our pretenses. The obvious failure to satisfy the minimum requirements of the world's peoples, including those below the poverty line in the United States, in final anaysis is a cultural refusal of people in power to know where their own long-term interests lie and to act accordingly. The have-nots are not forever going to live submarginally, at the edge of starvation or even in conditions of starvation.

Leaders in the rich-man's club, public and private (corporate), are all too willing to settle for short-term gains. They sarcastically ask not only what has posterity done for them, but also what have the poor and the wretched in this and other lands done for them? Why, they demand, should I share my bounty, or, better, why should I be interested in reorganizing the political economy—the constitutional order—to consider the needs of generations yet unborn and the world's have-nots? Let them, whether in the future or today, fend for themselves, is their reply.

Answers are easily found to such questions and attitudes. Those in positions of power in politics and economics are simply too stupid to realize that in an age of rapid social change, *they are their own posterity*. They do not comprehend that it is not their children or their children's children about whom they should be concerned, but they, themselves, the ostensibly sovereign individuals standing all alone and increasingly afraid in a world they never made. Never before in human history could such a statement be made. As with posterity, so too with the poor refuse of this and other lands; their demands, their minimum needs, will find expression and possible fulfillment in one way or another. They inevitably will press ever harder against the bastions of wealth and privilege.

Whether the rulers are also wicked poses other questions. If they are, and there is much evidence so to conclude, then they will not care about posterity, even including themselves, and certainly not the progeny of others. They will continue to settle for immediate short-term gains and will simultaneously attempt to ruthlessly suppress any discontent that crops up. The signs of such repression are already evident the world over, not excluding the United States.[23]

Given a choice between stupidity and wickedness, we should hope that it is the former. Even a stupid person is capable of some learning and can be compassionate, but a wicked person is evil and uncaring. (All too many political leaders today exhibit what may be called the smiling face of evil. Writing about Adolf Eichmann, Hannah Arendt described what she called "the banality of evil"—which was true enough.[24] But evil has other faces: "The new face of evil—blandly ordinary, commonplace, sincere—is not even a mask: for no mask is needed where there is nothing to hide, no guilt or shame, no awareness of guilt.")[25] We must, I believe, assume that humans are wicked by nature, and move from there. All history buttresses that conclusion. During the seventeenth and eighteenth centuries, "the theme of man's irrationality and especially of his *inner* corruption was no longer a speciality of divines; it became for a time one of the favorite topics of secular literature."[26] The men who wrote the formal constitution were fully aware of that corruption. Their remedy was to establish a system of checks and balances and (apparently) to allow people maximum freedom. The trouble with that solution is that, to paraphrase Thucydides, it permitted the strong and powerful to do what they wished, while the weak and powerless had to suffer what they must. The system guaranteed rule by the powerful. Two centuries later, the problems of governance remain the same but the fundamental question has become one of how to devise a governmental structure that will affirmatively help fulfill basic human needs. No government— no constitution—has yet attempted that massive task, but it must be done, and soon. This will of course require that the wicked (by definition) must, when they acquire power, be convinced in some way that it is in *their* own interests to help satisfy the needs of others.

How, then, to move? The challenge is staggering. When (if) an answer comes, it must be on three levels of inquiry. First, wickedness or evil in humans must be credibly explained, accompanied by suggestions for adequate ways to overcome it. Second, the goals of society as well as those of individuals must be articulated with clarity. And third, there must be a demonstration of the essential unity of mankind and nature and of the sense of intimacy with the cosmos. Religion was the vehicle by which these tasks were once accomplished, however imperfectly; but it is no longer sufficient to the need. Formal religion has evolved into a sterile form of superstition (even though tens of millions of Americans are nominal church members). All that is really available now is a primitive social technology and the artifact of the formal constitution. That's not much, and likely will not be enough to do the necessary.

[This generation of Americans is therefore confronted with a truly awesome task: how to deal effectively and fairly with the imperatives derived from the end of the 400-year boom and the coming of a global society. They can no longer rest content, secure in the belief that their political and economic institutions are up to the mark. They emphatically are not.]

[Representative democracy is not an accurate description of today's political order. Although propaganda sedulously spread in high school civics texts and by politicians in banal electoral campaigns pretend otherwise, popular sovereignty does not exist in the United States. This truth is seen, for example, in the operation of the iron triangles in Washington, D.C. As primary institutions of the secret constitution, they make a mockery out of the popular wisdom about representation and policy making. Nameless and faceless non-elected bureaucrats, public and private, couple with members of Congress (all too often, the members's nameless and faceless non-elected aides), striking compromises and coming up with proposed policies. Congress routinely rubberstamps those decisions. In all of this, the individual is lost.]

So, too, in economics: The consumer is not sovereign but is prey to the decisions made in corporate boardrooms about prices, investments, plant locations, and similar matters. The American economy is dominated by huge corporate combines that could not have been even remotely in the minds of the framers. In most industries, oligopolies control—as in automobiles, steel, petroleum, communications, and numerous others. Supposedly competitive companies in fact cooperate, at least subtly. Despite contrary rhetoric, the businessman fears competition and seeks to avoid it.

[As a consequence, the individual human being amounts to little or nothing in modern America. Politically and economically impotent, subject to an unceasing barrage of propaganda, he is the victim in law to the power of collectivities, both public and private. The core legal principle of a free enterprise system is contract, which in theory is an agreement between persons of approximately equal bargaining power. In fact, the natural person deals with corporations as a distinct inferior. Most agreements people conclude are not true contracts at all, because of the wide disparity in bargaining power. They are contracts of "adhesion"; one adheres to the terms of a sale or service on a take-it-or-leave-it basis. If taken, the agreement is usually on the company's terms, using standardized, preprinted forms. Reject it and go elsewhere, and the certain result is similar treatment from some other company. We live in a bureaucratized society and must of necessity deal with bureaucrats.

Thus individualism, as John D. Rockefeller noted at the beginning of the century,[27] is dead—as ideology, as political force, as economic entity, as the basis of private law. Replacing it is something that at times is called *communitarianism*.[28] Personal freedom is increasingly becoming freedom in a social organization, one that among other things helps to give identity to people. We are reverting to a form of feudalism, one in which status is again becoming more important than contract. The lone individual does not exist in family relations, neighborhood relations, state relations, social relations, or in the higher values of religion. Nowhere is the natural person left without guiding social groups, personalities, and principles. The individual spends his life as a member of a group or groups and is significant only in that way. Even Ralph Nader, the quintessential individualist, has now become a bureaucracy. Save for a very few, such as hermits, the autonomous person does not exist as such. This may be the hardest lesson that must be learned about life in the latter part of the twentieth century. The institutions characteristic of the 400-year boom have rapidly changed in substance, though not in form and certainly not in the rhetoric.

There is still another dimension to the end of the boom. We—all of humanity—are in a predicament, complicated and perplexing and novel. Less than 5,000 years after known Western history began, the "thinking reed" that is man has so managed to foul his own nest that it could become unlivable. Humans, as Dr. Harrison Brown has pointed out, are confronted with a number of terrible vulnerabilities.[29] Nuclear warfare grows ever more probable, and with it the end of civilization and perhaps of all life. A population explosion has occurred: five billion people now throng the planet, which is rapidly beginning to resemble a human anthill. By the year 2000, there will be more than six billion people. This will place intolerable strains upon time-honored ways of conducting affairs. If our institutions cannot really cope now, they will become bankrupt in the next quarter-century. The redundancy of workers is a problem: people in increasing numbers now face the terminal sense of the loss of work itself, and with it the loss of personal identity. Work has been central to the human condition for eons, but now many of the growing population are surplus to the needs

of the economy. The problem of mass higher education confronts us: an ⟨8–9⟩
educated *lumpenproletariat* is being produced, many of whom will surely
have dashed expectations.⟂

The inevitable consequence of these problems is a high potential for social
turmoil. Increasing demands for at least a rough equality of both opportunity
and condition add to the pressures. But such demands butt heads with the
idea of social limits to economic growth, a fact too little recognized. There
are some valued things, as the late Fred Hirsch showed,[30] that are in such
short supply that everyone's wishes cannot be satisfied. A caste system,
domestically and globally, means an enlarging chasm between the rich and
the poor. A runaway technology, has far too many unanticipated "second-
order" consequences.

All of these situations, and more, add up to the human predicament. The
vulnerabilities listed need not be documented here, for each is the subject
of a large and growing literature. Little, however, is being done, which
denotes a massive constitutional breakdown. Some scholars do not accept
the implications. Professor Julian Simon is one such person; he believes that
the idea of population overload is poppycock, asserting that people are "the
ultimate resource"—and the more the better.[31] Jonathan Swift, who satir-
ically advocated eating babies as a way of curbing population pressure in
Ireland, would have loved Simon.

Yes, an historical epoch has ended, and this generation must deal with
its implications. That the efforts made thus far are far too feeble is the
central theme of the next chapter.

CHAPTER 3

A SOCIETAL NERVOUS BREAKDOWN?

This is a new time in human affairs.... Our world is no longer the world into which we were born.... One great uncertainty of the future is its uncertainty.... What is new is that we have lost the option of ignoring our interdependent state—of ignoring the reality that we have become one world.

—Shridith Ramphal[1]

Americans—people the world over—may be careening toward a societal nervous breakdown.

Technology is out of control. No one seems to be able to tame it, and few wish to curb it.

The political system called pluralism is in disarray, increasingly unable to cope with a wide range of policy problems.

The economy stutters along. Trade-offs between inflation and unemployment grow more intolerable for the nation's growing ranks of the unemployable.

No one quite knows how to solve the long-term energy problem, the promise of unlimited energy from nuclear fission now having become dubious.

Environmental degradation continues almost unabated.

No one seems to know, and few appear to care, where society is headed—or should head. The old order is crumbling. But that idea is resisted, as something alien or even faintly subversive. Like Victorian maidens tubbing in their nightgowns, people generally are enveloped in a counterpane of faith that something will turn up to solve all human problems. There is a comparable faith in the arcane powers of technicians, who have replaced kings and priests as objects of awe and reverence.

Sixty years ago, at a time when fascism was coming to Europe, William Butler Yeats foresaw with uncanny prescience the shape of things present and things to come. He knew that a form of anarchy was on the loose, with the best people lacking all conviction and the worst filled with passionate intensity.[2] That anarchy deteriorated into fascism, which was, and is, the final solution of corporate capitalism to threats to its predominance. Yeats also anticipated what has become obvious today—that the cupboard of ideas is bare. Little, almost nothing, is forthcoming from the nation's intellectuals, whose ideas have divided into dozens of rivulets; in some areas, the mainstream of ideas has dried up altogether. We have thus reached a condition described by biologist and social critic Paul Ehrlich:

> If we do not soon get population growth under control; do not start to close the rich-poor gap; do not make substantial progress toward ridding the planet of such scourges as racism, sexism, and religious prejudice; do not cease the extermination of other life forms and learn to live with nature rather than trying to conquer it; then present trends will simply take us in 50 to 150 years where nuclear war could take us in 50 to 150 minutes. Ending the nuclear madness is the first step, but it is only the first step.[3]

Those trends are the focus of this chapter. In sum, they are the bane of uncontrolled technology and the social disease of factionalism.

Americans have a long-standing love affair with technology. They even invented the art of invention, perhaps the most important development of all.

Many benefits have been reaped: the level of material plenty, increased longevity, decline or eradication of some diseases, reduced hours of work, household conveniences, heat and light and air-conditioning to alleviate the discomforts of winter and summer, instant communication and rapid transportation are among the most obvious. All are familiar, and few wish to forgo them. Nonetheless, a haunting question must be posed and answered: do many technological advances—what some call progress—come at too high a price? Have unanticipated second-order consequences of some new technologies brought the nation and the world, as Ehrlich implies, to the brink of "doomsday"? Has humankind made a Faustian bargain with technology?[4]

Both the 400-year boom and the technological revolution, which occurred at roughly the same time, have exacted high prices. The boom enabled all people to believe that they, too, could share in Earth's bounty—which of course is all right but which requires, for its realization, rethinking of familiar institutions and practices. Unleashing atomic power was a tremendous technological feat, but it brought probable nuclear war as well as the as yet unsolved problem of dispensing with growing amounts of nuclear waste that will be lethal for 500,000 years. Perhaps the greatest price is the subtle intellectual one of the need for a fundamental paradigm shift, a basic alteration in deepset belief-systems. The dominant social belief-system of a given time is the fundamental way of seeing and thinking, of valuing and doing, based upon a specific view of reality. This is to be contrasted with physical belief-systems, such as those of Ptolemy and Newton, that sought to explain the material world. The concern here is with social affairs, although it is accurate to say that physical belief-systems (paradigms) can have spillovers into social affairs. Thomas Paine, the propagandist of the American revolution, is an example; he was greatly influenced by Newtonian views of the cosmos.

In the modern age, the dominant belief-system has these characteristics: industrialization as an ultimate good (no one has ever explained how the entire world can be industrialized); the scientific method as the means of ascertaining truth (which limits the human mind: truth is more than the product of laboratories); material advancement as the end of societal behavior (this is consumerism run amok); and the pragmatic temper regnant as the principal engine of social action. This mind-set has obvious shortcomings (some of which have been previously mentioned). The difference between the older belief-system and the new one may be simply stated. Within the relatively brief period of a few centuries the people's interest shifted from the inner world to the outer world; and all except one of the seven deadly sins—sloth—was transmuted into a virtue. Greed, avarice, envy, gluttony, luxury, and pride characterized and drove the new economy. A new society came into being, one in which new sources of power were closely linked to newly developed appetites. Neither government nor the church nor any other institution stemmed the tide. The consequence today is a congeries of steadily worsening public policy problems. Consider the following:

- public health measures that both reduce infant mortality and increase the life spans of people: This development has led to exponential population growth, which in turn places unbearable strains on both resources and politico-economic institutions.

- splitting the atom, followed by the hydrogen bomb: These actions have brought the threat of mass destruction, even the end of civilization, rather than enhanced personal and national security.

- greatly improved communication and transportation systems: The consequence is a shrinking planet, a global city (not, as Marshall McLuhan said, a global village), in which political volatility is the norm. Among other things, this development means that wars are more and more civil wars, which, with religious wars, are the bloodiest of all.

- environmental degradation: New methods of production, such as strip-mining coal, and the spoliation of croplands and tropical forests, have resulted in unknown impacts upon the world's climate.
- automation and robotics: These developments create monotonous and dehumanizing jobs. Even worse, they eliminate the need for much human labor. Mass man has become obsolescent, at precisely the time that population growth, in many parts of the world, seems to be out of control.

The list is not endless, but it is significant. The new social belief-system has manifest shortcomings, as Thomas Henry Huxley observed in 1876 when Philadelphia celebrated the centennial of the Declaration of Independence: "I cannot say that I am in the slightest degree impressed by your bigness or your material resources, as such. Size is not grandeur, and territory does not make a nation. The great issue, about which hangs a true sublimity, and the terror of overhanging fate, is what are you going to do with all these things."[5] What, indeed? A century later the question is even more portentous. Americans, however, have made their choice: they wish to expand on the "things" that perturbed Huxley. We worship today at the temple of technology, which is perceived as a god from which all material blessings flow. "You can't stop progress," the refrain goes with nauseating repetition. What is technologically possible will be done, and will be used, has been and is the law of American life.

That law is simply not enough, as anyone should be able to plainly see. Technological successes are both boon and (increasingly) bane. Technology must be tamed and harnessed if ever we are to achieve a sustainable society. Several fundamental failures of the modern dominant social belief-system may be identified.

Every person is not provided with an opportunity to contribute to the social good and to be affirmed by society in return. More and more people are surplus to the needs of the economy (which is central to the constitutional order). The median age of Americans creeps upward, which means that many older people do not die when others—the producers—think they should. The dreary fact is that we simply do not need much of the marginal labor—the young, the old, the uneducated, the stupid, as well as those who still fall outside the bounds of complete social acceptability (the blacks, for certain, and perhaps other ethnic groups as well). Although not so in ideology, the economy is Marxist in that it is characterized by economic determinism. The American businessman is a closet socialist, provided, of course, that socialist programs aid him (as they always have). The underclass is large and growing, a condition far from likely to change, which means that its members will exist merely on the periphery of society.

Power and justice are inequitably distributed. So, what else is new? might be the response to this. It has always been so, despite the myth to the contrary. The political, economic, and legal systems are skewed in favor of those who already have power and position. The disparity between those with power and wealth and those who do not have either was at least partially checked in the past by the opportunities brought by the 400-year boom, by a tradition of consequent social mobility, and by regulatory measures that helped to siphon off discontent. None, however, was significantly redistributive. The point is that all societies are oligarchically controlled. The oligarchy may be an elected one, as in the United States, but once in power the wishes of the majority of the people recede. As this volume is being written, Congress has authorized an undeclared war against Nicaragua—a surrogate war—even though the majority of Americans oppose the policy. This is not a new development; it has a long history, as Walter Karp has demonstrated, running at least as far back as the Spanish-American War.[6]

Technology is socially irresponsible. An unwritten but dominant postulate of the prevailing social belief-system is the idea that technology should be developed whenever someone can make a profit or whenever some new device can contribute to the nation's war-making capacity. Whatever is technologically possible will—nay, *should*—be done is the controlling principle. A physical principle—that something *can* be done—is therefore magically transmuted into a normative precept: it *should* be done. We thus are unthinking slaves of our own tools. Emerson was correct when he observed that things are in the saddle and ride mankind. The negative effects of new technologies are among the commonplaces of the day, but little and often nothing is being done about them. Technology is out of control, careening us toward some sort of "doomsday." "No one—not even the most brilliant scientist alive today—really knows where science is taking us. We are aboard a train which is gathering speed, racing down a track on where there are an unknown number of switches leading to unknown destinations. No single scientist is in the engine and there may be demons at the switch. Most of society is in the caboose looking backward."[7] The American constitutional order does not hold technicians to standards of public accountability. They moil away in their laboratories with little regard for the consequences of their inventions. This is so even though it must be emphasized that scientists and technicians are mere mercenaries in the battle of life. The technical elite is subordinate to the business elite. Our legal and political systems ensure that.

Goals beyond materialism and consumerism are not engendered. These goals are far from enough. The dominant social belief-system has largely solved many of the country's know-how questions but has yet to address the question of *what is worth doing.* We have a habit and a politics of greed and selfishness. "I'm all right, Jack" is the ruling maxim of those with material plenty, who command those who do not have it to pull themselves by their bootstraps and get it. Few think beyond the immediate and the personal; most Americans do not realize that we are all part of the "family of man," a family that is all in the same leaky planetary lifeboat and will sink or float together. The boat today is adrift, without sail or rudder or compass.

"Oneness" with nature is not inculcated. Since ancient Greece and Rome, humans have looked upon nature as something to be exploited without regard to consequences. This is a certain road to disaster. Humankind has yet to learn that it is not the master of all things. The dominant Judeo-Christian ethic derives from Aristotle, who observed that "plants were created for the sake of animals, and the animals for the sake of man"; and from Cicero, who maintained that humans are "absolute masters of what the world produces."[8] These long-held beliefs now pervade all of human society. They are dangerous to a high degree. Westerners for certain, and people elsewhere as well, do not identify with the environment, but seek to conquer and subdue it. We have not learned to respect and preserve the stability of natural ecosystems. This is a route that cannot be long continued, as Paul Ehrlich has shown.

Personal privacy is either dead or dying. Technological gimmickry has produced highly sophisticated surveillance techniques. There is no escape from them, nowhere to run and hide that is safe from their intrusions. Everyone today is an "actor"; when he enters a bank, a shopping mall, a subway, and perhaps even a public bathroom, he likely performs before an unknown and unseen audience. Data banks store the life histories and records of tens of millions of Americans. The United States has become a "dossier" society. Personal privacy, the central core of individual freedom and liberty, has become the victim of the technological age. Industrialized societies increasingly resemble giant computers, programmed by technicians who are the servants of those who wield real and effective political power. As Max Weber forecast, society has become rationalized and bureaucratized. This is spiritual death: "Specialists without spirit, sensualists without heart, this nullity [society] imagines that it has attained a level of civilization never before attained."[9] By making a Faustian bargain with technology, humans have sold their souls for material plenty. They have become the tool of their tools.

Today, however, there seems to be a dawning realization that every inventor opens Pandora's box with unknown consequences. But this result does not seem to perturb many Americans. In a famous expression, Karl Marx maintained that religion was the opiate of the masses. Today, this has changed: technology has become the opiate of both the masses and the educated public. Society may function like a "megamachine," as Lewis Mumford observed,[10] but few seem to care.

There is more. At the very time that humans cannot seem to cope adequately with the harmful side effects of physical technologies, the specter of greatly improved techniques of social technology looms ever larger on the horizon. We are already well into the age of biotechnology, of what Nobel Laureate Joshua Lederberg calls "algeny"[11]—changing the nature or essence of living things, including humans, through chemical and other means. The alchemist of the Middle Ages tried unsuccessfully to transform base metals into gold. The algenist of tomorrow will not suffer a similar fate. He will be able to "engineer" human beings, using ony present knowledge, such as recombinant DNA, which as Professor Ira Carmen has shown, both permits genetic engineering and poses difficult constitutional questions of its regulation.[12] Genetic engineers will employ "psychotropic drugs, aversive conditioning, electronic surveillance, Skinnerian behavior modification, and the collection, processing, and the use of personal information to institutionalize people outside the walls of institutions";[13] all of this, of course, in addition to recombinant DNA. The ideologist for this development is already in place: he is Professor B. F. Skinner, whose goal is the creation of "predictable" man, a person who conceives of freedom in Hegelian terms—doing what one is supposed to do. Skinner's *Walden Two* is a fictionalized account of the world he foresees—and desires.[14]

There is a large meaning in this for law and for constitutions. Technology is Janus-like. Its undoubted merits are matched, and perhaps exceeded, by its dark side. Science and technology are slowly, subtly, and "humanely" repealing the formal constitution. Millions of Americans are being subjected, without their knowledge or consent, to behavior modification and control through the use of law and the legal process for what is said to be the highest good: the welfare of a disembodied entity called society. A person's name has in substantial part become a number—his social security number—as Gian Carlo Menotti foresaw in *The Consul*. In all of this, the hidden side is who controls and who benefits most from society, hidden in the sense that the ultimate controllers and beneficiaries are able to define the axiomatic in public discourse and justify their privileged positions without serious dissent.

Were that all, the challenge to the human spirit would be daunting. But there is more, more that leads with seeming inevitability to a societal nervous breakdown. The cruel fact that time-honored institutions are in disarray has already been noted—they cannot ensure peace, control population, solve poverty, eradicate pollution, or tame technology. Something quite basic is out of kilter. An apt label for this increasingly perilous political condition is "factionalism," which exists on two levels—nationally (the relations of the United States to other nations) and domestically.

The United States was born at a time when nationalism began to be a sentiment that molded public and private life. It has since become one of the great determining factors of history. For about fifteen centuries after the life of Christ, the ideal in the Western world was of a universal world state. Politics and economics and religion were closely tied together. But simultaneously with the 400-year boom, the ideal was lost; its last vestige was the so-called Holy Roman Empire (which, as it often said, was neither holy nor Roman nor an empire). The nation-state emerged as the characteristic form of political order. Political power, rather than being divinely inspired, was said to emanate from the people as a body corporate. Popular sovereignty became a unifying slogan, even though little credence was given to it in fact. Then and today, it is a mere hortatory shibboleth without real content. It gives people the appearance of governing without the reality.

Nationalism today is a primitive type of tribalism; as such it is a positive barrier to decent and effective government. Why that is so cannot be neatly summarized. One reason surely is the religious fervor that surrounds the nation-state. The nation has replaced the church as the object of reverence and awe—seen, for example, in the outpourings of emotion that were displayed when the Iranian hostages returned in 1981 and that peaked in the summer 1984 Olympic Games. Patriotism has become a form of piety. The death of God may have been the foremost intellectual event of the nineteenth and early twentieth centuries, but since people seem to require something larger than themselves to be able to confront the vasty universe, the old-time fundamentalist faith has been succeeded by the civil or secular religion of nationalism. Some religious fundamentalists, such as Jerry Falwell and Pat Robertson, have merged their fundamentalism with nationalism.

In the United States, nationalism and localism have always been in tension. The question of whether America was truly a united state was not definitively answered until the Civil War had been fought and won on pure nationalistic grounds. By no means was that answer clear in 1789. But the nationalizing decisions of the Supreme Court in the early nineteenth century, joined by the unifying forces of modern technology, made the ultimate result inevitable. The Civil War merely settled on the battlefield what had been begun by business enterprise and new technologies. The organizing principle was, and still is, hierarchy. Technology leads to the consolidation of power. Federalism gave way to centralism, both in government and in business; a situation not at all likely to change.

It is far different in what at times is called the world community, where some 160 nation-states are now members of the United Nations. Federation, when present, is on ideological rather than geographical grounds, as in the North Atlantic Treaty Organization and the Soviet bloc. The centripetal force of political development in the United States is matched by a centrifugal force among nations. The European Common Market is the only true exception to that general rule.

Nationalism is both a religion and a disease. The United States, the nation with the soul of a church, has a national civil religion that is more widespread and more significant than orthodox sects. It has its hymns (anthems) and its sacred rituals (Thanksgiving Day, Law Day, Independence Day), and it has its prophets in those called (with overweening piety) the Founding

Fathers and its martyrs in Lincoln and Kennedy. (Strangely, no one remembers the other presidents who were assassinated—Garfield and McKinley.) The United States' mission has long thought to be special; as John Adams once stated: "I always consider the settlement of America as the opening of a grand scheme by Providence for the illumination of the ignorant and the emancipation of the slavish part of mankind all over the earth."[15] Some *chutzpah*, one might say, but Adams's creedal passion was and is the prevailing American ideology.

The state has thus become the religion; and although there is a separation of *church* and state in America (although less so than many realize), *religion* and the state have close and continuing connections. Ideological passions of one nation are matched by those of others—to the extent that nationalism may truly be called a pathological condition. Lord Acton was on the mark when he wrote that "the theory of nationality . . . is a retrograde step in history."[16] The creedal passions that swirl around nationalism make warfare all but certain. Nor is that all, as the Brandt Commission observed in 1983:

> The international community has made little headway in tackling its most serious problems—which began in the strained system of international economic relations and result in additional burdens on many developing countries. Prospects for the future are alarming. Increased global uncertainties have reduced expectations of economic growth even more, and the problem of managing the international imbalances of payments is increasing the threat of grave crises in international finance. *We have serious doubts as to whether the existing world machinery can cope with these imbalances and the management of world liquidity and debt.*[17]

The "world machinery" is the nation-state system, the cobbled-up multilateral arrangements created since 1945, and the activities—the *unregulated* activities—of multinational corporations.

The Brandt Commission stated the obvious: the economic and monetary system is not working properly (except for a relative few in the rich-man's club). The so-called Bretton Woods institutions—the International Monetary Fund and the World Bank—have become means by which the rich-man's club can retain its superiority and cream off the bulk of the world's wealth. They no longer suffice. New vision is required to plan and manage the future, a global vision that will transcend national boundaries and eliminate the poison of nationalistic "solutions." Self-interest must, if humans are to survive, be replaced by a concept of mutuality of interests, of meaningful cooperation among all the world's peoples. Nationalism is not only a retrograde step in history; it is fraught with such manifest dangers that it should be seen as a dangerous social disease.

The same may be said—perhaps doubly so—about domestic factionalism. Social groups, mainly economic, are dominant within the United States. By the prevailing political theory of pluralism, the groups interact and produce both the parochial good of the groups involved and the overall common good. The theory does not wash, as many political scientists now acknowledge—even though they have not come up with a viable replacement. Even Yale's Professor Robert Dahl, long an advocate of pluralism, has now concluded that the defects of the system are beginning to outweigh supposed benefits.[18] Pluralism has brought unjust inequalities among the people, the promotion of narrow interests by groups at the expense of the broader general good, a distortion of the public agenda (the way policies are made), and private control of public affairs. So says Dahl; his point is best seen in the growth of the supercorporations, which are both economic enterprises and political systems dependent upon the social order for their very existence. They are, in fact, public entities that ought to be governed in the same way as avowedly public organs.

The self-regulating market economy does not exist today; indeed, it never did save in the fantasies of some economists and the rhetoric of Chambers of Commerce. Corporate giants bear only a transitory and illusory resemblance to the comparatively tiny, competitive firms that under classical economic theory were subject to market forces. The "invisible hand" extolled by Adam Smith two centuries ago may have had some credence in the America of that time, when corporations were few and quite small, but it simply does not exist in modern corporate capitalism. The portents are constitutionally significant, as Professor Grant McConnell commented:

A substantial part of government in the United States has come under the influence or control of narrowly based and largely autonomous elites. These elites do not act cohesively with each other on many issues. They do not "rule" in the sense of commanding the entire nation. Quite the contrary, they tend to pursue a policy of noninvolvement in the large issues of statesmanship save where such issues touch their own particular concerns. . . . The distinction between public and private has been compromised far more deeply than we like to acknowledge. . . . The very idea of constitutionalism sometimes seems to be placed in question.[19]

McConnell surely was correct. To state his point in another way, factionalism has become the most corrosive pathology of the internal American constitutional order.

Factionalism thus is a social disease of the first magnitude, perhaps the most dangerous to the spirit and values of the formal constitution that exists today. Factionalism within the United States is matched by a like factionalism (nationalism) in the global order. Factionalism has direct and significant impacts upon the position of industrialized nations. Networks of collusive, cartelistic, and lobbying organizations are formed. Their consequence is inefficient economies and a growing ungovernability in politics.[20]

None of the framers foresaw such a development. The fifty-five men (at least, the thirty-nine who signed the formal constitution) wished to establish a system that would perpetuate a rule by those who already had wealth and privilege. James Madison, accordingly, is both the "father" of the formal constitution and in practical effect the Karl Marx of America's governing class. He invented his argument against majority rule, in *Nos. 10* and *51* of *The Federalist Papers*, for the benefit of those who were the main influences for a new constitution. What was at stake in the 1787 convention was the type of society that would eventually emerge, and the class which would control the levers of power. History gives a clear answer: Society was to be dominated, as it had been before 1787, by the moneyed and propertied class. The framers, to a man, were members of that class. These men got what they wanted, in the convention itself and in the series of judicial and congressional decisions early in the nineteenth century. They were to have a free hand in exploiting the nation's resources. Among other things, a complaisant Congress, in a fit of public generosity without parallel, turned over the "commons"—the resources of an untapped continent—to a favored few. Or, as Professor Wallace Mendelson observed: Supreme Court decisions "encouraged the flagrant corruption of state politics and reckless waste of natural resources. . . . Judicial protection of fraud in the Yazoo land scandal paved the way for the Robber Barons and their Great Barbecue at the expense of the American people."[21]

Madison was determined to erect in the formal constitution a protective screen for the minorities of wealth and status, which was to operate as an ideological blanket over a political order that would guarantee the liberties of the rich and privileged whose power and position, he thought, would likely not be tolerated indefinitely by a popular majority not hemmed in by constitutional constraints. He thus wished to splinter society (in *Federalist No. 10*) and then to fractionate government (in *No. 51*). The former meant that those with wealth, and thus with political power, would be socially dominant; and the latter meant that should a fractious majority manage to seize control of one of the branches of government it could be checked by the others. This was a sort of "fail-safe" procedure, under the operations of which Madison's and Hamilton's cohorts could not lose.

Only when other groups managed to surface, around the turn of the twentieth century, did the Madisonian plan begin to reveal serious shortcomings. So long as members of the business class, the manufacturing aristocracy, were able to control all of the branches of government, they had nothing to fear. But the system of the secret constitution that had operated mainly to their benefit began to unravel with the rise of trade unions, farmers' leagues, and other important social groups. As a consequence, pluralism began to decline and its faults to emerge at about the time that it was first recognized by Arthur Bentley in 1908.

Pluralism "worked" in the nineteenth century because only one important societal group existed: the business class. Today there are several. The result is the pathology of factionalism. No one, not even the president, can overcome the fragmentation of policies and create a consistent program for achievement of the general good. Coherence is lacking in the policy-making process. The president's institutional apparatus for establishing a rational policy is simply not possible under either the formal or the secret constitutions. Congress as a body is unable to govern adequately. *As an institution*, it has in large part lost the will to govern. Individual members, to be sure, participate in the iron triangles of the actual governing system. Madison's fractionated government still protects the rich and privileged, but it is also a system of "veto groups" in which others can at times protect *their* parochial interests. American politics in many respects has become less a battlefield for generalized policies than an arena in which single-issue pressure groups contend, often successfully, for promulgation of narrow policies.

A wave of euphoria swept over the United States in the early 1980s. President Ronald Reagan kept insisting, and Americans eagerly albeit unthinkingly believed, that they should again feel proud and stand tall. Sober reflection, however, forces the conclusion that today's optimism is not solidly grounded; it is more puerile than factual, as this and the preceding chapters have shown. We may well be experiencing a false dawn, but that emphatically does not mean that dawn will actually follow—the dawn of a new golden age. To the contrary, those who in recent years have been belabored for crying doom (unless countervailing measures were taken) will soon again be heard—and perhaps even heeded.

Inevitably.

Those who trust in God to rescue humans from their follies have nothing to go on except a blind and unthinking faith. And those who see in science and technology a means of escaping from the ecological trap that is slowly but surely closing are placing their faith on idols that stand on shifting sand.

"Whirl is king," and humanity finds itself living in the "29th day." Dr. Lester Brown related the story of the "twenty-ninth day" in a book with that title in 1978: "The French use a riddle to teach schoolchildren the nature of exponential growth. A lily pond, so the riddle goes, contains a single leaf. Each day the number of leaves doubles—two leaves the second day, four the third, eight the fourth, and so on. "If the pond is full on the thirtieth day," the question goes, "at what point is it half full?" Answer: "On the twenty-ninth day."[22] The global lily pond in which five billion people live in varying degrees of poverty or affluence may now be at least half full. The world is spinning out of control. Chaos masquerades as order. There is a demonstrable destructive logic to human systems. Already the terrible reactions to crises, near and far, are appearing. Crime stalks the cities of the world. Racism is rampant. The age of triage is upon us. Famines sweep through much of the southern half of the planet. Killing squads operate in most of the authoritarian nations. Terrorism is on the loose. Religious wars continue unabated. Population cannot be brought under control, peace cannot be assured, pollution is not controlled, and poverty is everywhere. These situations signify a societal nervous breakdown.

And yet there is a stoicism, even apathy among many. Why this is so is an important question, not yet answered. After all, the Lisbon earthquake was followed by Voltaire's *Candide*, showing that this was by no means the best of all possible worlds. No Voltaire is evident today, even after Hiroshima and Nagasaki, the baneful culmination of a science and technology run riot.

And there is no modern Tom Paine to generate enthusiasm in stirring language about the needs of the present and of the emergent future. We need another (updated) *Common Sense*, that enormously successful revolutionary pamphlet, one that speaks to the needs of today in much the same way that Paine spoke to the needs of the 1770s.

We are in for it, and the sooner we realize it the better, for only with realization can there come, if indeed it is possible for people to plan and control their future, some sort of rational resolution of the human predicament. William Irwin Thompson has suggested that a need exists for a Planetary Constitutional Convention.[23] He is correct: there will be some sort of world government at some time, perhaps not so far off, whether it comes by cataclysm, drift, or design and whether it is totalitarian, authoritarian, elitist, or democratic.

All of this requires a thoroughgoing confrontation of the basic dualism of the constitutional order. Of more importance, perhaps, we need to know what we want, as well as what we deserve, as human beings; and we also must come to know that all of us as individuals are segments of the greater whole that is the human race. We will fail, or perhaps succeed, together—not singly. Of that there can be no doubt.

PART II

TOWARD A SUSTAINABLE SOCIETY

We know we are on an unsustainable path. . . . We also know that there are no simple technological fixes. . . . Creating a sustainable society will require fundamental economic and social changes, a wholesale alteration of economic priorities and population policies.

—Lester R. Brown

The government of the United States—however well it may have served in the past century and a half, and however sound it may still be in its fundamental structure and functions—is nevertheless in conspicuous need of an exhaustive rehabilitation.

—Clinton Rossiter

CHAPTER 4

WHAT IS A SUSTAINABLE SOCIETY?

A postliberal world order is required: one that takes human rights seriously, as the first political concern.

—Christian Bay[1]

If we ask—as ask we should, as ask we must—what are the reasons for establishing governments, what would be an adequate reply? Much of the history of political thought is concerned with this question; even a cursory survey quickly reveals a number of basic, divergent ideas. This chapter briefly summarizes the most influential idea in the United States—that of John Locke, the intellectual "father" of both the formal and the secret constitutions—and offers a different viewpoint: that of a *sustainable society*, which is defined as "one that satisfies human needs and fulfills human deserts within environmental constraints."

About three centuries ago—the exact date is uncertain—Locke published his classic *Two Treatises of Government*. The *Second Treatise* is best known for Locke's defense of property as the ultimate value. After asserting that "Man in a state of nature" was free (an assumption for which he gave no proof), he went on to ask why a person would relinquish his freedom "and subject himself to the Dominion and Controul of any Other Power?" This question was answered by the statement that one's property was unsafe and insecure in a state of nature. Locke continued:

This makes him willing to quit a condition, which however free, is full of fears and continual dangers: and 'tis not without reason, that he seeks out, and is willing to joyn in Society with others who are already united, or have a mind to unite for the mutual *Preservation* of their Lives, Liberties and Estates, which I call by the general name: *Property.*

The great and *chief end* therefore, of Mens uniting into Commonwealths, and putting themselves under Government, is the *Preservation of their Property.*[2]

Society—the people being governed—thus look to known laws, impartial judges, and sure enforcement of the laws in order to preserve their property.

The question today is whether the Lockean prescription is any longer sufficient to the need. I think not: sustainability of society is a far better principle, one much more suited to the modern age. Locke was the political philosopher appropriate for America's age of abundance, a time that is now coming to a wheezing stop. Only by adhering to his expansive definition of property as including life and liberty as well as estates can it be said that he is relevant to the present-day situation. The United States, however, has never followed Locke that far: whereas property has always been protected by government, it has been and still is in the narrow sense of one's real estate and chattels and other forms of wealth / One of the arguments set forth subsequently in this volume is that the Lockean prescription should be followed in its entirety, that what are called entitlements and other claims on government should be perceived as a type of property. Should that be done, then the Lockean prescription would be brought up to date and made to fit modern circumstances./

[Locke's past intellectual influence is a point that need not be labored here. His expansive view of property as "lives, liberties and estates" received formal constitutional expression in the fifth amendment's protection against deprivation of life, liberty, or property "without due process of law" (a commitment on a high level of abstraction to the rule of law). Of more significance are his underlying assumptions. First, he appeared to believe that there would always be enough to go around, Earth's bounty being, if not endless, then at least sufficient to any foreseeable need. "In the beginning," he maintained, "all the World was *America*, and more so than that is now." Second, Locke asserted that "*All men by Nature are equal*," but did not follow through on his premise: "I cannot be supposed to understand all sorts of *Equality: Age* or *Virtue* may give Men a just Precedency: *Excellency of Parts and Merit* may place others above the Common Level: *Birth* may subject some, and *Alliance* or *Benefits* others, to pay an observance to those to whom Nature, Gratitude or other Respects may have made its due." The equality Locke espoused in general terms was that "every Man hath" an "*Equal* right . . . to his Natural Freedom, without being subjected to the Will or Authority of any other Man."[3] That, in net, was Locke the aristocrat, the person who viewed equality only in terms of those "above the Common Level."

His two assumptions are the underpinning of the development of both the formal and the secret constitutions. When one considers the consequences of constitutional decisions since 1789, it is clear that both of Locke's unarticulated beliefs have had an enormous influence. Today, however, they may be faulted.[The end of the 400-year boom has brought with it the knowledge that Earth is a finite planet, with finite resources, but with an ever-growing population pressing upon those resources. Locke's equality is of the moneyed and propertied, those who have always benefited most from the constitutional system. That such a view of equality is no longer sufficient to the need is becoming increasingly obvious.]

As Walter Lippmann argued in 1955, it is a gross mistake to believe that democracy differs from monarchy in essence. All governments have the same "necessary and natural duties": External security—the defense and promotion of the state's vital interests abroad—and internal order, security, and solvency. Lippmann went beyond Locke in his conception of property. He saw it as a "system of legal rights and duties" and believed that under changing conditions, "the system must be kept in accord with the grand ends of civil society." Drawing upon Sir William Blackstone's language for those "grand ends," Lippmann thought that property was not *a priori*, not anterior to society, but derived from society.[4] Political thought had come a long way from Locke, for Lippmann's views are almost diametrically opposite from his predecessor. Private property was considered to be a system of rights *and* duties—a giant step from Locke, who thought that those with title to property have "the sole and despotic dominion" over it. Locke's rampant individualism was transmuted by Lippmann into the notion that the rights of property are created by the state and therefore can be altered in the interests of wider, of community, values.

Another large intellectual step came in the 1970s when Professor John Rawls proposed his "Difference Principle" in his widely acclaimed *A Theory of Justice*. His was an effort to produce a better theory of property, something that Lippmann had called for. "Social and economic inequalities are to be arranged," wrote Rawls, "to the greatest benefit of the least advantaged." Further: "All social primary goods—liberty and opportunity, income and wealth, and the bases of self-respect—are to be distributed equally unless an unequal distribution of any or all of these goods is to the advantage of the least favored."[5] The equality principle had, with Rawls, run its full course.

The notes struck by Lippmann and Rawls provide the thesis for this chapter—that the *only* valid purpose of government in the modern age is the reasonable satisfaction of human needs and fulfillment of human deserts within environmental limitations. This will be called the government appropriate for a sustainable society.

What, then, is a sustainable society? Dr. Lester R. Brown maintains that it will differ from the present one in several respects: "Population size will be more or less stationary, energy will be used far more efficiently, and the economy will be fueled with renewable sources of energy."[6] Brown thus offers a beginning to thinking about sustainability; but much more must be taken into consideration. The following discussion cites the factors relevant to constitutions that seek a sustainable society: global relationships, population, technology, economy, nuclear war, national security, material resources, nature, and natural resources.

Since, as it has become truistic to mention, humanity today lives on Spaceship Earth, it is necessary to view the society pertinent to constitutionalism as planetary in scope. The nation-state may be the characteristic form of political order today, but none exists in isolation. Whether or not there is ever a formal global "declaration of interdependence"—something vitally needed—the increasingly close relationships, whether cooperative or adversarial or a combination of both, among nations is an undeniable fact. The unifying forces of modern technology have all but wiped out national boundaries. Constitutions of all nations must therefore confront the indubitable reality that today's policy problems have been expanded far beyond mere domestic affairs. Almost any issue worth noting has a larger-than-national aspect. Illustrations need not be multiplied. One will suffice: South Africa may wish to treat *apartheid* as a purely domestic concern, but it is obvious that it cannot do so.

Involvement in foreign affairs, of course, is not a novel development. All political units throughout human history have had to deal with others. What is new today is a growing realization that the entire globe is tightly knit together. This means that at least some degree of mutuality of interests exists. There is some recognition that Earth is a closely connected ecological system with finite resources, vanishing species, and an extremely fragile environment. And there is increasing awareness that irreparable harm can be done by selfish actions or neglect in an unregulated world. (That requires government.) Soon or late, that harm will fall upon the innocent and guilty alike. The sad fact is that such awareness is only slowly being translated into national policies. Acid rain from the United States may pollute the forests and lakes of Canada, but little or nothing is being done about it; the same damage is true for the forests of Germany and Switzerland and Norway, which are being destroyed by pollution from other nations.

Mutuality, therefore, is merely being verbalized, and then only partially. Nationalism the world over is neither trivial nor in decay. There are, in other words, certain interests that all humans share, but it would be foolish to believe that because of *shared* interests there is today a *commonalty* of interests: The interests of all human beings are simply not basically common. Humans do not live in a "world community," if that term is taken to mean that people the world over share common values. Sir Isaiah Berlin has said that a principal legacy of the Enlightenment was the traditional liberal tenet that the interests of all humans are basically common. "This naive belief," Dudley Seers maintained, "has been battered in the course of this century, especially since the constraints in energy and other resources emerged."[7]

Even so, that does not eliminate the requirement that any constitution in the modern age must in some way deal with *global relationships*. Humans do have a common interest in survival, which by no means is assured today for humanity as a species. The challenge to constitutionalists is to create a political and economic order that will ensure survival not only of the political units of the planet but, insofar as physiological limits permit, of the individual human persons. It is for this reason that the basic human need should be identified as that of security—security of self and of the collectivity to which he belongs. Today, as Richard Falk has written, "the state system is not able to deal with the agenda of human concerns very successfully."[8] Said another way, the present system of nation-states is not up to the task of satisfying human needs and fulfilling human deserts—that is, of maintaining societies that are sustainable. "The logic that controls the state system," Falk continues, "is no longer tolerable. It is too dangerous, wasteful, and stultifying. It inhibits the sort of economic, political, and cultural development that fulfills individual and collective potentialities at various stages of development."[9] Surely, Falk is correct.

Population will have to be stabilized. This is a fact that simply cannot be ignored (or refuted). As John Maynard Keynes wrote in 1920, "The time has already come when each country needs a considered national policy about what size of population, whether larger or smaller than at present, or the same, is most expedient. And having settled this policy, we must take steps to carry it into operation."[10] The goal should be for an "optimum" population, one that is not necessarily stationary, as Lester Brown suggested, but one that is in a state of shifting equilibrium with available and potential resources. The relationship between population size and availability of resources is one of the principal factors determining the types of institutions that societies establish.

Population, furthermore, has a direct bearing upon the transformation of America from a nation in which individualistic values were paramount (at least in the myth) to one in which the group is dominant. The urbanization of society, the collectivization of economic activity into huge corporate combines (a process that began after the Civil War), the change in nature of government to the National Security State, the rapid depletion of natural resources, the dangers from hostile ideologies and national power centers, the rise of mass "democracy," and the trend toward equality—all of these, and more, merge into a movement toward a new type of society, one in which the individual person is submerged into and overwhelmed by a congeries of collectivities. Population growth is both an efficient cause of this trend and a factor that makes that end inevitable. In sum, a society that does not have "a considered national policy" about population cannot be said to be sustainable.

An optimum population would be one that would best ensure the development of conditions (economic, political, and social) enabling humanistic values to be maximized. This is a task of the greatest complexity.

Population control of any type is controversial, as witness the brouhaha over the Supreme Court's decision legitimizing abortions. The ruling is fraught with extraordinarily difficult questions of morals and religion, of personal freedoms and natural rights, and touches the core of both individual and social well-being. Although many societies have had conscious population policies in the past (often for the purpose of reducing or, at times, of expanding their numbers), and some ten to twelve societies have some sort of population policy written into their constitutions today,[11] the population problem is planetary in scale. It is not simply a problem of one nation or one region or one continent. No longer, therefore, can nation-states pursue population policies alone.

This realization, of course, necessitates planning, and that means major governmental intervention into intimate personal relationships. But there is no alternative. And that is so, as Richard L. Meier wrote in 1959, even though "we have no idea whether solutions [to the population problem] will be found, or at what cost they may be put to use, but it does appear that, according to contemporary values, the alternative futures opening up for societies with excessive fertility are quite frightening. We cannot be optimistic and honest at the same time."[12] The question of what is "excessive fertility" overlaps with that of migration; both questions in turn have a direct relationship to the next point—whether technological changes, including automation and robotics, have now created a condition of population redundancy in most societies, including the United States.

Technology must be brought under greater social control. Today, it is both boon and bane, boon because it promises the means by which the material requirements of peoples the world over can be satisfied, bane because of the many unpredictable and unanticipated "second-order" consequences that have caused many of them to impact detrimentally upon the human condition. Whether the positive aspects of scientific and technological change will outweigh its negative features is far from certain. This is not to say that humankind could not counteract those deleterious second-order consequences, given the wit and the will to do so. What is certain is that science and technology can provide the only possible substitute for the 400-year boom. To do so, however, will take a measure of wisdom that few humans have thus far evidenced. Jacques Ellul's *la technique* dominates every field of human activity.[13] The consequence is that a technologically elite structure sits atop a technologically oriented society, while at the bottom are growing masses of people whose function is either to do the menial tasks that have not yet been mechanized or to drop into the expanding underclass.

Technology has resulted in population redundancy, both by improving death control techniques and by replacing humans with machines in the industrial system. The "population bomb"—Professor Paul Ehrlich's label[14]—has become as dangerous as the nuclear bomb. The basic tension between technology (and those it serves) and the bulk of the people has been well described by David F. Noble:

There is a war on, but only one side is armed: this is the essence of the technology question today. On the one side is private capital, scientized and subsidized, mobile and global, and now heavily armed with military-spawned command, control, and communication technologies. Empowered by the second Industrial Revolution, capital is moving decisively now to enlarge and consolidate the social dominance it secured in the first. . . .

On the other side, those under assault hastily abandon the field for lack of an agenda, an arsenal or an army. Their own comprehension and critical abilities confounded by the cultural barrage, they take refuge in alternating strategies of appeasement and accommodation, denial and delusion, and reel in desperate disarray before this seemingly inexorable onslaught—which is known in polite circles as "technological change."[15]

Noble was writing about the impact of technology on the work force. A consequence of improved death-control measures, accompanied by rising birthrates in much of the world and by structural unemployment, is that literally hundreds of millions of people throughout the world (including the United States) are superfluous and can no longer emigrate to underpopulated areas. "The threat of permanent economic superfluity," Professor Richard Rubenstein remarks, "now confronts millions of American workers."[16] Surely he is accurate: the *actual* unemployment rate in June 1985 was 14.7%, almost exactly double that of the *official* 7.3%.[17] Joblessness in the mid–1980s is at historically unprecedented levels for a time of supposed economic recovery and growth.

That rate, in net, is one aspect of the dark side of technology. But only one: there are others, such as the apparent fact that technology leads to the consolidation of political power. All of these developments have definite constitutional consequences, and all must be considered in constructing a sustainable society.

Technology, of course, has another—a benign—face. Technological developments, for the first time in history, offer humans a potential for escaping the dreary conditions of material want. Properly used, technology can provide, if not true abundance for all, at least sufficient material goods to satisfy the minimum requirements of human needs everywhere. In this sense, Emmanuel Mesthene has observed that technology "creates new possibilities for human choice and action but leaves their disposition uncertain. What its effects will be and what ends it will serve are not inherent in the technology, but depend upon what man will do with technology."[18] If that view is accepted, then once again a fundamental constitutional question is posed: how to tame or canalize technology into humane channels. This would be a mind-boggling endeavor, even though it may be vitally necessary. No society in human history has ever made a systematic effort to determine and assess the factors that help or restrain a person from establishing a career commensurate with his abilities, or even to live a full life equal to his biological potential. These factors determine the levels of an adequate scale of living and suggest what a sustainable physical and social environment ought to include.

The point, for present purposes, is this: a sustainable society is one that so controls technological change that human needs and deserts can be adequately fulfilled (within environmental constraints, of course, for it remains true that something cannot be made from nothing). Properly tamed and used, technology can help to bring a higher degree of prosperity, provide the basis for greater equality of condition, increase the potential for individual freedom, create a "leisure" society in which much traditional work is eliminated, and help solve such emergent problems as fresh and pure water throughout the world and cleaning up the polluted waterways, rivers and lakes and oceans, of the planet. What technology *cannot* do, however, is of greater import: it cannot make people wiser or more altruistic. Something more is needed; that "something" includes, but is not limited to, constitutional change.

The *economy* should be reexamined and restructured. If sustainability is the goal, as it should be, there will have to be fewer demands upon environmental resources and, correspondingly, much greater demands on people's moral resources. As will be demonstrated in the next chapter, the dimension of private governments must be recognized as an integral part of the American constitutional order.

In his State of the Union message to Congress in 1944, President Franklin D. Roosevelt saw the need for an Economic Bill of Rights:

This Republic had its beginning, and grew to its present strength, under the protection of certain inalienable political rights—among them the right of free speech, free press, free worship, trial by jury, and freedom from unreasonable searches and seizures. They are our rights to life and liberty.

As our nation has grown in size and stature, however—as our industrial economy expanded—these political rights proved inadequate to assure us equality in the pursuit of happiness.

We have come to a clear realization of the fact that true individual freedom cannot exist without economic security and independence. "Necessitious men are not free men." People who are hungry and out of a job are the stuff of which dictatorships are made.

In our day these economic truths have become accepted as self-evident. We have accepted, so to speak, a Second Bill of Rights under which a new basis of security and prosperity can be established for all—regardless of station, race, or creed.

Among these are:

The right to a useful and remunerative job in the industries, or shops or farms or mines of the nation;

The right to earn enough to provide adequate food and clothing and recreation;

The right of every farmer to raise and sell his products at a return which will save him and his family a decent living;

The right of every businesman, large and small, to trade in an atmosphere of freedom from unfair competition and domination by monopolies at home or abroad;

The right of every family to a decent home;

The right to adequate medical care and the opportunity to achieve and enjoy good health;

The right to adequate protection from the economic fears of old age, sickness, accident, and unemployment;

The right to a good education.

All of these rights spell security....

America's own rightful place in the world depends in large part upon how these and similar rights have been carried into practice for our citizens.[19]

The president was not really correct when he called those "rights" "self-evident." As of the mid–1980s, they are far from that.

Should such a Second Bill of Rights be put into effect, basic changes would be required in the formal constitution—and in the entire economic system. It is the saddest of commentaries upon the American constitutional order that not one of the rights FDR listed has, more than four decades later, become an actuality. The trend, as of today (1987), at any rate, is in the other direction. After the brief interlude of America's true golden age in the quarter-century after 1945, when statutory (not constitutional) "entitlements" began to proliferate, these claims against the collectivity called the United States are diminishing, quantitatively or qualitatively, at a rapid rate.

The requirement today is to translate human rights—as FDR listed them— into property rights, which have always been protected. Professor C. B. Macpherson has well stated the point: After noting that prior to the modern age there were never enough material goods to go around, he observes that there were rights to a certain standard of life enforceable by law or custom; he maintains that "these rights were seen as properties." More specifically and bringing the analysis up-to-date, Macpherson asserts:

In the twentieth century, one factor has changed: there is enough to go around, or will be if we make intelligent use of our knowledge of Nature, i.e., of our presently possible productive technology. So it now becomes possible to assert an equal right, for everyone, to a certain quality of life, certain liberties to develop and enjoy the use of our capacities. And it becomes possible to treat these rights as the earlier unequal rights were treated—as property, i.e., enforceable claims of the individual.[20]

Property has become so central to modern society that anything not so designated is likely to be relegated to an inferior position to it. With the present value-system, institutionalized in both the formal and the secret constitutions, human rights must be seen as property rights for the former to be generally realized. Whether or not FDR saw his Second Bill of Rights in such a light is unknown. What is known is that, as of 1987, those rights he listed have yet to achieve constitutional protection. It is quite likely that only in that way can a measure of economic justice—of distributive justice— be brought into full fruition.

The threat of *nuclear war* must be eliminated. No society can be called sustainable that teeters on the edge of annihilation, either from thermonuclear weapons themselves or from their "nuclear winter" aftermath.[21] The genie of the split atom cannot, of course, be put back in the bottle. Even so, the question of the employment of such weapons should be thoroughly examined to determine whether that uses comports with both international and constitutional law. "The doctrines which best repay critical examination," Alfred North Whitehead commented, "are those which for the longest period have remained unquestioned."[22] Since the first primitive atomic bombs all but obliterated Hiroshima and Nagasaki in August, 1945, few lawyers have questioned the "doctrine" that a nation-state may employ those ultimate weapons, in its absolute discretion, in warfare. In recent years, however, a growing number of legal scholars and others have begun critical analyses of the legality of nuclear weapons—at any time, at any place.[23] A constitution for a sustainable society will have to resolve the question once and for all time.

National security must be redefined. Today, it is principally concerned with military power, a view based on the assumption that the main security threats come from violence from other nations. Of course, that narrow conception cannot be ignored; nevertheless, there are nonmilitary national security dangers that may be as perilous as the more familiar ones. High on the list is environmental degradation throughout the world. Unless this is checked, and soon, biological systems will collapse, and the earth as it is now known will begin to resemble that of the ancient Sumerians and Mayans. Population excess, too, has ominous portents for societies everywhere. The key to national security is sutainability (as herein defined).

Existing and potential *material resources* must be more equitably distributed. This is not to say that equality of condition can ever be achieved, but it is to say that a determinate level of material well-being may be identified, below which humans everywhere should not fall. The crucial concern should be fairness or equity. The growing disparity between the affluent and the poor, Professor Lester Thurow tells us, is creating enormous strains on the body politic: "There are few examples of democratic societies that have managed to survive while tolerating extreme disparities in income and wealth."[24] Societal sustainability requires removing, insofar as possible, those differences.

The Biblical admonition that mankind should have dominion over everything that moves upon the earth (as well as matter that does not move, such as plants and minerals) must be replaced with a view that humanity has an inescapable "oneness" with *nature* and the natural world, and must act accordingly. Dominion under the tenets of Judeo-Christian theology has long been employed as a justification for relentless exploitation of the riches of the planet. This will have to be supplanted by an instruction, divine or otherwise, that humans must protect all of nature's creatures, large and small.

The finite nature of the planet Earth and its *natural resources* must be recognized. There *are* limits to growth. Anyone who thinks that economic growth can continue indefinitely, says Professor Kenneth Boulding, is either a madman or an economist.[25]

These several factors are more illustrative than exhaustive of the matters that must be considered in developing a sustainable society. The challenges appear to be overwhelming. Whether they can or will be adequately met is perhaps the central constitutional question of the day.

To achieve sustainability will require a major reordering of social priorities. Humanity is indeed on an unsustainable path, even though there is little evidence that the movers and shakers of the world recognize it. Whether they can be awakened is a question on which the jury is still out. Certainly, however, it is accurate to say that the difference between modern humankind and the cvilizations of the Mayans and the Romans, for example, is that the facts of nonsustainability are well known. Many perceptive observers know what should be done; they are the intellectual Paul Reveres who are trying to awaken both the populace and the elite to the manifiest dangers of the human predicament. The problem is both to spread that awareness and to engender the wit and will to do the necessary, as Professor Melvin Konner has concluded:

The dinosaurs ruled this planet for over a hundred million years, at least a hundred times longer than the brief, awkward tenure of human creatures, and they are gone almost without a trace, leaving nothing but crushed bone as a memento. We can do the same thing easily and, in an ecological sense, we would be missed even less. What's the difference? seems an inevitable question, and the best answer I can think of is that we *know*, we are capable of seeing what is happening. We are the only creatures that understand evolution, that, conceivably, can alter its very course. It would be too base of us to simply relinquish this possibility through pride, or ignorance, or laziness.[26]

That the transition, if made, to a sustainable society will require a continuing and even greater governmental presence should go without saying. Because, however, the modern age is typified by pervasive antigovernment attitudes, it is important to note that Konner is, at least implicitly, advocating the need for planned organizational behavior—a term that may be taken as a synonym for government. This may not be liked—indeed, it may be denigrated and abhorred—but in the world today there is no escape from politics, and thus from the continuing presence of government. The constitutional problem is not to reduce government but to employ it in an efficacious manner. However much the Friedrich von Hayeks of the world may decry the resort to what they call "statism," there is no escape from it.

The further meaning is that sustainability will necessitate major constitutional revisions. But for such changes to be effective will also require a change in human values. The two go together: "The argument over whether social change follows from changes in consciousness *or* changes in political structure obscures the fact that *both* must change if an alteration in either is to survive."[27] These ties make the central problem of the modern age doubly difficult.

I am suggesting, with Erich Fromm, that a sustainable society is one that "corresponds to the needs of man, not necessarily to what he feels to be his needs."[28] The question of human needs and deserts is only seemingly simple, even though much of the literature of American constitutionalism deals with it (under different labels). Needs are neither wants nor desires, although they can be. Deserts are more subtle, but are susceptible of determination.

Human needs—*basic* human needs—is a term in search of a definition. *Human needs* are defined here as "those things the satisfaction of which permits the self-fulfillment of the individual person in a social organization." Admittedly, this definition is too abstract, but it suffices as a general proposition. Although the emphasis is upon the individual, that individual is not an atomistic being alone and separate from other persons. People achieve significance only because they are members of some social entity; for present purposes, this is the United States of America. Professor Michael Walzer observes: "Every political community must attend to the needs of its members as they collectively understand those needs; ... the goods that are distributed must be distributed in proportion to need; and ... the distribution must recognize and uphold the underlying equality of membership."[29] The ultimate goal is personal self-respect or self-fulfillment—what some call recognition—in a social organization.

The contention is not that there should be equality of condition for everyone, but, rather, that a principle of minimum satisfaction of human needs should prevail. There is a level of physical and psychic satisfaction below which no one, anywhere, should fall. This is a watered-down version of Rawls's Difference Principle. In essence, the argument here is for a modern version of the wrongfully labeled and much maligned Leveller movement of mid-seventeenth century England. To explain that, a brief digression is in order. Who were the Levellers? What did they stand for? And why are they important in an essay on modern American constitutionalism?

Answers may begin by inviting attention to the maxim carved in the facade of the Supreme Court building in Washington: "Equal Justice Under Law." No one, certainly not the justices of the court, has ever given definitive content to it. The term, if it means anything, is a statement of an unrealized ideal rather than a description of reality. More significantly, it applies only to *formal* legal rights, that is, to "procedural justice." Rawls states the point: "Self-respect is secured by public affirmation of the status of equal citizenship for all," by which he apparently meant the civil and political rights set out in the Bill of Rights of the formal constitution.[30] Rawls continues: "The distribution of material means is left to take care of itself in accordance with the idea of pure procedural justice."[31] This is, roughly, a modernized version of what the Levellers advocated in England in the 1640s. It is not enough. Champions of pure procedural justice today, such as Ronald Dworkin and John Hart Ely, would only guarantee that people's demands will be heard and noted by the appropriate public officers.[32] But this will not do: It is offensive when, as often happens, a public official listens to a complaint and then ignores everything just said when making his decision. People are entitled to more than a mere hearing (or a vote, as Ely would have it); they also need something of the results they desired—provided, of course, that those desires fit into the overall scheme. "Guaranteeing people's formal legal status is not enough," Professor Robert Goodin correctly maintains, "to secure their self-respect. We must also stipulate something about substantive outcomes."[33] That is precisely where the notion of a constitution of human needs comes into play.

Equality to the Levellers was a procedural concept. A consideration of their ideas is important today because the framers of the formal constitution wrote on the assumption that there are always going to be more—more resources and more land—to satisfy the material needs of the populace. Western man's values have evolved in the context of a supposedly inexhaustible world where getting more of anything today did not preclude having more tomorrow. The Levellers did not demand equality of condition. They wanted the House of Commons, not the king or the House of Lords, to be sovereign; the Commons to be truly representative through universal manhood suffrage; and government to be decentralized to local communities. Economic reforms were advocated to further the interests of the "ordinary" person, as were complete legal equality, abolition of monopolies, opening the enclosures, abolition of conscription and billeting of troops in private homes, complete freedom of religion, major law reforms, and abolition of tithes (and thus no established church). It can readily be seen that much of what Levellers wanted found its way into the formal constitution, if not in the original document, then in the Bill of Rights. In his study of the movement, Theodore Calvin Pease wrote:

The Levellers invented political machinery of permanent value. They evolved the idea of a written constitution of paramount law as a limitation on the power of government. They devised machinery whereby the sovereignty of the people might express itself in the framing and acceptance of such written constitutions. Carrying their concept of government by law to the extreme, they designed the enforcement of their constitutions, like all other laws, through the courts.... For spreading their principles they designed a democratic party organization that suggests the committee of correspondence of the American Revolution.

... The Levellers stood for a number of judicial principles on which contemporary law was at best contradictory: trial by jury, the right of a prisoner to counsel and copy of indictment, his right to refuse to incriminate himself.[34]

No special insight is required to realize that much of the spirit and even of the letter of what the Levellers believed became standard American formal constitutional fodder. They adhered to the then revolutionary idea that the common people had the ability to do more than merely accept and carry out the political decisions of their social superiors. Their ideas have had an enduring significance in the development of Anglo-American legal and political institutions.

But the Levellers can be faulted, not in their specific ideas but in not realizing that constitutional (and thus, political) orders are by their very nature bifurcated. Furthermore, their concentration on "process"—on procedural justice—slighted substantive doctrines. Consider what their leader, John Lilburne, wrote in 1646: Men, merely because they were children of God, are "by nature all equal and alike in power, dignity, authority, and majesty"; civil authority, therefore, is exercised "merely by institution, or donation, that is to say, by mutual agreement and consent, given ... for the good benefit and comfort of each other."[35] In other words, governments derive their just powers from the consent of the governed, which means that every citizen must participate and give consent. As one of Lilburne's followers remarked:

Really I think that the poorest he that is in England hath a life to live as the greatest he; and therefore truly, Sir, I think it's clear, that every man that is to live under a government ought first by his own consent to put himself under that government; and I do think that the poorest man in England is not at all bound in a strict sense to that government that he hath not a voice to put himself under.[36]

That statement has, if not a modern ring, then one that was heard when the Declaration of Independence was drafted in 1776.

What would Lilburne advocate today? Would he and his followers demand that government undertake certain affirmative duties or obligations that go to the *substance* in addition to the *procedure* of rights? Not likely: The Levellers, as are those who are bemused by the ostensible glories of procedural due process of law as guaranteed by the formal constitution, did not proceed beyond procedural justice: "The equality [they] sought was equality before the law and equality of political rights."[37] That, to repeat, is only half the battle.

The term *Leveller* today is, of course, an epithet, an attempt to denigrate a movement that by present-day standards would be called wholly satisfactory by most constitutionalists. It was liberal in the John Stuart Mill sense. The Levellers can be faulted, however, both for not realizing that all constitutions are dual in nature and for not perceiving that their ideas of limited public government were based on an untenable assumption—stated by Yves Simon in this way: "Deliberation is about means and presupposes that the problem of ends has been settled."[38] The problem today is that the ends of governmental activity have *not* been settled. Their views of social justice were attenuated. Professor William A. Galston has well stated the point: "The traditional American penchant for political engineering or institutional tinkering is profoundly one-sided; democratic procedures are almost vacuous in the absence of collectively held moral convictions."[39] The meaning is clear: to succeed, a constitution must satisfy certain rights of the people beyond those recognized in the formal constitution. A new dimension to constitutionalism is indispensable.

Returning to the principal inquiry, what are the substantive rights that should be included within the concepts of human needs and human deserts? No easy answers exist, save on a high level of abstraction. Some generalized statements can be suggested, however, as a basis for meaningful thinking about both categories.

First, as to human needs, the contention here is that humans most fundamentally need *personal security*, which has two aspects: biological and psychological. Although some biological needs—food and shelter, for example—must be satisfied before psychological needs can be considered, the two classes will be discussed together. A constitution of human needs would be one that so structures society that everyone's personal security would be maximized. This may be called the *maximization postulate*. Implicit within it is the idea that personal security, the fundamental human need, can be satisfied only to the extent that the environment permits. But personal security is not an end in itself; rather, it is the essential prerequisite to achievement of self-respect (self-fulfillment). (The relevant society, moreover, will sooner or later have to be global in scope.)

Attainment of personal security is the ultimate standard by which public policies should be evaluated. Any government therefore gains legitimacy—has a valid claim to the right or title to rule—only to the extent that it makes provision for the conditions that allow personal security to be maximized.

Of course, greater specificity is required. A summary of what others have perceived as human needs will suffice. Abraham Maslow, by all odds the leading scholar in the field, has suggested the following hierarchy of needs:

- physical (such as air, water, food, sex, etc.);
- safety (the assurance of survival and of continuing satisfaction of basis needs);

- affection, or belongingness;
- esteem, by self and others; and
- self-actualization or self-development.[40]

Maslow considered these needs to be both instinctive and universal. He ranked them hierarchically (in order of "prepotency"): satisfaction of the first is necessary before the second can be addressed, and so on. To him, the human being is motivated by a number of basic needs that are "species-wide, apparently unchanging, and genetic or instinctual in origin." Needs, therefore, are both physiological and psychological.

Others have taken different tacks, most not nearly as specific as Maslow. Professor C. B. Macpherson rejects Maslow and maintains that Karl Marx provided a better model: "Labor in the broadest sense—creative transformation of nature, of oneself and one's relations with others. This, Marx held, was *the* truly basic human need."[41] Professor Marvin Zetterbaum reads Hobbes and Marx as maintaining "the primacy of recognition as a basic human need, if not *the* basic human need." To him, "man is thinkable as a being that is guided by nothing but a desire for recognition"; and he further commented, "we cannot escape the notion that the recognition and defense of self is *a* basic human need, if not *the* basic human need."[42] (This, of course, may be just another way of saying that personal and psychic security is the fundamental human need.)

To Professor Galston, the concept of need has a threefold classification: natural need, social need, and luxury. Natural needs are those "required to secure, not only existence, but also the development of existence." Developmental needs include adequate nurturance, adequate education, free and open institutions that permit a wide range of capacities, and friendships and social relations.[43] And Professor Christian Bay maintains that there are three ranges of basic needs: "physical survival and health needs, social belongingness and participation needs, and individual subjectivity needs."[44] Finally, Australia's Professor H. J. McCloskey asserts that "needs are things which ought, where possible, to be available, not withheld, prevented, and indeed, be supplied where necessary," and further that "where needs cannot be met, society or the world ought to be reordered as far as possible."[45]

No requirement exists to detail the precise nature of human needs. This volume in many respects is exegesis on the theme stated by McCloskey. Needs of course are complex, but they can be telescoped into the concept of personal security. I am, accordingly, proposing two things. First, humans the world over have a *constitutional right* to satisfaction of those needs that human action can reasonably be expected to fulfill. This, to be sure, is an "ought" rather than an "is" statement. It implies a fundamental systemic failure of global human institutions. Second, humans do *not* have a like right to the satisfaction of needs that the environment, broadly conceived, cannot accommodate.

Let me summarize: human needs theory is a significant part of philosophical and psychological literature. What is new, at least in a relative sense, is the application of the concept to politics and constitutionalism. Needs, moreover, are associative in nature and can only be attained through the operations of some collectivity. This implies the continuing necessity of a pervasive governmental presence. Since governments are the object of constitutions, human needs thus are directly relevant to any constitutional dialogue. This in turn makes it obvious that a fundamental reorientation of orthodox thinking about law and legal institutions is required. Constitutionalism in its historical sense of a limitation on government is no longer sufficient to the need; it must give way to one that recognizes an expanded view of the affirmative obligations of government. This is the burden of the next chapter. First, however, some discussion of human deserts is desirable.

What do people deserve? The question is not easily answered. Some may say that what a person deserves is largely a part of what he needs. That, however, is not necessarily so. Negative deserts (punishments) can hardly be called human needs, at least for those being punished. Possibly, however, there is a need—a psychological need—for people generally to know that malefactors are in fact subjected to the punitive power of the state.

Statements about personal deserts are seldom made by philosophers, legal or otherwise, whereas the theory of personal needs enjoys a considerable and growing literature. Professor Joel Feinberg has asked: "What is it to deserve something?" and proceeds to explain that a complete understanding of justice is impossible unless the complexities of personal desert are resolved.[46] If that is true—as it is—then constitutionalists must pay attention to human deserts.

The concept of *personal desert* involves more than rewards and punishments. Any comprehensive discussion of social justice would have to confront what Feinberg calls the "peculiar perplexities" of personal desert. The term is not pleonastic. Persons are not the only things that can be said to be deserving. Art and sculpture, for example, may deserve approval for being particularly well done; some human problems—for instance, the likelihood of nuclear war—may deserve careful analysis and examination; some species deserve to be preserved; and so on. Such statements have a great deal to do with social justice and with human needs, and thus with the realization of a sustainable society.

Desert, moreover, requires a basis. We should not, for example, say that a person deserves to be whipped "just for the hell of it"; and a claim that a person's desert is to be determined on the basis of whether his father was bald defies both logic and common sense. Both assertions lack an appropriate "basal reason" to justify them; the first rejects a basis for personal desert and is wholly capricious, and the second simply is a logical *non-*

sequitur. Such statements offend ordinary good sense and thus cannot be justified.

On the other hand, consider personal ability: is it a proper basis for desert? In one sense, the answer is yes; it deals with a determinate fact about a person. But is this enough? Is it either a good or sufficient reason that a person deserves some reward or accolade? The question has become controversial in recent years. It is one where values (or deserts) are in conflict, as several recent Supreme Court decisions attest.[47] Should there be a preferred admissions program in medical and law schools, whereby black Americans (admittedly qualified) are chosen over qualified whites because they are black? Should hiring and promotion policies follow the same route? In these cases, the Supreme Court has struggled with the enormously difficult task of reconciling conflicting deserts. There should be little wonder, therefore, that the justices were badly divided in their approaches to the issues in such cases—as, indeed, is much of American society. The question of "affirmative action" programs mandated by government is far from settled. The point stressed here is simply that when one begins to think about deserts, quite often the problem of choice between persons of equal deserts must be confronted—or at least choices when both candidates meet the established standards but one is higher in some respect (as in school grades) than the other. How those choices are made, and who benefits from them, is a central question today of both the formal and the secret constitutions, and is crucial to the concept of a sustainable society.

Desert is concerned with the modes of treatment that humans should receive from society (the state)—that is, what they *deserve.* Two types exist. The first is concerned with treatments with respect to persons deserving good or ill, rewards or punishments, praise or blame. Should Mr. Rummel be jailed for life by Texas for three minor crimes, none violent, totalling $229.00? Should Virginia incarcerate Mr. Hutto for forty years for a minor drug violation? Should Ms. Carrie Buck be involuntarily sterilized, again by Virginia, because she is considered to be mentally defective? In each of these instances, the Supreme Court said yes.[48] On the other hand, should the "well-known criminal," Richard Nixon, have received a full pardon from his chosen successor, plus all the benefits a generous Congress allots to former presidents? Do Woodrow Wilson and Harry Truman deserve to be called great presidents?

The second type of desert divides people not in accordance with rewards and punishments but in terms of those who deserve and those who do not. In philosophical terms, the first type of desert has been called retributive justice, whereas the second falls into the class of distributive justice. Competitive situations illustrate the latter class: prizes in contests and grades in schools, among others. "X deserves Y because of Z," with X being a person, Y a mode of treatment, and Z some determinate fact about X—such as being the winner of a chess game or a person who scores highest in a test.

What types of treatments do persons deserve from others? No quick or easy answer exists. But surely it is accurate to say that deserved treatments are closely connected with human needs, and that both are, or can be, subsumed under the concept of social justice. That is to say, a person, simply because of his humanness, deserves to have his basic needs satisfied insofar as the environment permits. Or, as Professor Thomas Grey has written, there is "a right in each person to have his basic material needs met by his society to the extent that he is unable to meet them by his own efforts."[49] The most fundamental human right, in sum, is that of having one's human needs satisfied (and deserts fulfilled). The trouble is that both the formal and the secret constitutions institutionalize a politico-economic order that has not in the past, does not now, and shows no likelihood in the future, of accomplishing that ultimate goal. Social justice has been and is slighted.

A word in conclusion about social justice: the question is far from an idle one. "Justice," James Madison wrote in *Federalist No. 51*, "is the end of government. It is the end of civil society. It has ever been and ever will be pursued until it is obtained, or until liberty is lost in the pursuit." But justice is not easily defined; it takes several forms: retributive, corrective, distributive, for example. As used here, the term *social justice* is employed as a synonym for a sustainable society.

Social justice is a form of distributive justice, concerned in its needs aspect with the way that benefits are allocated in society through its major institutions, and in its deserts aspect both with negative sanctions of human behavior (roughly: punishments) and with benefits conferred (one's "just deserts"). Social justice deals thus with the way that wealth is distributed, personal rights protected, and benefits divided among the people. (Much of formal constitutional law is concerned with precisely those matters.) In short, social justice is *suum cuique*, "to each his due." Or, as Dr. David Miller has argued, "The just state of affairs is that in which each individual has exactly those benefits and burdens which are due him by his personal characteristics and circumstances."[50] Among other things, this view means that equals should be treated equally, but that those who, for some reason, are lesser in status or stature than others, should be given a societal leg up in the race of life. (Affirmative action programs are an example.)

What, however, is a person's "due"? The question is complex, but some sort of answer is necessary. A reply can begin by making a distinction between the customary and the ideal in social affairs. What is customary means the accepted distribution of rights, goods, and privileges, as well as the conventional distribution of burdens and pains. These are thought by many to be both natural and just, and thus they ought to be—and, indeed, are—maintained by law. In short, "whatever is, is right," and therefore worthy of protection by the state and its apparatus (government). On the other hand, the ideal conception of justice looks to a system of rules and regulations of distribution that ought to exist (but probably never existed). Laws under this view are said to be just to the extent that they approximate the ideal. The distinction is between "conservative" and "prosthetic" justice. The former has the aim of preserving "an existing order of rights and possessions, or to restore it when any breaches have been made," whereas the latter has the goal of "modifying the status quo."[51]

A person's due, accordingly, may be perceived in one of two ways: either as protection of his present rights ("vested," as in property, rather than "civil") or as furtherance of the ideal of prosthetic justice. The term *rights* is used here in this manner: They "generally derive from publicly acknowledged rules, established practices, or past transactions; they do not depend upon a person's current behavior or other individual qualities. For this reason, it is appropriate to describe this conception of justice as 'conservative.' It is concerned with the continuity of a social order over time, and with ensuring that men's expectations of one another are not disappointed."[52] (This is an attenuated view of rights, as has been noted and as will be discussed in the next chapter.)

Social justice as rights (in its attenuated form) thus requires judges and others to protect the "is" in society—precisely what the Supreme Court and other courts have generally done throughout American history. The basic task of the judiciary in any modern industrial society is that of being an integral part of the governing coalition and thus helping to underpin the stability of the social order and protecting it from serious efforts to alter it. For that reason, the fundamental doctrine of American constitutional law has long been, and still is, that of "vested" rights, of which property rights are by far the most important. Much of the judicially announced constitutional law, historically and contemporaneously, revolves around that theme.

But in modern times, social justice as rights conflicts more and more with other perceived, albeit still inchoate, rights—those that have been labeled as human needs. The requirement now is to transmute the historical view of rights into one that sees human needs as human rights—and in turn, as Macpherson has argued, to consider such human rights as property rights. This will, of course, require substantial alterations in the constitutional status quo—the subject of the next chapter.

CHAPTER 5

GETTING THERE FROM HERE

Mankind makes a poorer performance of government than of almost any other human activity.

—Barbara Tuchman[1]

The problem is easy to state, but devilishly difficult to resolve. Ms. Tuchman surely was correct. But does this mean, as some politicians and commentators would have it, that the problem is one of getting government off the backs of people? Hardly. Enough is now known—at least, it should be known—for everyone to realize that government is emphatically not the problem. Far from it: rather, government is part of the solution. Without government there would be anarchy, and without some (rather large) degree of governmental participation in socioeconomic matters, the same large and growing disparities between rich and poor, advantaged and disadvantaged, would be certain to continue. The unregulated market so extolled by classical and neoclassical economists is simply not up to the mark of creating a sustainable society.

The real question is not to eliminate or even to greatly diminish the governmental presence. Few, in fact, truly believe that is should be. Those—for example, the officers in the Reagan administration—who advocate lesser government always leave room for an often undefined area in which it should operate. This is true even for the supposedly individualistic businessman, who takes the social structure and the governmental protections he enjoys for granted:

The organizer of industry who thinks that he has "made" himself and his business has found a whole social system ready to his hand in skilled workers, machinery, a market, peace, and order—a vast apparatus and a pervasive atmosphere, the joint creation of millions of men and scores of generations. Take away the social factor and we have not Robinson Crusoe, with his salvage from the wreck and his acquired knowledge, but the naked self living on roots, berries, and vermin. *Nudus intravi* should be the text over the bed of the successful man, and he might add *sine sociis nudus exirem*.[2]

The problem thus is to develop means by which government will become both more efficient and more accountable to the people—all of the people, not merely the favored few.

Professor James MacGregor Burns has pointed out that "it is precisely the system that does not work,[and that] what is 'deeply wrong in America' is rooted more in institutional and intellectual forces than personal ones. ... No leader—no matter how charismatic or politically skilled—will be able to govern effectively given the existing constitutional framework and informal networks of power."[3] That is exactly correct. Burns and Tuchman pose two fundamental questions. First, what are the reasons for the sorry record of human governance? Second, are there political (constitutional) changes that, if made, would help better that record? This chapter focuses on the latter question (the former is implicit in the exposition in the next chapter).

Three discrete questions are dealt with now: (1) What are, and what should be, the *obligations* of government in the modern age? (2) Can the *structure* of government be altered to produce better results? and (3) What *limitations* on government are there (and what should they be)? The question of whether America should have a formal constitution that provides for periodic revision will be considered in the next chapter. What follows is an exercise in the "ought" rather than the "is" of American constitutionalism.

The inquiry will focus on "getting there from here." The "here" was adumbrated in Part I of this volume; the "there" in the preceding chapter. Analysis can begin with some generalized statements. First, it is well to iterate that the American constitution, in both of its forms, is an evolving institution, following Darwinian rather than Newtonian ideas; it is a process rather than a fixed system, an open-ended flow of constitutive decisions. Constitutions therefore reflect the circumstances, the exigencies, of succeeding generations of Americans. Each generation has written and must, of necessity, write its own constitution. Today's generation does not differ. What is different now from the past is a dawning realization—thus far, not sufficiently widespread—of the imperfections of the Document of 1787 and the undoubted fact of extraordinarily rapid technological, and thus social, change, which soon or late will be translated into constitutional practices. The formal instrument drafted in 1787 may seem to be an immutable set of truths, but the appearance belies the reality. Change, continuing constitutional change, has been the norm since 1789 when the government made possible by the political immaculate conception in 1787 came into existence. Past constitutional alteration has, however, come in an incremental, *ad hoc* manner, through reactions to external forces, rather than in a planned way. Even the twenty-six amendments, including the Bill of Rights and the Civil War amendments, fit that description; they are constitutional Band-Aids, pasted on the outside of the basic structure in response to an immediate specific problem. At no time has there been a concerted general attempt to update what the framers wrought.

This method no longer suffices. *Systemic* reformation of the fundamental law is required. Leadership failures, Burns correctly tells us, are "increasing in frequency and seriousness" and "are now built into the system." This has grave imports for the citizenry: one consequence, as Burns implies, is that American society is not sustainable. The sword of constitutional deficiencies, however, cuts deeper than his concentration on the manifest failures of "the power to lead."[4] Today, we Americans must therefore write a new constitution for ourselves and "our posterity." In doing so, it is well to recall that all of us are our own posterity. People alive today must, by dint of inexorable necessity, grapple with constitutional problems of the first magnitude, in a social context that cannot be accurately predicted. The basic problems of governance do not change; they are the one constant. But the social context has been and is being so altered that their resolution must be sought anew.

Second, we must also remember that, as in the past, constitutional change of some type is certain to come whether or not we like or want it. The question is not whether alterations will be made in our fundamental law, but which ones, by whom, and who will benefit from them. Since we live, as physicist John Platt has remarked,[5] in an age of "the crisis of crises," and since law, including constitutional law, reflects the social milieu in which it operates, there can be little—there can be *no*—doubt that the constitution of tomorrow will differ markedly from that of today, just as today's is essentially dissimilar from that of yesteryear. The form and the facade may—likely will—be retained, but the substance will be altered. Inevitably. Great changes can and do come under old forms. Of course, any changes that retain the old forms will merely add to the institutional structure of the secret constitution, and thus would permit further enhancement of the power and prestige of the beneficiaries of America's unwritten fundamental law. The requirement, therefore, is for change in both of the old forms, the secret as well as the formal.

Third, the task of advocating substantial constitutional revision is not lightly undertaken. Inasmuch as the formal document is the chief artifact of America's civil religion, revered as such, any proposal for major alteration is certain to be met with derision or to be viewed as akin to secular blasphemy. This attitude, however, should not deter the inquiry, if for no other reason than, as George Bernard Shaw once commented, "All great truths begin as blasphemies." Once it is accepted, as it should be, that the formal constitution is flawed, and once it is perceived that the United States really has two constitutions (and that the secret is also flawed in that it does not provide for human dignity), then the idea that the primary task of government is to satisfy human needs and deserts is not the radical notion that on first thought it might appear to be. For that matter, if one gives the framers of the formal constitution their full due, it can then be said that they, too, were interested in creating a governmental structure by which human needs and deserts could be fulfilled. We thus can ask, once again, the question posed by Alexander Hamilton in *The Federalist No. 1*: are "societies ... really capable ... of establishing good government from reflection and choice, or ... [are they] forever destined to depend for their political constitutions on accident and force?" This question has never been adequately answered in the United States, although 200 years of constitutional history are considered by many to reply affirmatively to the first part of Hamilton's question. Certain it is, however, that American government as it has developed in two centuries was derived much more from "accident and force" than from "reflection and choice."

At least from their lights, and in the opinions of those who take an antiquarian view of American constitutional history, the men of 1787 did their job well, given the circumstances of the times. But the United States waxed strong and prosperous less because of the few thousand words the framers crafted in the constitutional convention than in spite of them. Only by ignoring, when deemed necessary, the letter or at least the spirit of the formal constitution has the nation been able to become what it is today. The many variations from the original model, coupled with the unique environmental conditions of nineteenth-century America, make it clear beyond doubt that Hamilton's question still awaits an answer. Whether, therefore, the American people are up to the task of designing a proper government—a government for a sustainable society—is not at all certain. In truth, the task has never been undertaken. But that is precisely the pressing need today.

Fourth, Hamilton's question must now be definitively answered, but in a set of environmental conditions far different from 1787, and not through replication of the impossible—the extraordinarily fortunate conditions that favored the framers and their immediate successors. There is no empty continent ripe for exploitation; and there is no new frontier of comparable importance. The framers were lucky, but did not follow through properly. Although they used their reason in an attempt to resolve seemingly intractable political problems, the context in which they labored meant that they had a unique opportunity to create a new society, one based on principles of social justice. After two centuries, any fair evaluation of what they wrought—the formal constitution, which, as has been said, permits the second, secret constitution to operate—can only conclude that the framers flunked their test. Social justice in the prosthetic sense has never characterized the United States.

Subsequent to 1789, moreover, human reason played at best a secondary role, secondary, that is, to the accidents and forces that were the main influence that molded the national development. The problem today is to achieve through the use of reason alone what no one—no nation—has ever been able to do: plan for and create a sustainable society. Or, as Nobel Laureate Herbert Simon has written, "Success depends on our ability to broaden human horizons so that people will take into account, in deciding what is to their interest, a wider range of consequences. It depends on whether all of us come to recognize that our fate is bound up with the fate of the whole world, that there is no enlightened or even viable self-interest that does not look to our living in a harmonious way with our total environment."[6] The challenge is difficult almost beyond measure. Whether it can be surmounted in a reasonably adequate way is far from clear at this time. The further meaning is that those in this generation of Americans are confronted with a task far more difficult than their ancestors faced two centuries ago.

Modern Western man arrogantly believes in the capacity of human reason to confront and resolve any problem that humans face. This is an article of faith—that humanity has the ability to deal with both the natural world and the affairs of men and women so that the human race will prosper. There is a pervasive belief that, once people set their minds to it, they, by using their reason, can solve any problem, overcome any barrier, fulfill any goal. The faith, while touching, is based on a mistaken reading of the American experience. It, however, is another heritage of the Enlightenment, somewhat analogous to the already mentioned idea that the interests of all people are basically common, one that has been so mauled by intellectual and physical developments during the past century that little credence can be given to it.

This is an added and all-important dimension to the political problem of getting there from here. But try we will, as try we should, as try we must. The bare bones, hard fact is that we can no longer rely on fortuities, fortunate or otherwise, to mold American constitutional development. But here, again, another well-nigh impenetrable barrier must be acknowledged—that really changing American thinking "has proved to be an almost impossible task over more than two hundred years."[7] Alexis de Tocqueville well stated the point in his classic *Democracy in America*:

I hear it said that it is in the nature and habit of democracies to be constantly changing their opinions and feelings. . . . But I saw nothing of the kind among the great democratic people that dwells upon the opposite shores of the Atlantic Ocean. What struck me in the United States was the difficulty of shaking the majority once an opinion is conceived of.... The public is engaged in infinitely varying the consequences of known principles rather than in seeking for new principles.[8]

But it is precisely those "new principles" of constitutional governance that are so vitally needed today.

So much for introduction. Much of what follows in this chapter is admittedly visionary. Unique times, however, demand unique responses. A reprise of tired, worn-out old ideas will not do. The basic problems of governance may not change, but today's reactions must. New institutions are required.

The first inquiry is into the concept of governmental *obligation*, or *duty*, (the terms are used synonymously). A relatively unexplored area of constitutionalism, most of the literature being concerned with either limitations on government or its structure, obligation is implicit nonetheless in all that government does. It is, for example, no semantic quibble to maintain that the notion of limitations on government—fundamental to the historic and orthodox conception of constitutionalism—carries with it the implicit view that government has an obligation to control itself. This, however, is not what is argued at the moment.

Although most discussions of constitutional obligation deal with the extent to which an individual owes duties to the state (to the collectivity), the emergent question that is increasingly being asked is the obverse: what are the affirmative obligations of the collectivity to individuals? "The great problem of political theory, especially for a period of two centuries after the Reformation, was to explain how any man, born 'free and equal,' could rightfully be under the dominion of any other man."[9] That is a statement of the obligation of the individual *to* the collectivity called society. The time has come to reverse that conception and to speak about the obligations *of* society to the individual person. Although the two facets of the concept are of course entwined, obligation should be perceived for what it really is—a two-way street.

Inherent in such a conception is this difficult problem: Although a person may be obligated to obey the commands of a particular government, is he similarly obligated to obey *any* type of government? I think not. A constitution of human needs must of necessity include the idea that a person is obliged to obey government only when certain "political" goods are furnished. Here, however, one must distinguish between legal and moral duty. Under the theory of the positive law, a person always has a legal duty to obey the law without regard to what it is. If he does not, then sanctions can be imposed by the state. The ready example as this is written is the positive law that imposes *apartheid* in South Africa. So, too, in the Soviet Union, where dissent is savagely repressed. One does not, however, have to accept the positive law in its entirety, but can validly maintain that a person's moral obligation or duty to obey the law runs only to those governments that furnish such political goods as can be equated with human needs. Professor Nannerl Henry explains:

A person's intention, as a member of a polity, to enjoy the benefits of that polity sufficiently obliges him to obey the authority that makes those benefits possible. His obligation continues as long as the sovereign is able to deliver the political goods, and no longer.

This argument . . . is the most basic form of what I propose to call the argument to obligation from the performance of political tasks, or the provision of certain essential goods and services. According to this argument, government performs a set of functions that we necessarily desire and *need* as human beings in society. Since obedience by subjects is essential to the performance of these functions, we ought to obey government.[10]

What are political goods? They may be compared to what economists call public or collective goods: "A common, collective, or public good," Professor Mancur Olson tells us, "is . . . any good such that, if any person . . . in a group consumes it, it cannot feasibly be withheld from the others of that group."[11] Such common or collective benefits, all of which, it is important to note, emanate from the state and its apparatus, government, include defense and police protection and the legal system generally—in sum, as Thomas Hobbes and David Hume maintained, "the provision of political order in the most minimal sense—security and protection—defense of citizens against external attack, and settlement of internal conflict."[12] Or, as Adam Smith, the classical economist, wrote, the duties of the sovereign include:

• Protecting the society from the violence and invasion of other independent societies;
• protecting, as far as possible, every member of the society from the injustice and oppression of every other member of it; and
• erecting and maintaining those public institutions and those public works, which though they may be in the highest degree advantageous to a great society, are, however, of such a nature, that the profit could never repay the expense of any individual or small number of individuals, and which therefore it cannot be expected that any individual or small number of individuals could erect and maintain.[13]

Well and good, one might say, but did Smith go far enough? Perhaps for his times (*circa* 1776) he did, but two centuries later his views fall short of the mark. Furthermore, it is not even enough to assert, as does Henry, that "the major task or purpose of government, the reason for its existence, is to provide goods . . . that are collectively valuable, but which cannot or will not be provided without common organization and coordinated direction of effort."[14] She lists such things as courts of justice and a legal system to settle disputes, aids to the economy, and contributions to the welfare of citizens in matters such as health and education. Henry is therefore closer to the argument here; nevertheless, something more is needed. That "something," as the English philosopher Thomas Hill Green phrased it, is "the obligation of individuals to each other as enforced by a political superior."[15] Professor J. Roland Pennock agrees: Political goods are those goods that "satisfy human needs whose fulfillment makes the polity valuable to man, and gives it its justification."[16] These include, he continues, security, welfare, justice, and liberty. His position is almost identical with that set forth in this chapter.

"The good life is the end of all social activity," Green asserted quite correctly.[17] This observation sets the tone for an outline of the type of obligations that a modern nation should have, the type of duties that a proper constitution should incorporate. Of necessity, the discussion that follows must be brief, more an adumbration than a comprehensive disquisition.

"Classical political philosophers from Aristotle to the Founding Fathers to Hannah Arendt," Professor John P. Diggins maintains, "have insisted that for a consitutional republic to survive it must return to its first principles."[18] He identifies liberal individualism and liberal pluralism as those principles. Well and good, so far as he goes, but he does not go far enough. Diggins fails to consider the social bases of such principles. They cannot— they never have—existed in an environmental vacuum. They are derivative from, rather than anterior to, a "constitutional republic" in the modern age. The true first principle, and, indeed, the only such principle today for such a republic has already been stated: to take such measures as are necessary and feasible to create a sustainable society.

This, to be sure, is at too high a level of abstraction. At a lesser level, the first principle of American governance in the present day may be subdivided into a triad of important constitutional doctrines: government—the state, the collectivity called society—has the obligation (1) to satisfy basic human needs and deserts; (2) to help create the conditions, environmental and otherwise, in which those needs and deserts can be fulfilled; and (3) to establish a system of accountability to the body politic so as to ward off aberrant and improvident exercises of governmental power. Each of these obligations is not now a part of either the formal or the secret constitutions; and each entails an entirely new governmental posture. How could they be put into effect? Only by major revisions in the present formal constitution; to that end, the following proposals are offered:

- *Congress shall have the duty to make all laws that are necessary and proper to provide for and maintain an environment conducive to the attainment of a sustainable society. This duty shall include, but is not limited to, measures designed* to achieve an optimum population, to control and defuse the threat of nuclear war, and to control environmental degradation.

- *Congress shall have the duty to make all laws that are necessary and proper to provide for and maintain the reasonable satisfaction of human needs and fulfillment of human deserts.* This duty shall include, but is not limited to, making provision for sufficient meaningful job opportunities for all who are able to work.
- *Congress shall have the duty to make all laws necessary and proper to check the excessive use of presidential and bureaucratic power.* This duty shall include, but is not limited to, establishment of a council of state within the office of the presidency, and provision for extensive use of the "legislative veto."

These proposals, written in constitutional language, call for a truly major alteration in the posture of government. They of course immediately present the problem of enforcement. To attain that end, the following further revision is proposed:

- *The Supreme Court shall have original jurisdiction to hear and determine the validity of allegations that Congress has failed in any of its duties. Any citizen eligible to vote in a federal election shall have a right to bring an action in the Supreme Court, the writ of which, if granted, shall run against Congress generally and the members specifically.*

The changes proposed here are the minimum essential to creation and maintenance of a sustainable society. Other alterations, going to the structure of government, are set forth later in this chapter. All of the proposed constitutional changes are based on the belief that orthodox theories and practices about the political economy, about constitutionalism, have become part of the problem rather than a means of providing ways to organize collective efforts and produce workable solutions to today's pressing policy problems. We surely do not wish to repeat what the ancient Romans allowed to happen; the Romans, as Herbert J. Muller recounts, did not adapt to changing social circumstances:

So Rome clung to its ancient political and religious forms long after they had lost their meaning, with a ritualistic reverence that disciplined and dignified its national life and that sapped its resourcefulness. While it cultivated the ideal of universal reason it remained devoted to a non-rational conservatism, which conserved irrational institutions.[19]

Precisely, Americans today are preserving their "irrational institutions," created for a far different nation, with inadequate realization that those institutions are at best ill-suited, at worst positive detriments, to dealing with the exigencies of the present and the emergent future. They cannot fulfill the first principle of governance—the satisfaction of human needs.

One other constitutional proposal merits mention at this time:

• *The limitations on governmental power set forth in the formal constitution shall apply not only to the organs of public government but also to any societal group that exercises substantial power over individuals. Such groups would include the supercorporations, the major trade unions, churches, farmers' leagues, professional associations, and any other group of comparable status. The result would be recognition in formal constitutional law of the group as the basic unit of society and of the fact of "private" governance (which thus far has been hidden in the interstices of the secret constitution).*

How can such changes as the foregoing be justified? Only the briefest of answers can be adumbrated here. Justification is ultimately predicated on necessity, not just for the disadvantaged but also for the advantaged. Sooner or later, social turmoil is certain to erupt among those lowest in the socioeconomic pecking order, unless steps are taken to alleviate their miserable conditions. The general movement toward equality—of opportunity, certainly, but merging into condition—has been a discontinuous theme running throughout American history since first stated in the Declaration of Independence. The movement in the formal constitution has consistently been toward a form of egalitarianism. Once loosed, as it is, the idea of equality cannot easily be stopped and turned around.

In some respects, furthermore, the proposed duties (save for that of the Supreme Court) would merely make constitutionally explicit what the national government has been trying to do in recent decades—at least before the so-called Reagan Revolution. The Employment Act of 1946 and the Humphrey-Hawkins Act of 1978, for example, were congressional attempts to legislate maximum employment policies for the nation. That they have thus far been relatively unsuccessful does not belie their significance. And the National Environmental Policy Act of 1969 was a first (halting) effort to ensure that Americans had an environmentally decent place in which to live. So, too, with the War Powers Resolution of 1973, a congressional effort to retrieve lost powers over the calculated use of violence by the president. Add Roosevelt's New Deal, which, as has been argued, may have been a means to save the system of corporate capitalism but which nonetheless did number some of the disadvantaged as beneficiaries of its programs.

These are illustrations of relatively recent congressional attempts to help satisfy human needs and deserts. That they have, thus far at least, proved to be insufficient to what is really required does not diminish the principal point to be seen: The United States crossed over a constitutional watershed in the 1930s: Government began to assume new obligations to the people. To date, its reach has exceeded its grasp; but that may be because the efforts were legislative, rather than constitutional, in nature. The New Deal reforms, although revolutionary at the time, were by hindsight mere incremental alterations, not at all solidified into the norms of the formal constitution. The requirement now is for something much more fundamental to be attempted.

[The Supreme Court, acting under existing procedures, could do this. As has been said, it could transmute human rights—those involved in basic human needs—into property rights. For example, the right of senior citizens to medical care, which is at least implicit in the Medicare program, could become "vested," a property right. So, too, with other so-called entitlements under the attenuated American version of the welfare state.]

Each of the proposed new obligations of government is, of course, worthy of at least a chapter and perhaps a volume of its own. Here, however, only a brief discussion is in order.

The United States has yet to seriously confront the population question. That this must be done, and soon, has already been suggested. A sustainable society cannot be constructed without a considered national policy about population size and distribution. As long ago as 1969, Robert McNamara, then president of the World Bank, called attention to the fact that the world's population was then three billion and would more than double in thirty-five years; and further, it would increase at a rate of one billion every eight years thereafter. McNamara believed that projections beyond those figures are unreal since "they will not come to pass because events will not permit them to come to pass. . . . Of that we can be certain. . . . What is not so certain is what those events will be. They can only be: mass starvation, political chaos, or population planning."[20] Who is to say that he was wrong, other, that is, than such purblind Micawberists as Julian Simon? As of 1986, the world's population passed the five billion mark, and already there is more than one instance of mass starvation as well as of widespread malnutrition, plus a growing incidence of political chaos. And yet, political leaders in the strong and wealthy nations of the world turn their heads aside: no true population planning is occurring. The time is short—it may already be too late—for anything meaningful to be done. For the United States not to face up to the population question, here and elsewhere, and do something *constitutional* about it is a failure of massive proportions, explainable only by an inherent stupidity or a willful blindness among those who exercise real power in the polity. Posterity—if there is one—will not think kindly about those men and women.

Nor has the American response to the nuclear peril been adequate to the obvious need. We have been fortunate that no nuclear bombs have been used since 1945. But the risk of either an accidental nuclear war or the first use of nuclear weapons growing out of a "conventional" conflict is ever-present. On more than one occasion during the past forty years American policymakers have seriously contemplated the employment of those ultimate weapons. The Cuban Missile Crisis of 1962 is perhaps the most obvious instance of this situation; but it was only one among several others. (It may be assumed that leaders in other nuclear-armed nations, including the Soviet Union, have done likewise.) As for an accident, in 1980 the malfunction of one silicon microchip costing 46¢ almost precipitated an exchange of missiles. There have been an untold number of other instances of mistakes and accidents that, if acted upon, could have triggered a nuclear war. Add the fact that at least half of the American nuclear forces "can be fired without the President's direct order" and it may easily be perceived that the awesome power of the bombs poses a clear and present constitutional challenge.[21] Here, again, this proposed duty or governmental obligation has not received a sufficient response. Rather than being defused, the nuclear peril grows ever closer day by day. If there are any survivors of a thermonuclear war, they, too, will not look kindly upon those in positions of power (the world over) today. (Further discussion of what might be done about the nuclear danger will be postponed until later.)

As with population and nuclear energy, the issue of environmental degradation seems to be beyond the ability of governments, as now constituted, to deal appropriately with it. The problem here, as with the others, is worldwide in scope; and will necessitate close and continuing cooperation among the nations of the world to resolve the manifold related problems that are involved. For example, no one seems to know how to stop the daily destruction of the tropical rain forests, even though there is agreement among scientists that their disappearance will have major impacts upon the climate and quality of life of other nations, including the United States. This is known, but the system does not respond. Whether it can be made to do so has become one of the pressing constitutional questions of the times.

The proposed congressional duty to take action to satisfy human needs has, as has been noted, its progenitor in the "entitlement" programs that are a heritage of the New Deal. When President Roosevelt advocated an Economic Bill of Rights in 1944, he thereby attempted to solidify those entitlements. The argument here is that the time has come to constitutionalize them. To do so would entail a major alteration in the economic system.

A focus on establishment of a constitutional right to a job will help to sharpen the discussion. This goal could be accomplished by a combination of congressional legislation and Supreme Court approbation of what Congress enacted. Congress has already edged up to the problem in the Employment Act of 1946 and the Humphrey-Hawkins Act of 1978; but they have been relative nonstarters so far as guaranteeing jobs is concerned. What is required is an affirmation of what a retired police officer and former marine once stated: "I don't think our system is all bad. . . . What I object to is, there's no planning. I don't care how much money it takes. They should put every guy that wants to work, to work."[22] Three economists echoed that idea, stating that serious attention should be paid to employment security and that there should be action that would affirm "every worker's right to be employed at some job or another—but not necessarily always at the same job."[23]

Since Congress has express power under the formal constitution to regulate commerce within the United States (and with foreign nations), there would be no hard-and-fast need for a constitutional amendment to accomplish this goal. Additionally, as will be shown later, the Supreme Court could, should the justices so desire, "enact" a constitutional right to a job into the formal constitution. Indeed, one justice, the late William O. Douglas, is on record as having said that "there is a constitutional right in this country for a citizen to have a job."[24] America is a labor society, which means that work is at the core of society. All aspects of life must conform to it—for example, education, vacations, and retirement. The purpose of education is to train people for work in the industrial structure. Vacations, which for most workers are relatively recent innovations, are periods of recovery and a time to rest and renew energies in order to be able to return to work better able to produce. Retirement, also a latter-day social phenomenon, is considered to be an earned rest after a lifetime of work. Even with the coming of the so-called information society, which bids fair to eliminate much of the need for labor, no one has yet produced a satisfactory substitute for work. People receive their identities from their jobs; they are significant in the eyes of others not so much for what they *are* as for what they *do*.

There are, of course, other human needs and deserts, but the way in which the nation confronts the employment problem is central to the others. People attain security from having work; work provides the necessary economic base for achievement of other human needs as Abraham Maslow, for example, listed them.

The recommended new constitutional obligation of Congress to rein in excessive use of executive and bureaucratic power has already been met, but only in part. For example, the War Powers Resolution of 1973 was a congressional effort to retrieve some of its lost powers over the use of violence. And the Administrative Procedure Act of 1946 was an attempt to control the exercise of bureaucratic power.

Neither piece of legislation, however, has proved to be sufficient to the need. Something more is required. That "something," in present discussion, is a proposal for establishment of a "council of state" within the office of the presidency. A similar proposal for widespread and systematic use of the "legislative veto," so as to help curb the bureaucracy, will receive only summary attention.

One of the primary aims of the constitutional framers was to establish a separate executive. Although popular wisdom has it that governmental powers were separated the better to prevent despotism, that at best is a half-truth. Under the Articles of Confederation there was no separate executive, which was seen as a great flaw. So the framers drafted Article II of the formal constitution, thereby establishing the president who was to have "the executive power" as well as several other more specific, yet ambiguous powers. Since 1789, the history of the presidency has been one of steadily aggrandized powers, so much so that today Americans may be said to be governed by an anomalous sort of executive hegemony. The president— rather, the office of the presidency with its several thousand functionaries— is *primus inter pares* within the national government.

Much of the enhancement of presidential power has occurred in this century. This has concerned a number of thoughtful observers, including Edward S. Corwin, Francis Wilcox, Averell Harriman, Hubert Humphrey, Benjamin Cohen, and Jeremy Stone.[25] There is no present need to set forth their proposals, save to say that each was a serious attempt to prevent the aberrant and improvident exercise of presidential power. Two centuries after the constitutional convention it has become clear that the framers erred in believing that there was no danger in a separate chief executive. There *is* danger, as the ensuing few pages will demonstrate. The focus will be upon the employment of nuclear weapons, the existence of which present the greatest hazard to people everywhere. "Presidential initiative without presidential debate is dangerous," observes Professor Charles M. Hardin.[26] And so it is; but neither the formal nor the secret constitutions provide for an adequate means of "debate."

In the past, debate, if it took place, did so among the president's so-called Kitchen Cabinet, augmented by a few trusted men from outside. During the Cuban Missile Crisis of 1962, President Kennedy convened an *ad hoc* "executive committee" to advise him. Neither "system" fills the need, simply because no one talks to the president "like a Dutch uncle."[27] There is an environment "of deference, approaching sycophancy."[28] A permanent "council of state" would be far preferable, one that would operate within the executive offices of the presidency. Simultaneously, Congress should create a joint committee on national security to oversee the operations of the council.

By no means is a council of state a novel idea. Oliver Ellsworth proposed one in the constitutional convention in mid-August 1787. But after considerable debate, the proposal was shelved. No vote on it was taken. Others of the framers who favored a council included George Mason, Benjamin Franklin, John Dickinson, and Gouverneur Morris. By laying the idea aside without a vote, the framers left it to future generations to decide whether a council was required.

Pluralizing the executive, accordingly, was very much in the minds of those who attended the Philadelphia conclave. And presidents throughout American history have found it desirable to call upon others for advice. Kitchen Cabinets and Kennedy's Ex-Com have been mentioned. The need today is to make those informal advice-givers into an institutionalized *advocatus diaboli* that would be a permanent part of the office of the presidency. The requirement is particularly urgent with respect to nuclear weapons. The time has come—indeed, it is long past—to respond to the challenge of Albert Einstein when he said that "the unleashed power of the atom has changed everything save our modes of thinking, and we thus drift toward unparalleled catastrophe."[29]

Our ways of thinking might be changed by establishing a permanent council of state, overseen by a joint committee of Congress. The need, according to Benjamin Cohen, one of FDR's closest advisers, is to devise means "to facilitate the wise and prudent exercise of presidential power."[30] A council would fulfill that need. Once chosen and properly staffed, it would operate as a permanent body within the office of the presidency, with the authority to take part in the decision-making process *before* important presidential decisions are made. It would, for example, have to be consulted on such questions as the "first use" of nuclear weapons. It would thus take a sober first thought on proposed plans and policies. The president, says George Reedy, one of President Lyndon Johnson's advisers, "is a form of king and no one argues with a king."[31] That is precisely the trouble with Kitchen Cabinets and informal advisers, and precisely what an established council of state would correct. The council would not be a peer to the president, for peers by definition are on the same level, but it would have powers to ask the hard questions and to argue with the chief executive.

Some observers have commented that the Supreme Court forces other governmental officers to take a "sober second thought" before proceeding on what they would like to do. A council of state would have exactly the same effect—but *before the fact*. The Court acts largely *after the fact*. The council, moreover, would not, as does the judiciary, forever be reacting to problems that have already erupted; it would be able to anticipate the emergence of problems as well as predict the probable impact of proposed policies. This would entail the rejection of *ad hoc*-ery—more specifically, of pragmatism—as the usual means of dealing with problems. Government routinely merely reacts to external stimuli and does little planning. It tries to put out fires that blaze up, rather than approach governance in a comprehensive way. This is the pragmatic temper regnant. The difficulty with this intellectual posture was well stated by Henry Kissinger (before he became a government official):

Pragmatism, at least in its generally accepted forms, produces a tendency to identify a policy issue with the search for empirical data. It seems in consensus a test of validity. Pragmatism is more concerned with method than with judgment. Or, rather, it seeks to reduce judgment to methodology and values to knowledge. The result is a greater concern with the collection of facts and figures than with the interpretation of their significance. . . . As long as our high officials lack a framework of purpose, each problem becomes a special case. But the more fragmented the approach to policy becomes, the more difficult it is to act consistently and purposefully. The typical pattern of our government process is therefore endless debate over whether a given set of circumstances is in fact a problem, until a crisis removes all doubts and also the possibility of effective action.[32]

Ad hoc government, if continued, could mean disaster—not only in the nuclear area but also in such matters as population and environmental degradation. This is the essential lesson to be learned from what transpired during the Cuban Missile Crisis. A primary mission of a council of state would be to develop the framework of purpose that Kissinger found so lacking in governmental decision making.

A persuasive case can be made for establishment of a council of state. Pluralizing the executive is a constitutional problem of the first dimension, in the world as it is today. The president could be, were such a council to be established, what Hamilton called an "energetic executive."[33] That it would be strenuously fought by any president should go without saying. Presidents do not like people to disagree with them. But the need is there; but it should be noted that, as Professor Theodore Lowi wrote in 1985, "Real reform in American presidential government will not come until there is a real change in points of view of powerful people. As in psychoanalysis, so in politics, coping is a solution, and it will not be found in techniques, but in awareness of the problem. Techniques will follow."[34] When those who control the institutions of the secret constitution recognize the nature of the nuclear and other perilous problems, only then will appropriate responses emanate from the institutions of the formal constitution. To date, the evidence is sparse indeed that the true nature of the perils confronting humanity has penetrated into the consciousness of enough Americans and certainly far from enough members of the Establishment. (Note: another way of pluralizing the presidency will be recommended subsequently—splitting the office into two, with one person being chief of state and the other being head of government.)

Since the foregoing and other putative obligations of the modern state are closely related to the structure of government, further discussion will be postponed until that subject has been presented. We turn now to the obverse of constitutional obligation: the time-honored idea of constitutionalism as *limitations* on government.

As it has been received and understood in the United States, the concept of constitutionalism is not only a part of the national myth system but it also has a normative content. Like religion, it is an effort to bring coherency to seeming chaos, supplying a set of beliefs revolving around the notion of limitations on governmental action that seek to canalize human behavior. Consider these orthodox definitions:

- *Friedrich Hayek*: Constitutionalism means that all power rests on the understanding that it is exercised according to commonly accepted principles, that the persons on whom power is conferred are selected because it is thought that they are most likely to do what is right, not in order that whatever they do should be right.

- *Daniel Bell*: The common respect for the framework of law, and the acceptance of outcomes under due process.

- *Charles McIlwain*: Constitutionalism has one essential quality; it is a legal limitation on government.

- *Carl Friedrich*: Only those parts of politics which can be expressed in legal rules can be reflected in a constitution. Behind the formal organization, an informal one will always operate. It is an essential part of the living constitution, which could not function without it.

- *Walter Murphy*: the fundamental value that constitutionalism protects is human dignity.[35]

If such views are accepted, only nations that seek and actually do limit government can be called constitutional.

Surely, however, that is not correct. Even a totalitarian nation has a constitution—for example, the Soviet Union's written one. That the USSR does not live up to what its constitution says may be taken to mean that the secret constitution of that nation is controlling over the written.

Constitutions and constitutionalism are both descriptive and prescriptive. But their prescriptions, their rules of fundamental law, by no means run in one direction only. The quoted definitions are illustrative of a heritage from the basically liberal, antiauthoritarian posture of the nineteenth-century constitutional state, the public law of which had two principal aspects: (1) positive law being changeable, vested rights receive special constitutional protections; and (2) citizens have correlative public rights, constitutional in nature, in the public sphere. The difficulty with this view is obvious: if anything has been learned about how written constitutions and their express limitations on government operate in reality, it is that they are relative to circumstances. A principle of constitutional relativity runs throughout American history. The limitations that the orthodoxy insists upon are more apparent than real. Government in the United States is now, has always been, and will continue to be precisely as strong as conditions necessitate. Necessity has always been the mother of constitutional law. (But this, emphatically, does not mean that constitutional change is not necessary.)

It was argued above that government should undertake certain affirmative obligations beyond those traditionally known. The argument now is that the putative limitations on government, those set out in the Bill of Rights, the Civil War amendments, and portions of the Document of 1787, should be put into full force and effect. That they have not been, either historically or contemporaneously, should be but is not common knowledge.

Soon after the constitutional convention adjourned in September 1787, Thomas Jefferson wrote to James Madison that a bill of rights was "what the people are entitled to against every government on earth, general or particular, and what no just government should refuse, or rest on inference."[36] But the framers had simply concluded that a written bill of rights was not necessary (which led George Mason to refuse to sign the new constitution). Alexander Hamilton argued in *The Federalist No. 84* that "the Constitution is itself, in every rational sense, a BILL OF RIGHTS." He failed to convince. In the first Congress that convened in 1789, Madison introduced the ten amendments that were to be called the Bill of Rights. Speedily ratified, they became part of the formal constitution in 1791. The basic idea was to find a means by which government would be obliged to control itself. Reasons of state thus were supposed to give way to, or at least be balanced against, reasons of freedom and human liberty. But not equality, it should be remembered, which entered the formal constitution only after the Civil War (in the fourteenth amendment).

The Bill of Rights and most other limitations on government, generally, are procedural rather than substantive. They assume, first, a democratic society; and second, that all that is necessary is to deliberate about means to achieve ends that have already been settled. Neither assumption holds water. Democracy, however defined, is at best a hopeless dream, particularly when the operations of the secret constitution are borne in mind. The framers feared it, and it has been realized since 1787 only in the rhetoric; reality has been, and is, otherwise. In much important constitutional litigation, moreover, ends rather than means are at the core of the dispute. The classic example, perhaps, is *Brown v. Board of Education* (1954),[37] the Supreme Court decision that began to accord black Americans procedural social equality. The ensuing thirty-plus years have demonstrated that procedure alone will not do the necessary "in the absence of collectively held moral convictions,"[38] precisely what is absent concerning the position of blacks in America. White Americans display little willingness to accept blacks in the mainstream of the national life.

The limitations in the formal constitution, furthermore, are often substantially undercut by the operations of the institutions of the secret constitution. To employ the same illustration: blacks have legal equality under the formal fundamental law but in fact are far from equal—in opportunity, in prestige, or in condition under the more important secret fundamental law. The problem this poses is to devise means to transmute the ideal epitomized in the formal document, as shown in the *Brown* decision and its progeny, into operational reality.

Other features of the express constitutional limitations on government merit mention. First, the proscriptions of the Bill of Rights tend to be more hortatory admonitions to government officers to behave decently in the circumstances than binding interdicts against governmental activity. Although, as in the first amendment (protecting freedoms of expression and religion), they may speak in absolute terms, by interpretation they have become mere relative commands. The interests of the state, of society, are always balanced against those of the individual person, with the balance routinely struck in favor of government. Second, those limitations have an evolving formal content; they have meant different things at different times since 1789. Through judicial interpretation, their meanings have changed and will continue to change through time. As Justice Felix Frankfurter once commented, "It is of the very nature of a free society to advance in its standards of what is deemed reasonable and right. Representing as it does a living principle, due process is not confined within a permanent catalogue of what may at a given time be deemed the limits or the essentials of fundamental rights."[39] Or, as Chief Justice Earl Warren opined in 1958, the eighth amendment (prohibiting cruel and unusual punishment) and, inferentially, the other parts of the Bill of Rights are to be construed in the light of "evolving standards of decency"[40] that are the hallmark of a civilized society. Third, only in recent decades—the process started slowly in 1925— has the Supreme Court held some (now, most) of the Bill of Rights applicable to the state governments as well as the federal government. Civil rights and civil liberties have thus been "nationalized" during the past sixty years. Fourth, constitutional limitations are presently applied against public government only, the justices thus far being unwilling to recognize the dimension of private governments. And that is so even though those governments, such as the supercorporations, have as great and perhaps greater effect on the rights and liberties of the citizenry as does public government. They are the "black hole" in American rights.[41] Finally, speaking generally, the civil rights and liberties set forth in the formal constitution do not seem to be highly valued by most Americans. They are "fragile and susceptible to the political climate of the time," assert Herbert McCloskey and Alida Brill. They conclude: "We are not convinced that the craving for freedom is inborn, much less that tolerance of others and the notion of reciprocity of rights are inclinations natural to everyone."[42] This means that we must face up to the fact of the manifest illiberality of many, perhaps most, Americans.

The net conclusion must be that the orthodox conception of constitutionalism is seriously faulty, that it requires rethinking both as it has evolved since 1789 and in the context of the problems of modern times. Can limitations on government that are expressed in the formal constitution be transmuted in some way into duties or obligations? This is one of the basic questions or fundamental challenges confronting constitutionalism today. The Supreme Court has shown some signs of edging toward answering that question in the affirmative. As long ago as 1937, the Court interpreted the due process of law clauses of the formal constitution, which speak in terms of negative limitation, in ways that said that the liberty protected by due process is "liberty in a social organization which requires the protection of law against the evils which menace the health, safety, morals, and welfare of the people."[43] In that statement by Chief Justice Charles Evans Hughes, the Court came as close as it ever has of reading principles of social justice, of the fulfillment of basic human needs, into the formal constitution.

Constitutions are also concerned with the *structure of government*. The formal constitution, in its main parts, does just that: it divides the national government into three branches and also splits the duties of governance between the states and the central government—in the system known as federalism. The governmental structure is the sole focus of attention of those, such as James Sundquist, James MacGregor Burns, and the Committee on the Constitutional System, who today are seriously concerned with the problem of constitutional change.[44] That this approach is seriously faulty is one of the main arguments of this volume.

When discussing any aspect of constitutionalism, one must begin with the world as it is, not as one might wish it to be. Any serious thought about what a constitution should do must pay close attention to how power is divided. At least four divisions of power are relevant: the system of nation-states, the separation of powers within the national government, federalism, and the fact of constitutional dualism.

The most prominent feature of the political world today is its division into 160-plus nation-states, each claiming sovereignty—the power of ulti-mate control—over a designated piece of territory. Some are huge and some are small unto insignificance, but all claim that common attribute of sov-ereignty. Even for the superpowers, however, sovereignty exists only in the positive law—that is, in the formal constitutions (written and unwritten). Delve below the surface of positivism and a bewildering web of interactions among nations quickly becomes apparent. These interactions tend to be economic and military, but other categories exist. Today, accordingly, no nation is truly sovereign in the sociological sense. Each depends in greater or lesser degree upon others, in a reciprocal set of relationships. Just like the industrial magnate who thinks he has made himself, nations throughout the world claim to be independent (sovereign), but they are far from being islands, entire to themselves; they cooperate far more than they conflict. They must deal with each other; there is no alternative. Natural persons attain significance as members of groups; and nations do likewise as part of a greater whole—an inchoate community of nation-states.

There is, furthermore, an obvious inequality among nations. Chief Justice John Marshall once asserted that there is a "perfect equality of nations";[45] but that can be true only in the formal sense (as in the one nation, one vote system of the General Assembly of the United Nations). Every nation may be equal in the eyes of international law but certainly some are much more equal than others. Nations are truly equal only in their interdependencies.

Their "perfect equality" is one of mutual dependence. That is so even for the present age of nuclearism.

Analogous divisions may be seen internally within the United States. The formal constitution splinters power, first, between the national and state governments; the states, second, in turn further split governing power into some 3,300 counties, almost a countless number of city governments, as well as an uncounted number of governing organizations with some type of political power. The greater New York City area, for example, has about 1,400 governing districts; and there are more than 100,000 taxing authorities in the United States. In addition, of course, is the triadic division of powers between legislature, executive, and judiciary that typifies both the national government and the states. A further subdivision, sometimes called a "headless fourth branch of government" may be discerned in parts of the federal bureaucracy.[46] Nor is that all: there is the significant division of powers between public and private governments, with the latter being recognized only in the secret constitution.

Both aspects of the basic divisions of political power—that in the "world community" and that within the United States—must be taken into account when considering what the structure of government should be. This means that the formal constitution should be altered in at least two fundamental ways: to take cognizance of the close relationships with other nations and to perceive the actual governing power of decentralized groups. Other divisions of power, such as federalism and the "separation of powers" in the federal government, also require attention.

The primary requirement, whether the focus is on planetary or domestic affairs, is to devise means by which some of the silences of the formal constitution can be filled with express, written provisions. One such gap is the relationship of the United States to the remainder of the globe. Although the formal constitution applies only in the territorial jurisdiction of the United States and its possessions—in general, it does not "follow the flag"— the secret constitution differs. Under Article VI of the Document of 1787, the numerous treaties and executive agreements to which this nation is a party are "the supreme law of the land." They are constitutive acts which in their totality make up a body of at least inchoate constitutional law that extends the constitution in operation far beyond the nation's borders. Inasmuch as power is the central concept of constitutionalism, a large body of law, law that is more than mere inchoation, exists in fact in the "world community." To cite but one example: the open "covert" war now being waged by the United States and its mercenaries in Nicaragua is power being exercised under the secret *external* constitution.

Even some of the attributes of political sovereignty have already been ceded by the United States to larger-than-national organizations. NATO is an example, the International Monetary Fund another, international commodity agreements a third, and the Organization for Economic Cooperation and Development a fourth. There are others, but they need not be listed to make the point. The list may not be endless, but it is significant. However much the perfervid "patriots" of the American Legion or the Daughters of the American Revolution may disagree, this country has already moved into a status of at least multinational, although far from worldwide, resolution of some of its important public policies.

The question is whether that significant beginning can be extended and formalized in the constitution. Professor Paul Freund once commented that any thoroughgoing commitment to larger-then-national institutions would require a constitutional amendment[47]—which may or may not be accurate. The essential point is that anyone who wishes to think seriously about the American constitutional order must, by dint of necessity, take the remainder of the planet into close and continuing consideration. However the question is resolved, constitutionalists cannot avoid attempting to place America in the world order. As the London *Economist* wrote in 1978, "It has seldom been more important to gear national policies to fit international goals, rather than the other way around."[48] Given the nature of new technologies of transportation and communication and given the fact that the entire globe is economically knit together, there can be no alternative to that conclusion.

By no means will such a transition come easily. People will not lightly give up their national allegiances and identifications. The trend at the moment seems to be directly opposite. People cling to the nation-state, on the apparent belief that the state—the "Good Old USA," "Mother Russia," "La Belle France," and so on—is in fact the source of all that is good. Nationalism is still the civil religion of this and other nations. People the world over have yet to perceive that there is no alternative to forgoing national identifications.

A sociological basis for a constitution that in some way would transcend a bankrupt nationalism may be found in the spread of corporate business throughout the world. Every American corporation of any consequence, as well as those from such other nations as Holland, Switzerland, Japan, West Germany, France, and Great Britain, operate to a considerable extent in other nations—whether in production or in distribution or in exploitation of natural resources. For the United States, this development is creating still another layer to the secret external constitution: the growing web of interactions among nominally private groups, often acting in concert with public government. What happened internally in the United States during the past century, when corporations grew larger and spread nationwide, is being paralleled externally. The meaning is clear: just as the supercorporations were one of the major factors altering traditional federalism in the United States, so, too, they have an effect in external economic—and thus in political—affairs. Corporations are helping to erase the boundary between what is domestic and what is foreign in the constitutional order.

We have seen that the primary characteristic of the formal constitution was divided political power. Lord Acton once remarked that "weighed in the scales of Liberalism, the instrument [the formal constitution] was a monstrous fraud." But, he continued, "by the development of the principle of federalism, it has produced a community more powerful, more prosperous, more intelligent, and more free than any other the world has seen." He also called the "principle of division ... the most efficacious check on democracy that has been devised."[49] Acton's notion that the principle of federalism led to the results he listed is not correct; it is an example of constitutional fetishism—attributing to constitutional principles a life far beyond what they actually have.

The framers did establish a national government with supposedly only limited, delegated powers, leaving the states with all other powers. Two centuries ago, the states were by far the stronger side of the federal system. But that, of course, was not to last. The legal basis for a strong national government was created during the two-thirds of the nineteenth century that culminated in the Civil War. Two strong chief justices—Marshall and Taney—so dominated the Supreme Court that public policy became nationalized in the formal law. The social basis came with expansion of the American empire westward, coupled with such technological advances as the railroad, the steamboat, and the telegraph. With the Civil War—fought, as Lincoln admitted, less to free the slaves than to save the Union—the United States became a true united state. The Union victory in the war eliminated forever the notion that sovereignty reposed in the states. Federalism has not been the same since 1865—not because of judicial decisions (although they helped), but because of the marriage of capital to technology to create the "trusts" (the forerunners of today's supercorporations). An economic basis was provided for a unified nation; a national common market evolved, with a decentralized political order sitting atop a centralized economic order.

Today, accordingly, the states exist more as administrative districts for centrally established policies than as sovereign entities. Those policies are established by public government (the federal government) and by the private governments of the giant corporations. Present-day federalism, as a consequence, tends to be more functional than formal. The truly important decentralized units in the polity are the corporate giants. The constitutional problem this poses is obvious: If Americans seriously desire a true federal system, they will have to think about telescoping the states into regional governments. The process has already begun, although in a halfhearted fashion. The interstate compact device, permitted by the formal constitution, is supplemented by commissions on interstate cooperation and by uniform legislation as a means by which the states have formed inchoate larger-than-state governing techniques. Two examples will show the emerging pattern. The Uniform Commercial Code, governing private contractual agreements, has been adopted by all of the states (with some variations)—a clear reflection of the national nature of the economy. And through computerized data collection, storage, and transmission, law officers throughout the nation are able to obtain instant information about the previous record of anyone arrested for any criminal violation, however minor. The fifty disparate states of the formal constitution are giving way to informal institutional (regional and national) arrangements, some of which may be said to be a part of the secret constitution. The states, moreover, are obviously subordinate to the federal government.

Cooperation, not antagonism, is the norm between the states and the national government. States are, as Hamilton said in 1787, a mere administrative convenience. This has long been known but never really acknowledged in the law of the formal constitution. The truly important units of local government are the supercorporations, which are the units of functional federalism. These organizations under the formal constitution are autonomous. A generation ago, Adolf Berle observed that "the power system emerging is in essence federalist. It contemplates autonomous economic organizations—corporations. It engenders loose relationships between those organizations, usually for the purpose of stabilizing or apportioning the markets."[50]

Economic federalism is a patent fact of American political life. This has significant consequences for the citizenry and for the idea of limitations on government. Professor Robert Hale stated the point well in 1952:

As far as individual liberty is concerned, it is just as important that legislative bodies should be able to protect persons from oppression at the hands of private groups which exercise power indistinguishable from that exercised by government as it is that courts should be able to protect them from oppression by officials whose power is more generally recognized as governmental.[51]

Or, as Alexander Hamilton commented in *The Federalist No. 79*, "In the general course of human nature, a power over a man's subsistence amounts to a power over his will." In 1908, Woodrow Wilson asserted that "the question of the relation of the states to the federal government is the cardinal question of our constitutional system"[52]—a sentiment that may have been accurate then, but it is no longer so. There are several such issues today, including the question of the relation of the nation to the remainder of the globe, the question of whether government (speaking for society) will undertake additional affirmative obligations to the people, and the question of recognizing the dimension of private governments.

As with federalism, so with the so-called separation of powers. The system established by the formal constitution has so broken down that Don K. Price bids us to "quit talking about the constitutional separation of powers."⁵⁸ The term is not now, nor was it really ever, an accurate description of how power is exercised in Washington, D.C. Several points merit emphasis. First, Congress as an institution has little stomach for undertaking the large responsibilities of governing. It willingly delegates large chunks of power to the executive branch, and also often stands mute when the executive assumes authority not granted by either the formal constitution or by Congress. As an institution, its participation in government has evolved (degenerated?) into that of endorsing decisions of the iron triangles of Washington or of following the presidential lead. Second, judicial independence is one of the principal myths of the constitutional order. Despite outward appearances to the contrary, federal judges are seldom at odds with either Congress or the executive. As Professor Martin Shapiro has remarked, "No regime is likely to allow significant political power to be wielded by an isolated judicial corps free of political restraints." When judges make law, as they do routinely, they are incorporated into the ruling elite. "The myth of judicial independence is designed to mollify the loser" in litigation, Shapiro maintains, and he further states: "One of the most important aspects of the social control practiced by courts is that of wedding the populace to the regime, of strengthening the people's perception of the regime's legitimacy and their sense of loyalty to it."⁵⁴ This is one reason why it is true that one is hard-pressed to identify *any* Supreme Court decision upholding personal freedoms when important societal matters are at stake—important, that is, as seen through the eyes of those who wield effective control in the body politic (often through the institutions of the secret constitution). Thus far at least, the liberties purportedly protected by the limitations expressed in the formal constitution are honored when their exercise makes little or no difference to the existing power structure of the nation.

If governing power is in fact shared in the federal government, usually it is in accordance with the norms of the secret constitution. Cooperation rather than conflict is routine, there being just enough of the latter to give the appearance of validity and thus to make alterations in the formal constitution desirable. Means should be devised by which the informal cooperative actions of the iron triangles can be expanded and made a part of the formal fundamental law. If that means moving in the direction of corporatism, no one should blink, for that is precisely the direction in which the evolution of the constitutional order is developing. Government needs to pull as one; means other than separated powers should be devised to check abuses of power. Washington lawyer, and counselor to President Jimmy Carter, Lloyd Cutler, agrees:

A particular shortcoming in need of a remedy is the structural inability of our government to propose, legislate and administer a balanced program for governing. ... The separation of powers between the legislative and executive branches... has become a structure that almost guarantees stalemate today. As we wonder why we are having such a difficult time making decisions we all know must be made, and projecting our power and leadership, we should reflect on whether this is one big reason.[55]

Cutler wishes to alter the governmental structure toward a parliamentary system.

The idea has merit. To be truly effective, however, such a change should be accompanied by other structural changes. Among these are the following six recommendations:

Serious consideration should be given to making Congress a unicameral body of not more than 100 members. As matters now stand, Congress consists of two large committees—the Senate, with 100 members, and the House, with 435 representatives—which simply are unable to act as a cohesive whole. Loyalties of the members run not to members' parties but to their local constituencies or to pressure groups. It is fair to say that Congress not only does not govern today, but does not want to govern. The American people have not been well served by the "system" of "representative government" established by the framers. A one-house Congress, properly staffed, would help alleviate that condition.

The presidency should be bifurcated. The United States is the only major nation in the world that combines in one person the duties of both head of government and chief of state. This means that removal of a president before the end of his elected term of office has become almost impossible. Impeachment is a meaningless scarecrow, despite the near impeachment of Richard Nixon. Several presidents in this century, in addition to Nixon, should have left office before their terms were up. The people's choice can become the people's curse—as has happened. Both Woodrow Wilson and Franklin Roosevelt were physically incompetent during the last year or so of their tenures. Herbert Hoover, Harry Truman, and Jimmy Carter had lost the confidence of the American people. But all except Nixon stayed on. A parliamentary style of government would be impossible without a provision for the head of government—the person similar to a prime minister— being removable by a vote of confidence by Congress. The new chief of state would be a person of known competence and prestige who would perform the ceremonial duties of the presidency.

Means should be devised whereby political parties, which are not even mentioned in the formal constitution, are able to control members of Congress. The head of government, as chief of party, would be in charge and would rule, as in Great Britain, unless on some extraordinary occasion he or she lost a vote of confidence. The two-party system is now an integral part of the secret constitution, having achieved that status by custom and usage and by Supreme Court decisions and congressional statutes.[56] Not that parties are called that; quite the contrary: in large part, although not entirely, they are considered to be private organizations. Their development since 1789 has, however, neatly albeit silently amended the formal constitution. No one can be elected president today unless he or she is a Democrat or a Republican. (Third parties, of course, are permissible, but they are constitutionally insignificant.) The basic problem is that party members pay little or no attention to the national party headquarters, and the loyalties of members of Congress attach, not to the party of which they are members or even to the president, but to those who contribute most to their electoral campaigns.

The fifty states should be telescoped into regional governments. No reason whatsoever exists for having a political subdivision called Rhode Island or Idaho or even Texas or California. If Americans indeed want a strong federal system, which many do, then the states (the regions) must of necessity have much more wealth and power. The nation could be divided into ten or twelve regions, each geographically contiguous within itself. If ten were formed, then each would elect ten people to the newly formed unicameral Congress. Economics and technology have bypassed the original state system, which was more an accident than a planned subdivision of political power.

The dimension of private governments, mainly that of the supercorporations, should be recognized in the formal constitution. Constitutional norms, both negative and affirmative, should be brought to bear against them. The close connection, the symbiotic relationship, between state and enterprise should receive constitutional recognition. Perceptive observers have known since at least the turn of the century that, as Professor Charles Lindblom wrote in 1977, "the large private corporation fits oddly into democratic theory. Indeed, it does not fit."[57] But the learned justices of the Supreme Court have thus far not seen fit to acknowledge the obvious.

The judicial role should be expanded so that the writ of the Supreme Court would run against both of the avowedly political branches of government, as well as private governments. (Of this, more below.)

By no means do these recommended structural alterations in government exhaust the possibilities of what ideally should be considered. But they are a start. Merely listing them, to be sure, points up the enormous complexities of the constitutional problem of the times. The conclusion can only be that the governmental apparatus conceived in 1787 is no longer adequate to present and emergent needs.

Even if adopted, furthermore, (a possibility that certainly is remote at best) by themselves these proposals merely replace certain procedural mechanisms with others. They do not confront the fundamental importance of the substantive norms—the affirmative obligations—to which government must adhere to attain a sustainable society. Changing procedural techniques, moreover, would not ensure that the proper people would be in positions of power and authority. Nevertheless, we should remember the counsel of Sir Karl Popper: "We should like to have good rulers, but historical experience shows us that we are not likely to get them. This is why it is of such importance to design institutions which will prevent even bad rulers from causing too much damage."[58] So we should, and that is what the framers of the formal constitution thought they had done. But the hard facts of American experience belie that goal for two reasons: First, the structure of government has proved to be a barrier to effective and accountable governance; and second, there is no guarantee that "too much damage" will not be caused, simply because of the operations of the secret constitution. If the framers thought about constitutional dualism, they made no public mention of it—or, could it have been that they knew that a secret or parallel constitution would operate but did nothing because they also believed that its operation would be to their benefit? One need not be a cynic to think that the latter was precisely what occurred in 1787 (at the convention), in 1789 (when the new government began to operate), and in ensuing years, when the propertied elite controlled the flow of official decisions.

In ending this discussion of the structure of government under the formal constitution, it is well to remember that the operations of the secret constitution often make a pretense out of what the framers wrought. Perhaps this is what Woodrow Wilson had in mind when he wrote in 1908:

> Government is not a machine, but a living thing. It falls, not under the theory of the universe, but under the theory of organic life. It is accountable to Darwin, not to Newton. It is modified by its environment, necessitated by its tasks, shaped to its functions by the sheer pressure of life. No living thing can have its organs offset against each other as checks, and live.... There can be no successful government without leadership or without the intimate, almost instinctive, coordination of the organs of life and action. This is not theory, but fact.... Living political constitutions must be Darwinian in structure and practice.[59]

So they should. Constitutions must—will—adapt to circumstances. Of that, there can be no doubt. Constitutional change is sure to come. The circumstances that were outlined in Part I will, soon or late, impact directly and heavily on the constitutional order.

The basic question is the direction that constitutional adaptation will take. Or, rather, what direction *should* it take? The above-mentioned additional governmental obligations and duties seem to me to be the minimum that are necessary. That is so even though it would be puerility compounded to believe that they will come into being. There are simply too many roadblocks in the ways that humans order their affairs to believe that they are ready to alter their dangerous and profligate ways. But the attempt should be made. The dialogue should begin.

Major problems, perhaps of an insuperable nature, remain. High among them is the question of enforcement: How can new affirmative obligations of government be put into effect? A mere paper promise in a written constitution is meaningless unless some way is available to transform it into operational reality. In addition, paper promises without the environmental conditions required to put them into effect are also meaningless, just as constitutional limitations become barren "parchment barriers" to adverse governmental action unless there is a spirit of liberty and of compliance abroad in the land.

Enforcement has always been a primary problem of a government that trumpets that it is one of laws, not of men. People tend to assume that if a law is passed either requiring or prohibiting something, it will be enforced by the public officers charged with that duty. This enforcement, however, is not the central point here. Rather, it is whether the proposed new obligations of Congress can be put into effect. The recommendation proffered is that the Supreme Court should assume a new role—that of hearing and deciding allegations that Congress has not fulfilled one of its express constitutional duties.

Constitutions and their limitations and obligations are not self-executing. Intervention of human agents is indispensable. Should a new constitution be written containing such additional affirmative obligations to the people as have been outlined in this chapter and be put into effect by Congress, there is no assurance that Congress would fulfill its new duties. What, then, can be done? The answer given here is that the Supreme Court, which as long ago as 1803 asserted that it was the province and duty of the judiciary "to say what the law is,"[60] should be the principal enforcement agency. This duty could be accomplished by enlarging upon the original jurisdiction of the Court. The formal constitution now reads (in Article III): "In all cases affecting ambassadors, other public ministers and consuls, and those in which a state shall be party, the Supreme Court shall have original jurisdiction." (That Congress by statute cannot enlarge upon that jurisdiction by statute has been accepted law since 1803.) This means that only a minute portion of the Court's present work is devoted to cases coming under the original jurisdiction provision. The Court today has an enormous workload; some, such as former Chief Justice Warren Burger, think it is far too onerous. If, therefore, its original jurisdiction were to be enlarged in accordance with the above-discussed recommendation, something else would of course have to go. (This suggests that there may be a need for *two* supreme courts, one to handle the types of cases that the present Court deals with and the other to serve as a tribunal that would hear and decide cases involving the new congressional duties.)

Historically and contemporaneously, the Supreme Court in saying "what the law is" tended to take a negative stance: It issued a series of "thou-shall-nots" to other governmental officers. The question now is how to permit it to say "thou shalt." This is by no means a novel proposition. During the past generation—the point of departure is perhaps the Little

Rock School Desegregation case, *Cooper v. Aaron* (1958)[61]—the Supreme Court not only overtly asserts that its specific rulings state a general rule but also has at times spoken in terms of affirmative constitutional duty. The suggestion, therefore, that the Court sit to hear and decide whether Congress has complied with certain express constitutional duties (obligations) newly inserted into the formal document is not nearly as radical as it might seem on first blush.

Let me explain. Inasmuch as the question of enforcement of constitutional obligations is crucial to the thesis of this volume, it is desirable to set forth at some length the outlines of a new and challenging role for the Supreme Court. The first inquiry is into the change in role of the Court during the past three or four decades from negative naysayer to affirmative commander. Although in some respects Professor Alexander Bickel was correct when he observed that *"Brown v. Board of Education* was the beginning"[62] of the new judicial posture, it is even more accurate to maintain that one of *Brown*'s progeny, *Cooper v. Aaron*, was the most important ruling of the Court during the tenure of Chief Justice Earl Warren.

In *Cooper*, a unanimous Court made a mutational legal leap by expressly asserting, for the first time in American history, that its decisions are "the supreme law of the land" and, as such, binding upon other governmental officers, federal and state. This assertion was a breathtaking grasp of governing power, fully as significant in its implications as the decision in *Marbury v. Madison* (1803), when the Court first asserted the authority to determine the constitutionality of an act of Congress. (Neither judicial review nor Supreme Court preeminence, it is important to remember, are set forth in the formal constitution. But they have now become so accepted that few challenge their basic foundation.) In *Cooper*, furthermore, the justices neatly accomplished the logically impossible—inferring a general principle (a rule of law) from one particular. In lawyers' language, therefore, constitutional decisions have become de facto class actions, with the "class" being the entire nation. The Court became a third, and highest, legislative chamber. National public policy is established through the medium of lawsuits, often generated by or against one person (as in *Roe v. Wade*, the 1973 abortion ruling).[63] Justice William Brennan acknowledged this in 1980 when he wrote that decisions in cases involving individuals "impose official and practical consequences upon members of society at large." He continued:

Under our system, judges are not mere umpires, but, in their own sphere, lawmakers—a coordinate branch of government. The interpretation and application of constitutional and statutory law, while not legislation, is lawmaking, albeit of a kind that is subject to special constraints and informed by unique considerations. Guided and confined by the Constitution and pertinent statutes, judges are obliged to be discerning, exercise judgment, and prescribe rules. Indeed, at times judges wield considerable authority to formulate legal policy in designated areas.[64]

Brennan was not quite correct: The Supreme Court is in fact, although not in theory, a third and *superior* legislative chamber, superior because it is interpreting the formal constitution and cannot be overruled by a mere statute. A constitutional amendment is required. Two centuries after the constitutional convention, where the notion of the Supreme Court as a "council of revision" was rejected, that tribunal is well on its way toward being not only an aristocratic censor of what government cannot do but also an oracle that issues edicts saying—at times—what government must do.

That position is an exponential leap from the original conception of the framers (insofar as their intentions can be determined). The full flowering of the idea was a long time coming—and we have yet to see just how far it will go—but the seed was planted as early as the *Marbury* decision in 1803. *Cooper* may be said to be a logical extension of *Marbury*. Instrumentalism came to law, as Professor Morton Horwitz has explained:

By 1820 the legal landscape in America bore only the faintest resemblance to what existed forty years earlier. While the words were often the same, the structure of thought had dramatically changed and with it the theory of law. Law was no longer conceived of as an external set of principles expressed in custom and derived from the natural law. Nor was it regarded primarily as a body of rules designed to achieve justice only in the individual case. Instead, judges came to think of the common law as equally responsible with legislation for governing society and promoting socially desirable conduct. The emphasis on law as an instrument of policy encouraged innovation and allowed judges to formulate legal doctrine with the self-conscious goal of bringing about social change.[65]

What was true of the common law was also true of constitutional law. Horwitz's last sentence describes remarkably well what the Supreme Court and other Courts have been doing for more than a generation. The mutational leap in *Cooper v. Aaron* had its antecedents in early American constitutional history. Although usually purporting to act *nomocratically*— "following existent rules"—the Court has been *telocratic*—"avowedly purposive and goal-seeking." With *Cooper*, telocracy became overt—and accepted within the polity.

The Court legislates—makes law—each time that it renders a constitutional decision (and often one interpreting statutes); and, indeed, as Justice Byron White observed in 1966, the Court cannot avoid doing so if it is to continue in its accepted constitutional mission.[66] It legislates for the people at large and for generations yet unborn (unless, as happens occasionally, it limits the thrust of its ruling to the facts of the case at bar). As "super-legislators," the justices therefore sit as a constitutional convention in continuous session, adapting the formal constitution to the exigencies confronting different generations of Americans. They may not be infallible—who is?—but they are final. Their rulings in effect amend the formal constitution, but not in accordance with the procedures for amendment set out in Article V.]

The precise turning point to overt constitutional telocracy came in Chief Justice Charles Evans Hughes's opinion in a minimum-wage case, *West Coast Hotel Co. v. Parrish* (1937).[67] Against a traditional argument that a state statute establishing minimum wages was an undue interference into the liberty of employer and employee alike, Hughes replied that the liberty protected in the formal constitution was "in a social organization" that used law to ward off some of the evils of industrialization. From being a limitation on governmental power, the due process clauses of the formal document became at least an invitation, and perhaps a command, for political action to ameliorate human distress. Hughes explained:

> The principle which must control our decision is not in doubt. The constitutional provision invoked is the due process clause of the fourteenth amendment, governing the states.... The violation alleged by those attacking minimum wage legislation is deprivation of freedom of contract. What is this freedom? The Constitution does not speak of freedom of contract. It speaks of liberty and prohibits the deprivation of liberty without due process of law. In prohibiting that deprivation, the Constitution does not recognize an absolute and uncontrollable liberty. Liberty in each of its phases has its history and connotation. But the liberty safeguarded is liberty in a social organization which *requires* the protection of law against the evils which menace the health, safety, morals and welfare of the people. Liberty under the Constitution is thus necessarily subject to the restraints of due process, and regulation which is reasonable in relation to its subject and is adopted in the interests of the community is due process.[68]

With that statement the Supreme Court changed the nature of liberty under the formal constitution. "From being a limitation on legislative power," Professor Edward S. Corwin commented, "the due process clause became an actual instigation to legislation of a leveling character."[69]

In effect, Hughes adopted without acknowledgment, and probably without knowledge, Thomas Hill Green's concept of positive freedom and of collective well-being. To Green, freedom meant "a positive power or capacity of doing or enjoying something worth doing and enjoying... in common with others."[70] Freedom thus depends on the "help and security" given by others, and which a person helps to secure for others. According to Hughes, who spoke for the Supreme Court majority, the liberty protected by due process is not only in a social organization but also requires the protection of law against social evils. The formal constitution became a true "living" constitution; and it has not been the same since *Parrish*. Governmental obligations, epitomized in the New Deal, helped to create a new type of government—the "positive state" as distinguished from the "negative, nightwatchman state" of the 150 years prior to *Parrish*. For that decision was quickly followed by one sustaining the National Labor Relations Act, which in turn led to a series of legislative entitlements that were judicially approved.

The seed of constitutional duty, planted by Hughes, lay dormant until the movement of black Americans for decent treatment under the institutions of the formal constitution brought irresistible pressures to bear upon the Supreme Court. An "indivisible" nation pledges "liberty and justice to all." This may be considered by some to be a mere hortatory slogan, a symbol; but we should remember that as Oliver Wendell Holmes taught, "we live by symbols."[71] The symbol today is becoming that of collective well-being, of the "general welfare" that is mentioned twice in the formal constitution. Green provided the philosophical basis for positive government, such as the social insurance programs that help to give the economic means for more people to be free. The duty of government in this conception is not so much to maximize individual liberty as an end in itself, but rather "to insure the conditions for at least a minimum of well-being—a standard of living, of education, and of security below which good policy requires that no considerable part of the population shall be allowed to fall."[72] It may readily be seen that Green is also the philosophical progenitor of a constitution of human needs. To this may be added the Declaration of Delhi of the International Congress of Jurists in 1960. The Congress, a group of lawyers from non-Soviet nations, concluded:

The International Congress of Jurists...recognizes that the Rule of Law is a dynamic concept for the expansion and fulfillment of which jurists are primarily responsible and which should be employed not only to safeguard and advance the civil and political rights of the individual in a free society, but also to establish social, economic, educational, and cultural conditions under which his legitimate aspirations and dignity may be realized.[73]

Again, this view is a recognition of the requirement for a constitution of human needs. It is a call for social justice.

But the problem, as yet unanswered, is how to transform the paper promises of Supreme Court decrees and congressional legislation into operational reality. Green wrote at a time—the late nineteenth century—when economic growth seemed to make his proposals possible; and he wrote only of the Western world, without regard to the teeming masses elsewhere. The statement of the International Congress of Jurists came at a time when the expectations and demands of those teeming masses were beginning to press ever harder on Western institutions, as the Brandt Commission recognized.[74] Modern governmental institutions were created and developed during a seeming age of abundance, well before the coming age of frugality, and thus well before the appearance of what has been called a "zero-sum society."[75] This label seems appropriate for an economy, a society, that approximates · a "steady-state" position, one in which economic growth does not keep up with either population increase or the rising expectations of people long caught short in the race of life. The proposal therefore that Congress assume a new constitutional duty of helping to create the environmental conditions favorable to maintenance of a sustainable society must be weighed against the fact of what has previously been called the end of the 400-year boom.

The Supreme Court surely has a role here. We have already seen how the Court during the past four decades has issued affirmative commands to the American people to unify their society socially as well as educationally. *Brown v. Board of Education* and its progeny characterized a new beginning for the Court, a point emphasized in the early 1960s when the justices decreed that all votes should count equally (one person, one vote) in the election of state legislatures and the federal House of Representatives.[76] The voting cases caused Justice Felix Frankfurter to state his dismay that states could be judicially ordered to follow the formal constitution's prescription of equal protection of the laws, on pain of having judges do the job of reapportionment of legislatures if necessary. In effect, Frankfurter thought that the remedy, if any, lay in the state legislatures—which meant, of course, that malapportioned voters should go to the very people who benefited from the prior system, the state politicians, and ask them to vote themselves out of office—a well-nigh classic example of judicial purblindness. So, too, with Justice John Harlan, who grumbled in 1964 that the one person, one vote decisions were based on a mistaken view "that every major social ill in this country can find its cure in some constitutional 'principle,' and that this Court should 'take the lead' in promoting reform when other branches fail to act."[77] This, again, is a clear case of judicial myopia: how could Harlan possibly have believed that the formal constitution is a self-executing document and that people should await the admittedly "slow workings of the political process"? The political process was not merely "slow"; it was stalled in the voting cases. The formal constitutional command of equal protection of the laws—which, of course, is an ambiguous provision—simply was not working, either for black Americans (the *Brown* situation) or for urban voters (the one person, one vote cases). When some formal constitutional institution refuses to live up to its responsibilities, what are people to do? The Frankfurter-Harlan "remedy" is no remedy at all.

Their views simply do not wash, as any perceptive observer of the Supreme Court knows (and as all students of the Court's history should know). The Court has always had the power and authority to say what the law *is*, and since at least the *Brown* decision in 1954, to say what the law *should be*. For that matter, even when saying what the law is, the justices cannot avoid choosing between two (or more) conflicting principles of approximately equal weight; and in so doing, must make law (say what the law should be). (This has been called the Principle of Doctrinal Polarity, which all cases that reach the Supreme Court exhibit in greater or lesser degree.) This polarity is to be seen, to mention another well-known example, in the way that the Court prescribed a little code of criminal procedure in *Miranda v. Arizona* (1966).[78] Although that lawsuit on its face seemed to concern only Miranda and the state of Arizona—when Miranda had been caught in the toils of the criminal law administration of that state—the Supreme Court wrote broadly and issued a new general command to apply to people in Miranda's situation. The *Miranda* opinion can travel under several labels: it can be called a legislative enactment by the de facto third legislative chamber, a "backdoor" advisory opinion issued by the Court majority (even though since the 1790s the Court has adamantly refused to issue true advisory opinions), or a weakened type of constitutional amendment—weakened because *Miranda* can be overruled by the Court—that extended the sixth amendment's right to defense counsel back from the trial to the arrest and investigatory stages of the criminal law process. *Miranda* followed on the heels of other criminal law decisions, *Gideon v. Wainwright* and progeny,[79] which in effect ordered government to furnish attorneys to indigents who had been caught and accused of crimes. Another outstanding and still controversial ruling came in 1973 when a Court majority legitimized abortions during the first trimester of a woman's gestation period.

Nor were these decisions all. Some lower court judges in the federal system, as well as some state supreme courts, also began to locate affirmative duties in the lean language of the formal constitution and in state constitutions. It was a judicial revolution of the first magnitude, as significant as was the Supreme Court's assertion of the power to second-guess other government officers in *Marbury v. Madison* (1803). There is, in sum, a growing willingness of some (but far from all) judges to intervene actively in governmental administration, and not only to identify affirmative duties of government but also to command obedience to judicial decrees. As Professor Nathan Glazer commented, "The courts have truly changed their role in American life" and have reached deeper into the lives of people than "they ever have in American history." Glazer claims this role is against "the will of the people,"[80] a sentiment that simply is not correct. Remedies are required for long-felt ills; and if, as with black Americans, the outwardly political branches of government will not extend them, people are left with only the judiciary. Impotent politically, these people see judges as their final hope to work "within the system" and to better their condition. This belief may be what led Justice Lewis Powell to assert, shortly before his nomination to the Supreme Court, that "the judiciary may be the most important instrument for social, economic and political change."[81] Interest groups of all ideologies view the Court as being able to decide important issues of public policy.

In this sense, it may well be that the new role for the courts is the final, desperate hope of an increasingly shaky system of American constitutionalism for salvation from its own inequities and inconsistencies. The new type of litigants believes the incessant rhetoric about democracy and the rule of law, so such persons call upon an oligarchic judiciary to further their ends. This situation may be a paradox, but it is a fact. It is a paradox, also, because the Supreme Court historically operated as the protector of property and privilege. That could continue, but only if the Court were to follow signals of the past three or four decades so as to enlarge the group of beneficiaries of their decisions. The justices should realize that extending some gains to the disadvantaged will help to drain off social discontent—and thus would permit the propertied and privileged to retain their positions. This situation, to be sure, as Robert H. Jackson maintained in 1941, would be "government by lawsuit."[82] But constitutional decisions, he went on to say, "are the stuff of power politics in America." Constitutional interpretation, Frankfurter once remarked, "is not at all a science, but applied politics."[83]

All of this explanation serves to buttress the previous contention of the myth of judicial independence. As part of the political process—using that term in its best rather than an invidious sense—judges have become equal in title and equal in origin with the legislature and the executive. This, of course, is not to say that "the universe will obey the judicial decree"[84]: to the contrary, edicts will be obeyed only to the extent that they conform to the *zeitgeist*. The Supreme Court in this respect does not differ from either Congress or the president. It cannot go off on frolics of its own. What the justices can do is to keep their "radar" tuned to prevailing public opinion. And they can, as they did in *Brown v. Board of Education*, become the conscience of the people; they can erect standards toward which the population should aspire.

The justices of the Supreme Court have become a latter-day version of Plato's philosopher-kings—what Judge Learned Hand derided as a group of "Platonic Guardians."[85] The label is unimportant. What is important is the undeniable fact that the justices make up the law as they go along, and in so doing they cannot avoid ruling on the wisdom of disputed governmental actions. Although, furthermore, it is true that they cannot reach out and rule on a case not before the Court—they must await the accident of litigation—it is also true that once they decide to rule they can make their constitutional interpretations as broad or narrow as they wish. This means that, despite the alleged rule against issuing advisory opinions, the justices, as noted, do so in an indirect or "backdoor" manner, "legislating" for the nation at large and for the future. With its immense docket—on the order of 5,000 cases are filed each year—the Court can, and does, pick and choose from among the cases, deciding only those issues that it thinks are of national importance. Despite an occasional aberration, it does not deal with the trivial disputes, trivial, that is, from a national rather than personal sense (for all cases are far from trivial for at least one of the litigants).

There is a further meaning for the Court as a group of philosopher-kings: the constitution is not a mere lawyer's document, and the justices should be drawn from more than the legal profession. Morris Raphael Cohen called attention to what should be but is not obvious: "We cannot pretend that the United States Supreme Court is simply a court of law. Actually, the issues before it generally depend on the determination of all sorts of facts, their consequences, and the value we attach to these consequences. These are questions of economics, politics, and social policy which legal training cannot solve unless law includes all social knowledge".[86] But since the beginnings, lawyers have monopolized the judiciary, including the Supreme Court, even though most judges are narrow-minded specialists with little or no background for making wise social judgments. Writing in 1881, long before he joined the Supreme Court, Oliver Wendell Holmes anticipated Cohen:

The very considerations which judges most rarely mention, and always with an apology, are the secret root from which the law draws all the juices of life. I mean of course what is expedient in the community concerned. Every important principle developed by litigation is in fact and at bottom the result of more or less definitely understood views of public policy; most generally, to be sure, under our practices and traditions, the unconscious result of instinctive preferences and inarticulate convictions, but nonetheless traceable to views of public policy in the last analysis.[87]

By no means do lawyers have a monopoly on the type of learning and experience necessary to adequately perform the awesome duties of the Supreme Court, either at present or with, as recommended, enhanced functions. We should no longer indulge in the pretense that the Court is merely another court of law.[88]

The Supreme Court is a very special type of court—if, indeed, it is a court at all in its constitutional decisions. Although encased in the trappings of legalism and imprisoned, in part at least, by the shortcomings of the adversary system, it is in fact America's ultimate faculty of political theory. This has long been so (although little recognized in the literature). As long ago as 1924, the institutional economist John R. Commons could observe, quite accurately, that the justices were "the first authoritative faculty of political economy in the world's history."[89] Commons merely invited attention to what should have been obvious.

All of this has not come without controversy, to be sure. Thomas Jefferson once complained that Chief Justice John Marshall had made the formal constitution "merely a thing of wax" that the Court "may twist and shape into any form they please."[90] Or, as Justice Holmes commented decades later, "We are very quiet here, but it is the quiet of a storm center."[91] So it is: The Court is the target of pressure groups' tactics, and its decisions are often met with strident disapproval from a moiety of the populace. The abortion decisions are a prominent example of such rulings.

The Court has long been viewed *and* accepted as an authoritative spokes man for national values. As such, it has no counterpart in any modern government. But it can be compared to the oracles who in ancient times helped humans to find their way in the face of an unknown and threatening future—precisely what Americans confront today. The Delphic Oracle, for example, provided help on "substantive" issues—what people should or should not do. "The mere fact that Delphi provided a center for enquiry on many subjects was of incalculable significance in the Greek world."[92] So, too, with the Supreme Court: its impact is immeasurable in a quantitative sense but what it says (and does not say) is equally significant in modern America.

Although the analogy should not be pushed too far, the Delphic claim that the Oracle was without "deceit" seems similar to the idea of the Court as ultimate constitutional interpreter—the notion, self-asserted, of Supreme Court infallibility. The Delphic priests, like Supreme Court justices, had no organized religious system and no established church, but they did have close and continuing contacts with local priests (in the case of the Court, contacts are with the American bar). "The supremacy which Delphi long maintained over its rivals and all other methods of divination was largely the outcome of an accumulated prestige, and was little supported by dogma or ecclesiastical organization."[93] So it is with the Supreme Court, where the justices make decisions by some sort of judicial divination. The litigable parts of the formal constitution are "empty vessels" into which a judge "can pour nearly anything he will."[94] As Chief Justice Earl Warren candidly admitted, "We, of course, venerate the past, but our focus is on the problems of the day and the future as far as we can foresee it." The Court, said Warren, has the awesome responsibility of often speaking the last word "in great governmental affairs." He went on: "It is a responsibility that is made more difficult in this Court because we have no constituency. We serve no majority. We serve no minority. We serve only the public interest as we see it, guided only by the Constitution and our own consciences."[95]

Since, however, the formal constitution is no guide at all—it being only by an indefensible fiction that decisions can be logically derived from its text—the justices have only their consciences, their personal philosophies, to divine what the results should be in constitutional cases. This is where we are today. No one should blink, therefore, if the Court extended its reach to encompass the imposition of affirmative duties upon Congress and the president.

This chapter has outlined some alterations that seem desirable in the formal constitution. As sweeping as they are, they only suggest half the battle. Changes must also come in the secret constitution. This, in the last analysis, necessitates that the basic value system of Americans requires re-evaluation. The focus of the next chapter will deal in part with that question.

CHAPTER 6

THE ROADBLOCKS

It is the first step in sociological wisdom to recognize that the major advances in civilization are processes which all but wreck the societies in which they occur—like unto an arrow in the hands of a child. The art of a free society consists first in the maintenance of the symbolic code; and secondly in fearlessness of revision, to secure that the code serves those purposes which satisfy an enlightened reason. Those societies which cannot combine reverence to their symbols with freedom of revision, must ultimately decay either from anarchy, or from the slow atrophy of a life stifled by useless shadows.

—Alfred North Whitehead[1]

Extraordinary conditions demand extraordinary, even unique, remedies. Some desirable institutional alterations in the formal constitution have been proffered. Whether these can come into being is far from likely—although that does not detract from their desirability. Formidable obstacles to their realization can be easily identified. This chapter outlines some of the most important "roadblocks." The basic theses are that the norms of the secret constitution should be brought into consonance with those of the formal constitution and that the principal goal of both fundamental laws should be the reasonably adequate satisfaction of human needs.

First, it is highly improbable, and perhaps impossible, that a system of constitutional dualism can be wholly eliminated. The secret constitution will continue to operate, but those who control its institutions must in some way take steps to ensure that their actions jibe with the enduring values of the formal constitution. This is a roadblock of substantial and perhaps

135-6

insuperable proportions. How it is resolved will in large part determine the shape of things to come in the United States. (Of this, more below.)

Second, the fallacy of Micawberism must be dispelled. There are many who will quickly invoke the cliché, "If it ain't broke, don't fix it," when confronted with arguments for constitutional change. (The answer to that charge, of course, is simple: fix it before it breaks. Just as preventive medicine is the best type of medicine, so it is with governments, even though the idea has not been accepted. Those who invoke the cliché should be certain that American constitutionalism is a winning game—and who can really say that, given the shape of things domestic and global?) Barbara Tuchman, for example, concludes her *The March of Folly* with a counsel of despair: "If John Adams was right, and government is 'little better practiced now [the late eighteenth century] than three or four thousand years ago,' we cannot reasonably expect much improvement. We can only muddle on as we have done in those three or four thousand years, through patches of brilliance and decline, great endeavor and shadow."[2] But it—the constitutional structure—*is* broken, broken almost as badly as were the Articles of Confederation in 1787, and it simply will not do to maintain that people have no alternative but to continue to "muddle on." The times are too perilous, too fraught with unparalleled dangers, to permit an unplanned drift into the future. We can no longer put off trying to answer, this time in conditions far different from two centuries ago, Alexander Hamilton's incisive question about whether humans are capable of creating good governments by design and choice or whether they are forever relegated to being the butt of accident and force. The blind, unthinking faith in the powers of science and technology to rescue humankind from its self-imposed follies, through a series of as yet unknown technological fixes, simply will not do the necessary. It is folly compounded to think otherwise.

The invisible chains of Micawberism must be broken: It is fatuous to believe that something will magically turn up to solve humanity's problems, absent a sustained, comprehensive and *directed* human effort. How this can come about is not at all clear. Perhaps some truly major crisis will be necessary: "If there's ever gonna be change in America, it's gonna be 'cause every community in America's ready for it—and boom! There's gonna be a big tidal wave, and it's gonna crash down on Washington, and the people are finally gonna be heard."[3] Such a tidal wave may be seen historically in the Great Depression of the 1930s, when the hunger and misery of tens of millions of Americans finally forced the federal government to take action. Despair was turning into violence and the nation teetered on the edge of at least partial anarchy. The social tidal wave first hit the presidency (President Franklin D. Roosevelt), then Congress, and finally the Supreme Court—all of the primary institutions of the formal constitution. The nation, generally, saw quite clearly that things could not be allowed to drift and that nothing was bound to turn up to resolve the miserable conditions of so many people.

The New Deal programs were the consequence. Although the United States was a late-bloomer as compared with some European nations, those programs made up the American version of the welfare state. That they did not solve the fundamental problems of economic distress is well known. But they did buy some time. Only, however, the advent of a military economy, before, during, and after World War II, and consequent high governmental expenditures for national security concerns, were able to lift the country from the morass into which it had sunk.

There is a lesson in social dynamics here: Only a situation that is widely perceived to be a crisis will dissipate and ultimately eliminate the mindless faith in Micawberism. Dr. Willis W. Harman has concluded that the *problematique* of humankind can be met. "We have to be on guard against the belief that experts have all the answers," he maintains. "Fundamental change in societies has always come from vast numbers of people changing their minds just a little."[4]

The nuclear threat may be such a crisis that little by little is changing the minds of large numbers of people. To quote George Kennan: There is, he said,

a growing appreciation by many people of the true horrors of nuclear war; a determination not to see their children deprived of life, or their civilization destroyed, by a holocaust of this nature; and finally..., a very real exasperation with their governments to ignore the fundamental distinction between conventional weapons and weapons of mass destruction and prevents them from finding, or even seriously seeking, ways of escape from the fearful trap into which the cultivation of nuclear weapons is leading us.[5]

Should that exasperation be expanded to include other human needs, then the puerile adherence to Micawberism might wither away. Whether the political leaders liked it or not, they would have to react to the pent-up demands of the people the world over.

It can happen. It did in the 1930s. Witness, furthermore, the present-day's growing ferment in the Third and Fourth Worlds for better conditions of life—in South Africa, in the Philippines, in Latin America, in sub-Saharan Africa. People are on the march, and it will behoove those who would be their leaders to determine the direction the march is taking and try to get out in front and lead.[6] Even in the United States, the last bastion of corporate capitalism, discontent is growing about the widening gap between the "haves" and the "have-nots." This condition cannot last, simply because it is absurd, absurd that people anywhere should be out of work and hungry and homeless. The tidal wave of discontent is certain to swell, no doubt slowly at first, but inexorably, until something is done in a meaningful sense. If, as was said in the Civil War, the nation could not survive half-slave and half-free, so it is today: the nation—certainly the spirit of the formal constitution—will not survive with a dwindling minority being affluent and with growing numbers of the impoverished.

Third, the "American disease is a roadblock to change." The past may be only prologue to the present and the future; but the future, because of as yet unknown scientific and technological changes, cannot and will not be a mere extension of the past. A major turning point in the human condition requires, as Arthur Koestler has argued, a like transition in the human mind and the human psyche.[7] Human folly, Barbara Tuchman tells us, is "the self-destructive act carried out despite the availability of a recognized and feasible alternative"[8]—precisely where *homo sapiens* finds itself today in almost the entire range of public policies. "The present generation is the hinge of history," biophysicist John Platt asserts.[9] So it is: Change, massive social change, is pandemic. This is certain to have a major impact upon the political and economic—the constitutional—order. Whether those inevitable changes will follow desirable paths depends upon two factors: (1) the adequacy of constitutional institutions, and (2) the correct set of human values. The factors go hand in hand; both are important and are so interlocked that their separation, save for purposes of discussion, is impossible. This bond has created the crucial problem, labeled by Professor George Lodge, the "American disease":

> The American disease is a pathological condition, deriving from a severe development crisis in the evolution of American society. It is a psychotic condition, characterized by the denial of reality and the inability to develop solutions to the problems being forced upon the community by a new and unfamiliar environment. In its extreme manifestations, the American disease has the symptoms of schizophrenia, a condition for which there is essentially no cure; but in fact, the disease more closely resembles the ailment of a troubled adolescent whose grief at growing up causes him to deny reality, or to cope with it through wishful thinking or a regression into immature, counterproductive behavior.
> *The treatment of the American disease will necessarily include a rebuilding of the foundation of our society.*[10]

Exactly. Lodge thereby posed the fundamental constitutional question.

We live today, Lodge maintains, with the remnants of an outmoded and exploded ideology. Few persons want to make the necessary transition. Most have a mindset with three elements—"the creedal passion to stay with the old, the inefficient and illegitimate transition to the new, and our confusion about the bases of authority."[11] Lodge concludes that little is known about the disease and that there is no known remedy for it—which is not really correct. The disease, as he describes it, is known to all who want to see and to understand the human condition, and the remedy is obvious, at least on a high level of abstraction. There must, in sum, be changes in human values and in political institutions. Both kinds of changes are necessary, and must proceed in parallel lines. The time has come, as Lodge suggests, for Americans to outgrow their adolescence and to deal effectively with the twin requirements of a constitution of human needs: changes in constitutional institutions and in values.⌉

Fourth, the "arrogance of humanism must be recognized." The challenge confronting *homo sapiens* is awesome, unique in human history. Whether it will be met in a reasonably adequate fashion is far from certain. "The question," Professor Robert Heilbroner observes, "is how we are to summon up the will to survive—not perhaps in the distant future . . . but in the present and near-term future, while we still enjoy and struggle with the heritage of our personal liberties."[12] Only those who profess belief in the well-nigh infinite capacity of the human mind to detect and solve problems will believe that the challenge will be met⌈ Complete faith in humanity's ability to direct its destiny, Professor David Ehrenfeld has cogently argued,[13] is dangerously fallacious. Surely he is correct./ There may be little chance that the future can truly be engineered—at precisely the time that the need is greatest for that to be done. That is so even though the majority of educated people are convinced—on faith, it seems, for it is against the overwhelming weight of the evidence—that there is no trap, including the closing ecological trap, that people cannot reason their way out of once they put their minds to it.

Humans do not steer the planet Earth in its orbit; nor can they. Nature will not provide the corrective remedy to societal ills, however; if it is to be done, humans must provide it themselves.⌉ "Biological evolution has let us down; we can only hope to survive if we develop techniques which supplant it by inducing the necessary changes in human nature."[14]

But still, the human spirit abides. Many people are searching for valid answers or for ways to help extricate the species from the morass into which it is immersed. Koestler's despairing remedy is for the development of a drug that would eliminate blockages in the human brain that impede its proper use—mystic insights, philosophic wisdom, creative power. "To use our brain to cure its own shortcomings" was to him "a brave and dedicated enterprise."[15] In that view, Koestler seems to have anticipated the coming of what may be called the ultimate technological fix—the use of cloning, of genetic engineering, to create not only new life-forms but to alter the behavior of present life-forms.[16] Still in a relatively primitive stage of development, genetic engineering—what Dr. Joshua Lederberg labeled as "algeny"—may well be the wave of the future.[17]

If so, the question, age-old but still present, of who watches the watchmen (the genetic engineers) immediately obtrudes. Koestler raises but does not adequately answer the question. He writes:

To hope for salvation to be synthesized in the laboratory may seem materialistic, crankish, or naive; but, to tell the truth, there is a Jungian twist to it—for it reflects the ancient alchemist's dream to concoct the *elixir vitae*. What we expect from it, however, is not eternal life, nor the transformation of base metal into gold, but the transformation of *homo maniacus* into *homo sapiens*. When man decides to take his fate into his own hands, that possibility will be within reach.[18]

Koestler did not foresee the advent of algeny, but his suggestion that a drug be produced to alter the human mind is a progenitor of what genetic engineers are doing today. "For the first time in history, humanity is able to convert living material into new shapes and forms, to redesign existing organisms, and to engineer wholly new ones genetically. It is a time that marks a qualitative break from our entire past relationship with nature."[19] This has extraordinary, far-reaching implications. What is emerging, says Jeremy Rifkin,[20] is a new concept of nature, with cybernetics as the organizing framework, computers as the organizing mechanisms, and living tissue as the organizing material. This scenario is no fantasy: In 1980, the Supreme Court ruled that new forms of life, engineered in laboratories, are patentable.[21] That historic decision lent legal legitimacy to the revolution in bioengineering technology, a revolution, Rifkin contends, that will prove to be as important to humanity as the use of fire.

The biotechnological revolution is well upon us. It, too, may be a part of the arrogance of humanism. But it is one whose final consequences are wholly unpredictable. It is also one that illustrates how technology has outrun law, for there is no adequate regulatory machinery in existence to keep it within humane bounds.

Fifth, the inadequacy of human reason is a roadblock. There is a type of fatuous optimism that holds that if people think hard enough and are of good will, all human problems can be solved. Although the formal constitution was essentially a product of the Age of Reason (the eighteenth century), that sort of mindless optimism has long been known to be faulty. This is true even though much of the literature about formal constitutional law is bottomed on the premise that law today is a rational process, understandable as such, and administered as such. That notion is simply wrong: Reason, at most, is instrumental. It cannot determine where humans should go, but it does have utility in telling them how to get to predetermined goals. How those goals are identified is not a function of reason.

Belief in the power of reason has been traced to the ancient Greeks, who are generally considered to be the discoverers of rationality in human affairs and of rational inquiry into the nature of the universe, of what constitutes the good life for humankind. To the Greeks, reason was the highest human faculty, and the exercise of reason the best life. Rationality came into full bloom with the Stoic school, about the third century B.C., and was adopted by many Romans. As Marcus Aurelius, emperor and Stoic, wrote in his *Meditations*: "Reason and the reasoning art—philosophy—are powers sufficient to themselves and for their own work. They start from a first principle which is their own, and make their way to the end that they set before them."[22]

It is, however, the first principles, the premises, from which reason proceeds that are all-important. Reason by itself cannot produce those principles. They must, of necessity, come from elsewhere. They must, that is, be accepted on faith. Even the natural sciences, the so-called hard sciences, proceed in that way, as Professor Henry Margenau has informed us: "Deductive science (in contradistinction to descriptive sciences like geography or botany) begins with fundamental, unproved propositions which are verified only in their several consequences. The scientist does not seek to prove these axioms; rather, he accepts them provisionally, judiciously but without proof, hoping that their consequences agree with the facts. Nor is his attitude toward them one of avoidance or tolerance. He cannot get going without them."[23] So it is with constitutionalism: John Locke, among others, proceeded from certain fundamental, unproved propositions—as does, for that matter, anyone who writes seriously about the role and function of constitutions and of governments.

Within the legal system, especially the judicial process, reason has a sharply limited role. Lawsuits are adversary in nature; the system is based on the assumption that if certain procedures are followed, then some sort of justice will result, justice in the sense that the decisions reached will be seen as at least tolerable and perhaps even desirable. This premise, however, is at best a limited use of reason. Moreover, the assumption on which the adversary system is based, at least in constitutional cases, is likely to be seriously faulty. As has been noted, it is the ends—the results—that are at issue, and procedure alone in the absence of collectively held societal goals is meaningless.

Sixth, human affairs, furthermore, display, as Dr. Andrew Bard Schmookler has shown, a destructive logic rather than the play of reason. This is the problem of power. Reason is the polar opposite of power. Schmookler, in his seminal *The Parable of the Tribes*, bids us to attend to the central fact of power in the global political arena:

Imagine a group of tribes living within reach of each other. If all choose the way of peace, all may live in peace. But what if all but one choose peace, and that one is ambitious for expansion and conquest? What can happen to others when confronted by an ambitious and potent neighbor? . . . The irony is that successful defense against a power-maximizing aggressor requires a society to become more like the society which threatens it. Power can be stopped only by power, and if the threatening society has discovered ways to magnify its power through innovations in organization or technology (or whatever), the defensive society will have to transform itself into something more like its foe in order to resist the external force.[24]

Therefore: power rules human destiny. This, of course, is not a new insight. Thucydides and Plato's Thrasymachus said much the same in ancient Greece.

Nevertheless, Schmookler's is a magisterial, persuasive argument that humanity is mercilessly ruled by the struggle for power. His study is a grim, even terrifying explanation of human history. If accurate, it denotes the demise of humanism and of the ideas of the Enlightenment. (In many respects, those ideas—of rationality, of the commonalty of humankind, and the like—were derivative from the 400-year boom. With its end, their end came also.) Schmookler stands in direct line with others who have altered for all time the place of *homo sapiens* in the universe—in an intellectual sense. Galileo and Copernicus smashed Ptolemaic cosmology and caused thoughtful people to realize that they were merely inhabitants of a minor planet in a minor star system, among millions of other star systems. Darwin demonstrated that humanity is not at the center of the natural world, by showing that the species was not the product of special creation but the probably fortuitous result of an immensely long biological evolution. Freud had an analogous impact: humans are not masters of their destinies, but, rather, the product of unconscious drives; "rational man" is at least a partial myth. And Schmookler has now demonstrated that humankind's last intellectual underpinning—history is the result of its own doing—is simply not true. History, he maintains, is one long chronicle of the imperatives of power, a process that is usually indifferent to specific human aspirations. A grim picture, that, one that brings to mind John Donne's complaint at the dawn of the Copernican revolution: " 'Tis all in peeces, all cohaerance gone."

The human mind, save for that of a few, has yet to catch up with the implications of what Galileo and Copernicus taught, and there is a like refusal to accept the full implications of Darwin's and Freud's insights. The same fate may befall Schmookler. Yet his ideas, as well as those of his progenitors, will not die. They will percolate through the minds of those who perceive human matters true, who penetrate the mythology of a given age to see those matters holistically—as they actually are.

Schmookler's challenge is essentially to the constitutional order of a planet subdivided into 160-plus nation-states, each claiming sovereignty over patches of land of greater or lesser size. *The Parable of the Tribes* bids us to remember William Butler Yeats's prescience of sixty years ago: "Mere anarchy is loosed upon the world."[25] Is there a way out of the intellectual trap in which humanity is caught? Schmookler ends his study on a note of optimism: "As our power to do evil has grown, so has our ability to do good. Every day, all over the earth, millions of people struggle in countless ways to deflect the course of human destiny from the abyss. And not without effect. For the century that has brought global conflict has witnessed the germination of the seeds of global cooperation."[26] So it has, although one would be unwise to place too much emphasis on the idea of cooperation. Even so, any problem that humans have the power to make for themselves, they surely have a like power and ability to resolve in some sort of reasonable fashion. To believe otherwise would be to sink into the Slough of Despond, from which there is no exit.

Schmookler's parable is a powerful challenge to the status quo. Can humankind so alter existing systems and attitudes that serve power into systems and attitudes by which power is canalized in ways to serve basic human needs? He writes:

This book is a work of diagnosis, dwelling upon the pathological to illuminate the etiology of the problems that afflict us. Diagnosis is, however, only a first step. It is also necessary to prescribe a course of treatment, a means of achieving the wholeness civilization now lacks.... Even in dwelling upon the negative, it can have a positive effect, for effective treatment requires good diagnosis. The better we understand the root causes of our systems ... the more likely will our good intentions lead to good results....

If redesign of the system is one side of the challenge facing us, ignition of the spirit is the other. The dulling of our feelings ... is why we are in danger of failing in the tasks our civilization presents us.[27]

"Redesign of the system" is a problem in constitutionalism; "ignition of the spirit" is the problem of human values. We are all strangers in a strange land, for which both a map and a compass are required. The compass points in the direction of the satisfaction of basic human needs; it is the question of which values a constitutional order should pursue. The map is the constitutional structure required to follow that path. They must proceed together.

Let us revert for a moment to the question of how much human reason can play in ordering human affairs. It must be remembered that reason is entirely instrumental. The goals or ends of human endeavor must be selected by other means. Recall what Nobel Laureate Herbert Simon wrote: "Success depends on our ability to broaden human horizons so that people will take into account, in deciding what is to their interest, a wider range of consequences."[28] We have elsewhere called attention to what was called the Principle of Reason-Directed Societal Self-Interest,[29] which, although not recognized as such in the legal and political literature is nonetheless a fact that has been followed, however reluctantly and partially, throughout American history. It is, to give it another label, the Principle of Minimal Satisfaction of Human Needs. Reason plays a limited part here: those who wield effective control in the polity have made, when considered necessary, just that amount of social adjustment that will serve to siphon off enough discontent to enable the societal status quo to be maintained. Token or cosmetic gains are extended under the formal constitution, as with black Americans, while under the secret constitution no real redistribution of wealth, prestige, or social power occurs. The system abides, although it is based on continued economic growth.

There is an important lesson here. One may infer that, even if Schmookler is correct, there is enough resiliency in the human spirit and enough intelligence in the human intellect to enable *homo sapiens* to recognize that humans must, by dint of inescapable necessity, work together. It may take a widely recognized crisis, as has been said. But it cannot be repeated too often that the crisis is already here—on a number of fronts.

Seventh, periodic formal constitutional change must be made easier. Inasmuch as law is more a reflection than a molder of events, and since the United States is characterized by extremely rapid social change, the necessity for a means whereby desirable periodic constitutional revisions can be made becomes obvious. The framers made formal constitutional alteration extremely difficult. The only express way is to follow the tortuous procedures set forth in Article V: an amendment requires a two-thirds vote of each house of Congress and ratification by three-fourths (thirty-eight) of the states. It is truistic to maintain that the Article V provisions have not been adequate to the need; some other means had to be developed to adapt the formal document to the exigencies faced by succeeding generations of Americans. This change has been accomplished mainly by Supreme Court decisions, some especially significant congressional statutes, and some presidential actions. Article V thus is seldom followed (its other proviso for another constitutional convention, to be convened when two-thirds of the states wish it, has never been invoked). Save for the Bill of Rights (the first ten amendments) and the fourteenth amendment (added in 1868), only three or four of the other fifteen amendments are of a substantial nature. (These include the sixteenth, permitting a federal income tax; the nineteenth, authorizing female suffrage; and the twenty-second, limiting the president to two terms in office.)

Are the procedures of Article V and the secret constitution's means of updating the formal constitution sufficient to present-day and future needs? These techniques allow for only *ad hoc*, incremental alterations, when the requirement surely is for something more comprehensive and sweeping. Should, therefore, another convention again be assembled, with the stated purpose of making the Document of 1787 (and the secret constitution) current with modern conditions? Further: should the new formal constitution contain a provision for progressive updating of the document as social conditions change? The answer given here—admittedly controversial—is "yes" to both questions.

That there should be another constitutional convention, and soon, is a proposition that has become so obvious as to need no extended argument. Noted previously is the fact that conditions today, when perceived clearly and truly, bear marked resemblances to those of 1787. If Americans could write a constitution then, surely they can do so today. Those who fear another convention—their numbers are many—display a depressing lack of confidence in the ability and capacity of the American people to order their own affairs, as well as a faith, almost religious in its intensity, that all will be well because something is bound to turn up that will resolve all social tensions. Opponents of another convention are wrong on both scores.

The case against a new convention and major revision of the formal constitution has been well stated by Professor Dean Alfange:

I am unregenerate enough to remain unconvinced—not because I don't see much of the same desperate need that you do for new values and new ways of thought, but because I don't see how we can discover those new values through re-examination of constitutional provisions. The horse still comes before the cart. New values may guide us to new constitutional principles, but without those values being in place to begin with, the new Constitution will inevitably be an embodiment of our current modes of thought. If we cannot transcend the status quo through politics and legislation, we are not likely to do so through constitution-making because the process will be guided by the same political and legislative considerations that determine current policy. Moreover, if we put the status quo in the Constitution, where we can't change it, we won't be better off; we'll we worse off.[30]

That is eloquent. But is it accurate? The answer surely is that Alfange is correct only in part. The interaction of values and law, of course, is important. But Alfange merely restated the question rather than answer it.

Values are important—of that there can be no doubt. Nor can William Galston's position that constitutional procedures are vacuous in the absence of collectively held moral convictions be denied. But that position is only half an answer. Values are meaningless without the political (constitutional) means to make them effective. In like manner, of course, political change in a social vacuum, in the absence of a change in values, would be ineffective. The question, thus, is not whether the horse must precede the cart, as Alfange maintains, but rather, it is to determine how the two—value change and political change—can proceed along parallel lines.

At one time, perhaps before the Reformation, the Church could be the source of values. That fact changed with the rise of the nation-state to dominance. "Political disputes today," Jacques Ellul explains, "are what disputes between Christians were in the sixteenth century." Or, in similar language of Robert Nisbet, "From about the sixteenth century the national state became much the same kind of haven for man that the Church had been from the time of the fall of Rome in the West."[31] As Fyodor Dostoevsky so cogently related in The Legend of the Grand Inquisitor, because people require a faith in something, a belief that someone is in control, it is easily perceivable that values, such as they are, emanate more from the state today than from any theological institution. The implication of this is important: changes in law can help create a new moral climate. Law may not be omnicompetent but it can be the "conscience of a sovereign people."[32] To the extent that black Americans have improved their status in recent decades—and they have, even if mainly in the formal constitution—it was their use of law and the judicial process that turned the corner to better treatment.

This improvement has large significance for changes in other values. This is not to say, to be sure, that law and legal change can alone do the necessary.

But they can help, if only Americans summon the will to do so. That will may well be derivative from the fact that morality in America is largely a matter of following rules, with the rules coming from the state in some type of law. As Professor Alexander Bickel commented, law is the "value of values," and "we find our visions of good or evil in the experience of the past, in our tradition, in the secular religion of the American people."[33] As has been noted, this secular religion is Americanism or patriotism, one that views the formal constitution as its chief artifact. Perhaps the law has a "specious morality," as Professor Sanford Levinson has argued, but that is really not the point. Rather, it is that a "nation with the soul of a church"[34] can, through its official law-making organs, help set the moral climate of the country.

New laws and new ways of thought can be discovered through changes, particularly in the fundamental law of the formal constitution. When in 1954 the Supreme Court declared racial segregation to be contrary to the mandate of the fourteenth amendment's equal protection of the laws clause, the justices thereby erected a moral standard toward which the nation should aspire. The justices found something lurking in the interstices of that amendment that no previous Court had identified, and they changed for all time the nature of American society. Is that, in Alfange's terminology, a new value? The answer can only be yes. Which, then, was the horse and which was the cart? The answer seems obvious. And that is so even though developments since 1954 have not fulfilled the spirit or the letter of that landmark decision. Oracular pronouncements by the Supreme Court—such as those made affecting the status of black Americans or the possibility for women in the first trimester of pregnancy to get an abortion on demand—are not only statements in political (constitutional) theory but also articulations of moral positions.

Why is there a great fear of another convention? The basic concern seems to be that single-issue zealots would domininate it—those, for example, who want to outlaw consensual abortions or mandatory busing of schoolchildren to attain racial integration, or those who wish to authorize prayers in public schools. Some people think that the Bill of Rights would be jeopardized. These fears have some validity, but not much. They can be countered.

The arguments to counter them begin with the already-stated realization that each generation writes its own constitution, although not in a planned, rational manner. Reaction to exogenous circumstances has had most to do with past constitutional change. Adjustments were made in an *ad hoc*, "pragmatic" way. Short-term solutions were sought. No long-range planning was done, or even considered. This method no longer suffices. The formal constitution was predicated in a faulty paradigm. The result, in Harlan Cleveland's language, is that "we are living in tomorrow's world today, still using yesterday's ideas."[35] We should always remember, furthermore, that the 1787 convention was itself a "runaway" meeting; the delegates far exceeded their assigned mission.

Moreover, anything that another convention produced would have to be ratified by thirty-eight states, itself a major barrier to any deleterious alteration. Although it is true that the 1787 conclave ignored the provision in the Articles of Confederation calling for unanimity for any change, it is highly unlikely that the same thing could happen today. The spread of literacy and the impact of the mass media would militate against changing the three-fourths rule to make changes in the formal constitution.

Of course, it is theoretically possible that another convention would propose repeal of the Bill of Rights. Even given, however, the low status of popular support for civil rights and liberties, documented by Herbert McClosky and Alida Brill,[36] it strains credulity to believe that people generally would accept such fundamental alterations in the constitution. If the United States is in such a marasmic state that the Bill of Rights, or any part of it, could be repealed, no one should think that the parchment barriers of a written constitution would prevent what determined majorities might want to do in any given set of circumstances.

There are benefits to be derived from the great national debate sure to be generated by convening a new group of men and women to consider alterations to the constitution. This is what occurred in Canada a few years ago, when a new constitution was being drafted.[37] Americans would be forced to think long and hard about what type of nation they desire and how it should be governed. There are worse things. Indeed, surely it is valid to say that one of the chief responsibilities of citizenship is to confront such questions and to deal with them in a thoughtful way. As Levinson has said:

> The point is that the Constitution is not a menu of self-evidently good things but a document and set of understandings that structures our political lives for ill as well as good. If the thirty-fourth state does endorse a convention, we should not recoil in fright but instead make every effort to assure that state legislatures send thoughtful men and women to it.... But we should not only take the prospect of a convention seriously, we should welcome it, albeit with fear and trembling. For it would give us the opportunity to define the country we wish to be and to determine whether our current structure of government allows us to be that country. If we do not ultimately trust our fellow citizens to rise to such an occasion, then we should accept the demise of our experiment in self-government.[38]

Surely that view is correct. Surely, too, there are millions of Americans who would labor tenaciously and effectively for a new and better constitution.

There would, of course, be opposition to creation of a constitution of human needs. Principally, this opposition would come not from the single-issue "crazies," those who have tunnel vision and perceive only one major public policy problem (such as abortion, school busing, school prayers, or a balanced budget). Rather, the opposition would emanate from those who have always profited most from the operations of our constitutional order—the moneyed and the propertied—who would resist such a basic alteration because they likely would perceive it as jeopardizing their positions of power and privilege. This means, as has been suggested, that these people must have the perspicacity to perceive where their long-term interests lie and thus to know that the disadvantaged will, soon or late, rise up against a system that keeps them in penury and want. The people are on the march the world over, as Willy Brandt has warned,[39] so there is really no feasible alternative to taking serious steps to rectify some long-felt ills and to come to terms with nature.

By no means do American have a perfect constitution. Nor do they have a special insight into revealed truth about how humans are best governed. There is no quick fix—technological or political or legal—by which increasingly apparent and dangerous social pathologies can be cured. We must confront and fully understand the fact that constitutions are always in flux, and try to act, within the limits of human reason, to do something rational about both of our fundamental laws. The human being has, perhaps with overweening hubris, labeled itself as *homo sapiens*. The time has come—indeed, it is long past—for humans everywhere, and particularly American constitutionalists, to live up to that label—to be, that is, truly sapient. A move toward developing a constitution of human needs would be a major step in that direction. The worst possible course of action would be to continue to drift along, secure in the pathetic faith that Americans are God's chosen people and that someday, somehow, something will turn up to enable us and others to emerge from the swamp in which we are now immersed. The time is short and the water rises: The task must be tackled—and soon.

EPILOGUE: ALTERING THE CONSTITUTIONS IS INEVITABLE

Most Americans fail to appreciate the extent to which they have accepted a passel of constitutional fictions. Although these are not entirely false, neither are they historically sound.... When Alexis de Tocqueville discussed the U.S. Constitution, he found it "frightening to see how much diverse knowledge and discernment it assumes on the part of the governed. The government of the Union rests almost entirely on legal fictions."

—Michael Kammen[1]

This volume has been an essay predicated on the premise that America has a system of constitutional dualism. This fact simply cannot be burked in any discussion—*serious* discussion—of American constitutionalism. Arguing for ratification of the formal constitution, Alexander Hamilton in *The Federalist No. 85* maintained that it should be approved because it could always be changed by subsequent amendments. He was only partly correct. The formal document has been amended, but only twenty-six times. Further, as has been noted, other means were devised to keep the constitution current with the exigencies facing succeeding generations of Americans. Finally, and of greatest importance, Hamilton failed to mention—although surely he knew of its existence, even then—the secret constitution and how it would have to be modified.

That the formal constitution has changed in the two centuries since 1787 is undeniable. The secret constitution has been altered much less: the same class of people are highest in the social and political pecking order today as they were 200 years ago. The pretense is that the United States is a democracy, with popular sovereignty in control. Reality differs. Some of the reasons for that conclusion have been set out in Part I. Much, of course, remains to be said. Since, however, this essay is an adumbration rather than a comprehensive treatise, time and space do not permit more than a few closing remarks.

First, the fact that half, or more, of those eligible do not vote is clear evidence that something is badly awry in the constitutional order. No government can truly call itself legitimate—in the sense of having the right or title to rule—when the national leader (the president) is elected by only a smallish minority of the citizenry. More and more people apparently have come to realize, intuitively at least, that such a government is not really credible or legitimate—in a nation that insists it is a democracy.

Second, emerging from the constitutional convention in September, 1787, Benjamin Franklin is said to have told a curious bystander, "We have given you a republic, sir, if you can keep it." The republic has been kept, mainly in its formal sense, for two centuries. This has served a hidden function: those who control the levers of power in the institutions of the secret constitution have found it to be desirable and useful to allow "the people" to believe that they are sovereign and that government follows their desires. So the formal constitution endures, even though it is related to today's actual constitutions, living and secret, only in symbolic ways. The formal constitution has lasted, furthermore, because it was drafted at a time when a unique set of environmental conditions made it highly improbable and perhaps impossible for it to fail.

Third, the formal document as written was based on "the theory," as Justice Oliver Wendell Holmes once remarked, that it was "an experiment, as all life is an experiment."[2] At its outset in 1789, it was a leap into the dark future. The framers, and thus Americans in general, have been extraordinarily fortunate. The constitutional experiment came at the precise time in history, and in the precise part of the planet, that it could not fail—although it came close, as the War of 1812 attests. As James Russell Lowell observed in 1888, "After our Constitution got fairly into working order it really seemed as if we had invented a machine that would go of itself, and this begot a faith in our luck which even the civil war itself but momentarily disturbed."[3]

Fourth, the United States and the world are so basically different from the way they were in the latter part of the eighteenth century that serious attention must be paid to whether Americans any longer want to keep their constitutional system. If that view is considered to be utopian because it simply is not possible to alter the system, the reply can only be, as John Platt remarked, that "the present generation is the hinge of history.... We may now be in the time of the most rapid change in the whole evolution of the human race, either past or to come.... The world has now become too dangerous for anything less than Utopia."[4] Similar warnings have, of

course, long been heard—Isaiah, Jeremiah, Cassandra, Spengler, Ehrlich.
One ought, therefore, to be cautious about making such assertions about
the modern age. Nevertheless, there are good and sufficient reasons for
considering the present times to be unique. These have already been noted—
the nuclear peril, the population bomb, the slow but seemingly inexorable
closing of the ecological trap, Schmookler's principle of the destructive logic
of human systems. We are truly teetering on the edge of the abyss of what
Koestler called "genosuicide."[5]

Once that abyss is perceived, then it follows that the true utopians, to
employ the term pejoratively, are those who believe that the United States
can continue to drift along with its time-honored institutional structure,
making only incremental adjustments in the law and theory of the constitution. Constitutionalism by drift is a sure road to disaster, either in the
few minutes of a nuclear exchange or in the slower but no less deadly
decades of continued population growth and environmental degradation.
Today's Micawberists—their names are legion—may not think of themselves as unheeding and unthinking utopians, but that is precisely what they
are. At one time, perhaps, Americans could think in utopian fashion: that
is what the framers of the formal constitution did. Their type of thinking
is no longer valid.

Fifth, we should, therefore, heed Professor John Diggins's advice to resort
to "first principles."[6] We must, that is, think long and hard about the goals
and purposes of the collective endeavor called society. As the late Scott
Buchanan once observed, "We must make a new beginning by defining
again for ourselves those parts of our Constitution that have become corrupt
and stultifying in our own political behavior. A good beginning might be
made by reading the writings of John C. Calhoun, who very early saw the
fateful possibility of neglect and misuse of our political system."[7] This
possibility prompted Calhoun to propose something akin to a continuous
constitutional convention, something that Americans have partially attained—although not in the way that Calhoun advocated—in the modern
role of the Supreme Court. Even with its present-day enhanced posture,
however, the Court is not sufficient to the manifest need.

Sixth, that the proposals in this volume fall beyond what is now politically
possible is not a sufficient reason not to think seriously about them. Changes
have occurred in the past 200 years in the relationship of government to
the citizenry. It will not do, therefore, to dismiss the proposed constitution
of human needs out of hand. In the 1930s, most lawyers and political
thinkers sneered at the New Deal programs—which wrought a constitutional revolution—as obviously unconstitutional and so wildly impractical
as not to merit serious discussion. It took a depression and mass discontent
to vary that social picture. Like changes could come about once it is perceived, and it must be at some time, that the "crisis of crises"—the social
climacteric—in which we are now so deeply immersed is as deleterious

(likely, more so) to the health and welfare of the polity as was the Great Depression.

Seventh, I have not mentioned some obvious flaws in the formal constitution, flaws that simply serve no useful purpose today. They are the vermiform appendixes of the body politic. Included, among others, are the second amendment on the right to "keep and bear arms"—not, as the National Rifle Association would have it, an absolute right, but only because a well-regulated militia was once considered to be a necessity; the third amendment's proscription against quartering of troops in private homes; the provision for an electoral college as the means of choosing the president and vice president; and the prohibition (in Article I, Section 10) against the states granting letters of marque and reprisal. All of these, and more, should be jettisoned; this point is beyond argument.

Eighth, Americans have choices to make, and soon, and the only question is not whether they will be made, but how, by whom, and for whose benefit. It is far too late in the evolution of the species and of the nation that those changes, when made, can be solely for the benefit of a favored few. People the world over are restless; they are seeking different resolutions to age-old problems of governance. No longer are the many willing to accept only the crumbs that drop from the tables of opulence of the few. This is true both *of* nations, as in the so-called North-South division,[8] and *within* nations, as in the simmering discontent in America's underclass. Those who control the levers of power in both the formal and the secret constitutions can no longer ignore that hard fact. They will have to make adjustments in the status quo, not from some newfound attitude of altruism, but because to do so is in *their* interest. Altruism has never been a characteristic of ruling elites, so it is incumbent on the many to make it apparent to the willfully blind that present-day roadblocks to establishment of a sustainable society, one in which human needs receive reasonably adequate satisfaction so far as the environment allows, must be surmounted. The alternative is far from pleasant, as the current situation in South Africa evidences. For anyone to believe that the growing underclass in the United States (and elsewhere) will continue to remain relatively quiescent is at least utopian and even quixotic.

Social change, the rapid change so characteristic of the modern age, means political and legal change. Unavoidably. Whether Americans can summon the wit and will to direct those changes toward attainment of a sustainable society, while surely necessary, is far from certain. But they should try. After all, they really have no choice, for constitutional alteration will come whether or not it is liked or planned for. We need a new republic, one suited to the demands of the present day and the foreseeable future. It will not do to make some relatively minor procedural alterations, as James Sundquist and James MacGregor Burns have advocated.[9] Constitutional Band-Aids are not sufficient to the manifest need. We must look toward the substantive nature of a sustainable society. "There is no escape from politics. As a

consequence of ecological scarcity, major ethical, political, economic and
social changes are inevitable whatever we do."[10]

Let's do it right.

A beginning can be made by resolutely confronting the manifold problems
of the present day and equally resolutely facing up to those of the emergent
future. In doing this, it must be recognized that it is fatuous beyond measure
to believe that what was written in the late eighteenth century can govern
the present. Keep what is good of what the framers wrote, and discard the
rest. That this recommendation means that the changes must be planned
for should be self-evident, but is not—except to a few. This, in net, means
the continuing presence of government. And that, in turn, means that attention must be paid to the constitutional order. Ours is the age of the
planned society, as any number of post-World War II developments attest.
No other way is possible.

NOTES

PROLOGUE: CONSTITUTIONAL DUALISM

1. Quoted in W. Bagehot, The English Constitution 59 (1867) (pagination from 1963 paperback ed.).

2. B. Crick, In Defence of Politics 76 (2d ed. 1972).

3. Dahl, *Power, Pluralism and Democracy: A Modest Proposal* 3 (a paper delivered at the 1964 annual meeting of the American Political Science Association). See also S. Keller, Beyond the Ruling Class 71–72 (1963); P. Bachrach, The Theory of Democratic Elitism: A Critique *passim* (1967).

4. P. Burch, Elites in American History: The New Deal to the Carter Administration 388 (1980).

5. For preliminary discussion, see Miller, *Pretense and Our Two Constitutions*, 54 George Washington Law Review 301 (1986).

6. W. Bagehot, supra note 1, at 61.

7. W. Wilson, Congressional Government 30 (1885).

8. W. Karp, The Politics of War (1979). Karp wrote particularly of how the United States got into the Spanish-American War and World War I.

9. W. Reisman, Folded Lies: Bribery, Crusades, and Reforms 12 (1979).

10. D. Price, America's Unwritten Constitution (1983).

11. W. Reisman, supra note 9, at 12–13. An application of Reisman's model may be found in R. Neely, How Courts Govern America (1981).

12. H. Vaihinger, The Philosophy of "As If": A System of Theoretical, Practical and Religious Fictions of Mankind (C. Ogden trans. 2d English ed. 1935), at p. *xli*.

13. R. Michels, Political Parties: A Sociological Study of the Oligarchical Tendencies of Modern Democracy 401 (1915).

14. F. Neumann, The Democratic and the Authoritarian State 8 (1957).

15. D. Price, supra note 10, at 9.

16. See G. Adams, The Iron Triangle (1981); D. Cater, Power in Washington (1964); Heclo, *Issue Networks and the Executive Establishment*, in The New American Political System 87 (A. King ed. 1978); D. Price, supra note 10, at 93.

17. 198 U.S. 45 (1905).

18. The Federalist No. 79. It should be noted that Hamilton was writing about the judiciary and the need to keep judges independent, not about industrial workers. Nonetheless, his observation is relevant here.

19. R. Neely, supra note 11, at 19.

20. C. Lindblom, Politics and Markets 356 (1977). Much that appears in Lindblom's book is relevant to the present volume.

21. Schechter Poultry Corp. v. United States, 295 U.S. 495 (1935). See also Panama Refining Co. v. Ryan, 293 U.S. 388 (1935).

22. G. Poggi, The Development of the Modern State: A. Sociological Introduction (1978).

23. C. Lindblom, supra note 20, at 171.

24. See The Papers of Alexander Hamilton, Vol. X (H. Syrett ed. 1966). See also J. Miller, Alexander Hamilton and the Growth of the New Nation 289 (1959).

25. H. Brayman, Corporate Management in a World of Politics 57 (1967).

26. Schmitter, *Still the Century of Corporatism?*, 36 Review of Politics 85 (1974). See A. Miller, Politics, Democracy, and the Supreme Court 79–97 (1985).

27. A. Shonfield, Modern Capitalism: The Changing Balance of Public and Private Power 231 (1965).

28. Ibid. See also A. Miller, The Modern Corporate State: Private Governments and the Constitution (1976).

29. M. Parenti, Inventing Reality: The Politics of the Mass Media (1986). See also N. Postman, Amusing Ourselves to Death: Public Discourse in the Age of Show Business (1985); B. Bagdikian, The Media Monopoly (1983).

30. For discussion, see Griffith, *The Political Constitution*, 42 Modern Law Review 1 (1979). See also A. Miller, Toward Increased Judicial Activism: The Political Role of the Supreme Court (1982).

31. See the unsigned comment, now known to be written by Holmes, *The Gas-Stokers' Strike*, 7 American Law Review 582 (1873).

32. Ibid.

33. C. Lindblom, supra note 20, at 189.

34. D. Miller, Social Justice 20 (1976).

35. Raphael, *Conservative and Prosthetic Justice*, 12 Political Studies 149, 155 (1964).

36. D. Miller, supra note 34, at 26.

37. K. Young, Sociology: A Study of Society and Culture 898 (1942).

38. B. Skinner, Beyond Freedom and Dignity 34 (1971).

39. A. Huxley, Brave New World Revisited (1958).

40. Lamar, *The First American West: Jamestown, 1607–1699*, 74 Yale Review 64, 77 (1984).

41. M. Kammen, People of Paradox 56 (1972).

42. 1 Records of the Federal Convention (M. Farrand ed. 1927), quoted in M. Parenti, Democracy for the Few 44 (3d ed. 1977).

43. H. Zinn, A People's History of the United States 98–99 (1980).

44. Ibid.

45. 10 U.S. 87 (1810).

46. See M. Josephson, The Robber Barons (1934); R. Lustig, Corporate Liberalism: The Origins of Modern American Political Theory, 1890–1920 (1982); C. Lindblom, supra note 20, at 174: "Alexander Hamilton's *Report on Manufactures* put government in an active supportive role for business."

47. 14 U.S. 304 (1816).

48. 17 U.S. 316 (1819).

49. 19 U.S. 264 (1821).

50. 22 U.S. 1 (1824).

51. 5 U.S. 137 (1803); 17 U.S. 518 (1819).

52. The term *heterarchy* is borrowed from J. Ogilvy, Many Dimensional Man (1977). See also Michael, *Neither Hierarchy nor Anarchy: Notes on Norms for Governance in a Systemic World*, in Rethinking Liberalism 251, 259 (W. Anderson ed. 1983).

53. C. Beard, An Economic Interpretation of the Constitution of the United States 324 (1914).

54. *Letter from Thomas Jefferson to Samuel Kercheval*, July 12, 1816, quoted in W. Douglas, Stare Decisis 31 (1949).

55. Quoted in L. Berg, H. Hahn, and J. Schmidhauser, Corruption in the American Political System 11 (1976).

56. D. Dowd, *Comparative Economic Development of the West and South*, in Slavery and the Southern Economy 244, 252 (H. Woodman ed. 1966).

57. 95 U.S. 485 (1878).

58. J. Pole, The Pursuit of Equality in American History 193 (1978).

59. *Letter from President Lincoln to Horace Greeley*, Aug. 22, 1862, reprinted in 5 Collected Works of Abraham Lincoln 388 (R. Basler ed. 1953).

60. 67 U.S. 638 (1863).

61. Santa Clara County v. Southern Pacific R.R., 118 U.S. 394, 396 (1886). See Corporations and Society: Power and Responsibility (W. Samuels & A. Miller eds., 1987).

62. Butler, *America's Armed Forces "In Time of Peace": The Army*, Common Sense 6 (Nov. 1935), quoted in S. Lens, The Forging of the American Empire 270–71 (1971).

63. B. Tuchman, The Proud Tower: A Portrait of the World Before the War 1890–1914, at 409 (1966) (quoting letter from Judge Taft, July 8, 1894, to his wife).

64. W. Wilson, The New Freedom 36 (1914).

65. 2 Public Papers of Woodrow Wilson 376 (1925).

66. Standard Oil Co. v. United States, 221 U.S. 1 (1911). See T. Arnold, The Folklore of Capitalism (1937).

67. W. Wilson, supra note 64, at 449–51. (emphasis added)

68. Olney's letter to the railroad president is reproduced in L. Jaffe, Judicial Control of Administrative Action 12 (1965).

69. Smyth v. Ames, 169 U.S. 466 (1898).

70. Letter from Justice Miller to William Pitt Ballinger, Dec. 5, 1875, quoted in C. Fairman, Mr. Justice Miller and the Supreme Court 374 (1939).

71. See A. Miller, supra note 28, *passim.*

72. Quoted in Hitchens, *Anthony Wedgwood Benn: Can He Put England Together Again?*, Mother Jones, Nov. 1981, at 14.

73. Bernstein, *The New Deal: The Conservative Achievements of Liberal Reform,* in Towards A New Past 264–65 (B. Bernstein ed. 1968). See P. Conklin, The New Deal 72 (1967): "The enemies of the New Deal were wrong. They should have been friends.... The New Deal underwrote a vast apparatus of security. But the meager benefits of Social Security were insignificant in comparison to the building system of security for large established businesses."

74. W. Leuchtenburg, Franklin D. Roosevelt and the New Deal 1932–1940, at 336, 346–47 (1963).

75. The history is traced in A. Miller, The Supreme Court and American Capitalism (1968).

76. See Miller, *Social Justice and the Warren Court: A Preliminary Examination,* 11 Pepperdine Law Review 473 (1984), reprinted in A. Miller, Politics, Democracy, and the Supreme Court 201–26 (1985).

77. 347 U.S. 483 (1954); 349 U.S. 294 (1955).

78. The classification between manifest and latent beneficiaries is borrowed from R. Merton, Social Theory and Social Structure 115–22 (rev. ed. 1968).

79. See Miller, supra note 76. See also B. Schwartz, Super Chief: Earl Warren and His Supreme Court (1983).

80. J. Ellul, Propaganda (1964).

81. N. Postman, supra note 29, at 155.

CHAPTER 1: CONSTITUTIONAL MYTHOLOGY

1. May, *Political Myth and Liberal Morality,* in Rethinking Liberalism 283, 287 (W. Anderson ed. 1983).

2. R. Tugwell, The Emerging Constitution (1974).

3. See Reforming American Government; The Bicentennial Papers of the Committee on the Constitutional System (D. Robinson ed. 1985).

4. J. Burns, The Power to Lead (1984).

5. Quoted in J. Robertson, American Myth, American Reality 345 (1980).

6. For an argument that we should return to government under the Articles of Confederation, see W. Williams, America Confronts a Revolutionary World (1976).

7. Gladstone, *Kin Beyond Sea*, 127 North American Review (1878). As Professor Michael Kammen has demonstrated, Gladstone's encomium has often been quoted out of context. See M. Kammen, A Machine That Would Go of Itself 162–63 (1986).

8. Justice Johnson's assertion may be found in Elkinson v. Deliesseline, 8 Federal Cases 593 (1823).

9. W. Karp, The Politics of War (1979).

10. See M. Shapiro, Courts: A Comparative and Political Analysis (1981); J. Griffith, The Politics of the Judiciary (1977); Miller, *The Politics of the American Judiciary,* 49 Political Quarterly 200 (1978).

11. D. Price, America's Unwritten Constitution 135 (1983).

12. W. Wilson, Constitutional Government in the United States (1908).

13. For a brief discussion, see Miller, *The Constitutional Law of the "Security State*," 10 Stanford Law Review 620 (1958). See also A. Miller, The Modern Corporate State: Private Governments and the American Constitution (1976).

14. Quoted in A. Nevins, John D. Rockerfeller 622 (1940).

15. This segment from Lincoln's famous Gettysburg Address is erroneous because the nation, as known today, did not come into existence until the formal constitution was drafted in 1787, duly ratified, and a new government took office in 1789. The nation was not dedicated to equality among men. Slavery was recognized, and others—women, indentured servants, Indians, men without property—were at best second-class citizens.

16. S. Roane, *Letter to the Editor of the Richmond Enquirer*, June 18, 1819, reprinted in G. Gunther, John Marshall's Defense of McCulloch v. Maryland 130 (1969). See also Monaghan, *Our Perfect Constitution*, 56 New York University Law Review 353 (1981).

17. N. Machiavelli, The Discourses (first published in 1531).

18. On civil religion, see American Civil Religion (R. Richey & D. Jones eds. 1974).

19. See, for example, Huntington, *The Democratic Distemper*, The Public Interest, No. 41, Fall, 1975, at 9.

20. In McCulloch v. Maryland, 17 U.S. 316 (1819).

21. *Letter to Samuel Kercheval*, July 12, 1816, quoted in W. Douglas, Stare Decisis 31 (1949).

CHAPTER 2: AN EPOCH ENDS

1. W. McNeill, The Great Frontier: Freedom and Hierarchy in Modern Times 58–9 (1983).

2. R. Rubenstein, The Age of Triage (1983).

3. See A. Schmookler, The Parable of the Tribes (1984); F. Capra, The Turning Point: Science, Society and the Rising Culture (1982): "...we are trying to apply the concepts of an outdated world view—the mechanistic world view of Cartesian-Newtonian science—to a reality that can no longer be understood in terms of these concepts. We live today in a globally interconnected world, in which biological, psychological, social, and environmental phenomena are all interdependent." p. 15–16.

4. See J. Simon, The Ultimate Resource (1981); Are World Population Trends a Problem? (B. Wattenberg and K. Zinsmeister eds. 1986).

5. R. Kuttner, The Economic Illusion: False Choices Between Prosperity and Social Justice (1984).

6. Christian Science Monitor, Feb. 10, 1975, at 5.

7. D. Moynihan and N. Glazer, Beyond the Melting Pot (1953).

8. Quoted in W. Williams, America Confronts a Revolutionary World: 1776–1976, at 25. (1976).

9. Ibid.

10. T. Hobbes, Leviathan (1651).

11. A. Schmookler, supra note 3.

12. B. Tuchman, A Distant Mirror (1978).

13. See F. Capra, supra note 3, at ch. 1.

14. M. Weber, *Die Protestantische Ethik und der Geist des Kapitalmus*, first published in Archiv fur Sozialwissenschaft und Socialpolitik Statistik, Vols. xx, xxi. For discussion, see R. Tawney, Religion and the Rise of Capitalism 261–63 (1926) (pagination from 1947 paperback ed.).

15. R. Tawney, supra note 14, at 234.

16. Weber, *Social Psychology of World Religions*, in From Max Weber 271 (H. Gerth & C. Mills eds. 1958).

17. F. Turner, The Frontier in American History (1920).

18. W. Webb, The Great Frontier (1952).

19. H. George, Progress and Poverty c. 8 (1879).

20. See the several essays in Corporations and Society: Power and Responsibility (W. Samuels & A. Miller eds., 1987).

21. See, for example, W. Brandt, Arms and Hunger (1986).

22. Compare A. & P. Ehrlich, Earth (1987) with W. Ophuls, Ecology and the Politics of Scarcity (1977) and R. Miles, Awakening from the American Dream (1976).

23. See A. Miller, Democratic Dictatorship: The Emergent Constitution of Control (1981).

24. See H. Arendt, Eichmann in Jerusalem: A Report on the Banality of Evil (1963).

25. A. Montagu & F. Matson, The Dehumanization of Man 3 (1983).

26. A. Lovejoy, Reflections on Human Nature 15 (1961).

27. Quoted in A. Nevins, John D. Rockefeller 622 (1940).

28. For discussion, see G. Lodge, The American Disease 43–50 (1984).

29. H. Brown, The Human Future Revisited (1975).

30. F. Hirsch, Social Limits to Growth (1976).

31. J. Simon, The Ultimate Resource (1981).

CHAPTER 3: A SOCIETAL NERVOUS BREAKDOWN?

1. Quoted in The Manchester (England) Guardian, Sept. 26, 1983, at 15.

2. See his poem, *The Second Coming* (1923).

3. Ehrlich, *The Nuclear Winter: Discovering the Ecology of Nuclear War*, 5 Amicus Journal 20, 30 (Winter 1984).

4. See Weinberg, *Social Institutions and Nuclear Energy*, 177 Science 27 (1972); McDermott, *Technology: The Opiate of the Intellectuals*, in Technology as a Social and Political Phenomenon, (P. Bereano ed. 1976).

5. Quoted in D. Boorstin, The Republic of Technology: Reflections on Our Future Community 1 (1978).

6. W. Karp, The Politics of War (1979).

7. R. Lapp, The New Priesthood: The Scientific Elite and the Uses of Power 29 (1965).

8. See J. Passmore, Man's Responsibility for Nature (1974).

9. Quoted in W. Mommsen, The Age of Bureaucracy: Perspectives on the Political Sociology of Max Weber 99 and *passim* (1974).

10. See, for example, L. Mumford, The Myth of the Machine: The Pentagon of Power (1970).

11. See J. Rifkin, Algeny (1983).

12. I. Carmen, Cloning and the Constitution (1985).

13. P. Schrag, Mind Control *xi* (1978).

14. For a scholarly account of his views, see B. Skinner, Beyond Freedom and Dignity (1971). See also C. Lasch, The Culture of Narcissism 154–86 (1979).

15. Quoted in P. Smith, The Shaping of America (1980).

16. Lord Acton, Lectures on Modern History (1906).

17. Independent Commission on International Development Issues, Common Crisis North-South: Co-operation for World Recovery 2 (1983). (emphasis added.)

18. R. Dahl, Dilemmas of Pluralist Democracy (1982).

19. G. McConnell, Private Power and American Democracy 339 (1966).

20. See M. Olson, The Rise and Decline of Nations (1982); Transnational Relations and World Politics (R. Keohane & J. Nye eds. 1972).

21. W. Mendelson, Capitalism, Democracy, and the Supreme Court 24 (1960).

22. L. Brown, The Twenty-Ninth Day 1 (1978).

23. W. Thompson, Evil and World Order c. 8 (1976). See also R. Falk, The End of World Order c. 11 (1983).

CHAPTER 4: WHAT IS A SUSTAINABLE SOCIETY?

1. Bay, *Thinking About Human Rights: A Contribution to Postliberal Theory*, in Rethinking Liberalism 269, 280 (W. Anderson ed. 1983).

2. J. Locke, Two Treatises of Government Book II, c. IX, Sec. 123 (1681). (emphasis in original)

3. Ibid., at Sec. 49, Sec. 54. (emphasis in original).

4. W. Lippmann, Essays in the Public Philosophy 94–6 (1955) (pagination from 1956 paperback ed.). Said Lippmann: " ... private property can never be regarded as giving to any man an absolute title to exercise 'the sole and despotic dominion' over the land and resources of nature. The ultimate title does not lie in the owner. The title is in 'mankind,' in the people as a corporate community. The rights of the individual in that patrimony are creations of the law and have no other validity except as they are ordained by law." Pp. 92–3.

5. J. Rawls, A Theory of Justice 75–8 and *passim* (1971).

6. L. Brown, Building a Sustainable Society 247 (1981).

7. D. Seers, The Political Economy of Nationalism 155 (1983).

8. R. Falk, The End of World Order 235 (1983).

9. Ibid., at 268.

10. J. Keynes, The Economic Consequences of the Peace 8 (1920). See, for preliminary discussion, Miller & Davidson, *Observations on Population Policy-Making and the Constitution*, 40 George Washington Law Review 618 (1972), reprinted in A. Miller, Social Change and Fundamental Law: America's Evolving Constitution c. 6 (1979).

11. These societies include Ecuador, Yugoslavia, China, the Philippines, Panama, Peru, Turkey, Portugal, Mexico, Vietnam, and Thailand. It should be mentioned that most of these constitutional provisions refer also to family planning. Letter from Center for Population and Family Health, Columbia University, Nov. 8, 1984.

12. R. Meier, Modern Science and the Human Fertility Problem 63 (1959).

13. See J. Ellul, The Technological Society (J. Wilkinson trans. 1964) (paperback ed.); Ellul, *The Technological Order*, in The Technological Order: Proceedings of Encyclopedia Britannica Conference 10 (C. Stover ed. 1963).

14. P. Ehrlich, The Population Bomb (1971). See also P. Ehrlich, A. Ehrlich and J. Holdren, Ecoscience: Population, Resources, Environment (1977).

15. Noble, *Present Tense Technology*, 3 democracy no. 2, at 8 (1983).

16. Rubenstein, *The Elect and the Preterite*, 59 Soundings 357, 359 (1976). See also Dahrendorf, *The End of the Labor Society*, World Press Review, March, 1983, at 28: "There is no cure for today's unemployment."

17. Council on International and Public Affairs, The Underbelly of the U.S. Economy: Joblessness and Pauperization of Work in America (Special Report No. 4, August 1985).

18. E. Mesthene, Technological Change: Its Impact on Man and Society (1970).

19. F. Roosevelt, *State of the Union Message*, 90 Congressional Record 57 (78th Congress, 2d Session, Jan 11, 1944). (emphasis added).

20. C. Macpherson, The Rise and Fall of Economic Justice 84 (1985).

21. See Ehrlich, *When Light Is Put Away: Ecological Effects of Nuclear War*, in The Counterfeit Ark: Crisis Relocation for Nuclear War 247 (J. Leaning & L. Keyes eds. 1984); Sagan, *Nuclear War and Climatic Catastrophe: Some Implications*, 62 Foreign Affairs 257 (1983).

22. A. Whitehead, Adventures of Ideas (1933), quoted in Miller, *A Note on the Criticism of Supreme Court Decisions*, 10 Journal of Public Law 139 (1961).

23. See, for example, Nuclear Weapons and Law (A. Miller and M. Feinrider eds. 1984).

24. L. Thurow, The Zero-Sum Solution 112 (1985).

25. Cited in R. Miles, Awakening from the American Dream: The Social and Political Limits to Growth 11 (1976).

26. M. Konner, The Tangled Wing: Biological Constraints on the Human Spirit 435 (1982).

27. J. Ogilvy, Many Dimensional Man 7 (1977). (emphasis in original)

28. Fromm, The *Psychology of Normalcy*, 1 Dissent 43 (1954), quoted in Fitzgerald, *Introduction*, to Human Needs and Politics x, xi (R. Fitzgerald ed. 1977).

29. M. Walzer, Spheres of Justice 84 (1983).

30. J. Rawls, A Theory of Justice (1971).

31. Ibid.

32. R. Dworkin, Taking Rights Seriously (1977); J. Ely, Democracy and Distrust (1980).

33. R. Goodin, Political Theory and Public Policy 90 (1982).

34. T. Pease, The Leveller Movement 359 (1916).

35. Quoted in G. Sabine and T. Thorson, A History of Political Theory 446 (4th ed. 1983).

36. Quoted in ibid.

37. T. Pease, supra note 34, at 359. See also G. Sabine and T. Thorson, supra note 35, at 445.

38. Y. Simon, Philosophy of Democratic Government 123 (1951).

39. W. Galston, Justice and the Human Good 279 (1980).

40. Maslow, *A Theory of Human Motivation*, 50 Psychological Review 394 (1943), reprinted in A. Maslow, Motivation and Personality c. 5 (1954).

41. Macpherson, *Needs and Wants: An Ontological or Historical Problem?*, in Human Needs and Politics 26, 34 (R. Fitzgerald ed. 1977).

42. Zetterbaum, *Equality and Human Need*, 71 American Political Science Review 983, 986 (1977).

43. W. Galston, supra note 39, at 164.

44. Bay, *Thinking About Human Rights: A Contribution to Postliberal Theory*, in Rethinking Liberalism 269, 277 (W. Anderson ed. 1983).

45. McCloskey, *Human Needs, Rights and Political Values*, 13 American Philosophical Quarterly 1, 7 (1976).

46. J. Feinberg, Doing & Deserving: Essays in the Theory of Responsibility *passim* (1970).

47. For example, Fullilove v. Klutznick, 448 U.S. 448 (1980); Steelworkers v. Weber, 443 U.S. 193 (1979); University of California Regents v. Bakke, 438 U.S. 265 (1978); Defunis v. Odegaard, 416 U.S. 313 (1974).

48. Rummel v. Estelle, 445 U.S. 263 (1980); Hutto v. Davis, 445 U.S. 947 (1980); Buck v. Bell, 274 U.S. 200 (1927).

49. Grey, *Property and Need: The Welfare State and Theories of Distributive Justice*, 28 Stanford Law Review 877, 897 (1976).

50. D. Miller, Social Justice 20 (1976).

51. Raphael, *Conservative and Prosthetic Justice*, 12 Political Studies 149 (1964).

52. D. Miller, supra note 50, at 26.

CHAPTER 5: GETTING THERE FROM HERE

1. B. Tuchman, The March of Folly 4 (1984).

2. L. Hobhouse, The Elements of Social Justice 140–41 (1922).

3. J. Burns, The Power to Lead: The Crisis of the American Presidency 101 (1984).

4. Ibid.

5. J. Platt, Perception and Change c. VII (1970).

6. H. Simon, Reason in Human Affairs 108 (1983).

7. R. Reeves, The Reagan Detour 10–11 (1985).

8. Quoted in ibid., at 11.

9. Pennock, *Introduction*, to Political and Legal Obligation *xiii, xiv* (J. Pennock and J. Chapman eds. 1970).

10. Henry, *Political Obligation and Collective Goods*, in Political and Legal Obligation, supra note 9, at 263, 269. (emphasis supplied)

11. M. Olson, The Logic of Collective Action c. 1 (1965).

12. Henry, supra note 10, at 275–76.

13. A. Smith, The Wealth of Nations, Book V, c. I, parts 1–3, quoted in Henry, at 275.

14. Ibid.

15. T. Green, Lectures on the Principles of Political Obligation 29 (1941) (reprinted from Green's collected works; the lectures were delivered in 1879–80).

16. Pennock, *Political Development, Political Systems, and Political Goods*, 18 World Politics 415 (1966).

17. T. Green, supra note 15, at *xviii*. The quotation comes from A. D. Lindsay's introduction to Green's book.

18. J. Diggins, The Lost Soul of American Politics 4 (1984).

19. H. Muller, The Uses of the Past 222 (1952).

20. Address by Robert S. McNamara, President of World Bank Group, University of Notre Dame Commencement, May 1, 1969, quoted in Miller & Davidson, *Observations on Population Policy-Making and the Constitution*, 40 George Washington Law Review 618 (1972).

21. For discussion, see Miller and Cox, *Congress, the Constitution, and First Use of Nuclear Weapons*, 48 Review of Politics 211, 423 (1986).

22. Quoted in S. Terkel, American Dreams Lost and Found 232 (1981).

23. S. Bowles, D. Gordon & T. Weisskopf, Beyond the Waste Land: A Democratic Alternative to Economic Decline 275 (1983). See also L. Thurow, The Zero-Sum Society (1980).

24. Quoted in B. Schwartz, Super Chief: Earl Warren and His Supreme Court—A Judicial Biography 184 (1983). Justice Douglas made the quoted remark in a Supreme Court conference.

25. Discussed in Miller and Cox, supra note 21.

26. C. Hardin, Presidential Power and Accountability: Toward a New Constitution 66 (1974).

27. G. Reedy, The Twilight of the Presidency (1971).

28. Ibid.

29. Quoted in J. Schell, The Fate of the Earth (1982).

30. Cohen, *Presidential Responsibility and American Democracy: How to Guard Against the Aberrant Exercise of Presidential Power* 23 (1974 Royer Lecture, University of California Berkeley, May 23, 1974; unpublished typescript).

31. G. Reedy, The Presidency in Flux 16 (1973).

32. H. Kissinger, The Necessity for Choice (1961).

33. The Federalist No. 70.

34. T. Lowi, The Personal President 212 (1985).

35. F. Hayek, The Constitution of Liberty 181 (1960); Bell, *The End of American Exceptionalism*, 41 Public Interest 193 (1975); C. McIlwain, Constitutionalism: Ancient and Modern 21 (revised ed. 1947); Murphy, *An Ordering of Constitutional Values*, 53 Southern California Law Review 703, 758 (1980).

36. Quoted in H. Arendt, On Revolution 143 (1963).

37. 347 U.S. 483 (1954).

38. W. Galston, Justice and the Human Good 279 (1980).

39. Wolf v. Colorado, 338 U.S. 25, 27 (1949).

40. Trop v. Dulles, 356 U.S. 86 (1958).

41. See D. Ewing, Freedom Inside the Organization *passim* (1977).

42. H. McClosky and A. Brill, Dimensions of Tolerance: What Americans Believe About Civil Liberties 4 (1983).

43. West Coast Hotel Corp. v. Parrish, 300 U.S. 391 (1937).

44. See J. Burns, supra note 3; J. Sundquist, Constitutional Reform and Effective Government (1986). On the Committee on the Constitutional System, see Reforming American Government: The Bicentennial Papers of the Committee on the Constitutional System (D. Robinson ed. 1985).

45. The Antelope, 23 U.S. 66 (1825).

46. See, for example, Strauss, *The Place of Agencies in Government: Separation of Powers and the Fourth Branch*, 84 Columbia Law Review 573 (1984).

47. Freund, *Law and the Future: Constitutional Law*, 51 Northwestern University Law Review 187, 194 (1956).

48. *Moving the World Uphill*, The Economist (London), April 29, 1978, at 89.

49. Lord Acton, Lectures on Modern History 295 (1906) (pagination from 1960 paperback ed.).

50. A. Berle, Power Without Property: A New Development in American Political Economy (1959).

51. R. Hale, Freedom Through Law (1952).

52. W. Wilson, Constitutional Government in the United States (1908).

53. D. Price, America's Unwritten Constitution 135 (1983).

54. M. Shapiro, Courts: A Comparative and Political Analysis (1981).

55. Cutler, *To Form A Government*, 59 Foreign Affairs 126 (1980).

56. See J. Sundquist, supra note 44. See also L. Fisher, The Politics of Shared Power: Congress and the Executive (1981).

57. C. Lindblom, Politics and Markets 356 (1977).

58. K. Popper, Conjectures and Refutations 344 (1963).

59. W. Wilson, Constitutional Government in the United States (1908).

60. Marbury v. Madison, 1 Cranch 137 (1803).

61. 358 U.S. 1 (1958).

62. A. Bickel, The Least Dangerous Branch: The Supreme Court at the Bar of Politics (1962).

63. 410 U.S. 113 (1973).

64. Richmond Newspapers, Inc. v. Virginia, 448 U.S. 555 (1980).

65. M. Horwitz, The Transformation of American Law, 1780–1860, at 30 (1977).

66. Miranda v. Arizona, 384 U.S. 436 (1966).

67. 300 U.S. 379 (1937).

68. Ibid., at 391. (emphasis added).

69. E. Corwin, Liberty Against Government 161 (1949).

70. 3 T. Green, Works: Miscellanies and Memoirs 371 (3d ed. (1891). See Miller, *Toward a Concept of Constitutional Duty*, 1968 Supreme Court Review 199.

71. O. Holmes, Collected Legal Papers (1920).

72. G. Sabine, A History of Political Theory 674 (1937).

73. International Congress of Jurists, The Rule of Law in a Free Society 3 (N. Marsh ed. 1960). See Thorson, *A New Concept of the Rule of Law*, 38 Canadian Bar Review 239 (1960); Miller, *An Affirmative Thrust to Due Process of Law?*, 30 George Washington Law Review 399 (1962), reprinted in A. Miller, Social Change and Fundamental Law: America's Evolving Constitution c. 4 (1979).

74. The Brandt Commission's official title was Independent Commission on International Development Issues; it issued two reports: North-South: A Program for Survival (1980) and Common Crisis North-South: Co-operation for World Recovery (1983). Some of its background papers are reproduced in The Brandt Commission Papers (Selected Background Papers Prepared for the Independent Commission on International Development Issues, 1978–1979 (1981). See also W. Brandt, Arms and Hunger (1986).

75. L. Thurow, The Zero-Sum Society (1980).

76. Reynolds v. Sims, 377 U.S. 533 (1964); Wesberry v. Sanders, 376 U.S. 1 (1964). See R. Dixon, Democratic Representation: Reapportionment in Law and Politics (1968); R. McKay, Reapportionment (1965).

77. In Reynolds v. Sims, supra note 76 (dissenting).

78. 384 U.S. 436 (1966).

79. 372 U.S. 335 (1963). The Gideon precedent was extended in Argersinger v. Hamlin, 407 U.S. 25 (1972).

80. Glazer, *Towards an Imperial Judiciary*, 41 Public Interest 104 (Fall 1975), criticized in Miller, *Judicial Activism and American Constitutionalism*, in Constitutionalism 333 J. Pennock and J. Chapman eds. 1979). See also Miller, *In Defense of Judicial Activism*, in Supreme Court Activism and Restraint (S. Halpern and C. Lamb eds. 1982).

81. Powell, *Attack on American Free Enterprise System* (a memorandum dated Aug. 23, 1971, submitted to the U.S. Chamber of Commerce), quoted in A. Miller, Politics, Democracy, and the Supreme Court 281 (1985).

82. R. Jackson, The Struggle for Judicial Supremacy (1941).

83. Frankfurter, *The Zeitgeist and the Judiciary*, in Law and Politics (A. MacLeish and E. Prichard, Jr. eds. 1939).

84. The quote comes from B. Adams, The Theory of Revolutions 213 (1913), quoted in A. Mason, Security Through Freedom 149 (1955). Adams continued: "No delusion could be profounder and none, perhaps, more dangerous." P. 219.

85. L. Hand, The Bill of Rights (1958).

86. M. Cohen, Reason and Law 73–4 (1950).

87. O. Holmes, The Common Law 35–6 (1881).

88. For discussion, see A. Miller, Toward Increased Judicial Activism: The Political Role of the Supreme Court (1982); Miller, *Some Pervasive Myths About the United States Supreme Court*, 10 St. Louis University Law Journal 153 (1965).

89. J. Commons, Legal Foundations of Capitalism 7 (1924).

90. 15 The Writings of Thomas Jefferson 278 (A. Libscomb and A. Burgh eds. 1904–07), quoted in L. Levy, Against the Law: The Nixon Court and Criminal Justice 447 (1974).

91. O. Holmes, Collected Legal Papers 292 (1920). See D. O'Brien, Storm Center: The Supreme Court in American Politics (1986).

92. H. Parke and D. Wormell, The Delphic Oracle 416 (1956).

93. Ibid., at 420.

94. Quotation from Judge Learned Hand, in The Spirit of Liberty: Papers and Addresses of Learned Hand 81 (I. Dilliard ed. 1953).

95. *Retirement Address of Chief Justice Warren*, June 23, 1969, reprinted in 395 U.S. *x-xii*.

CHAPTER 6: THE ROADBLOCKS

1. A. Whitehead, Symbolism—Its Meaning and Effect 88 (1927).

2. B. Tuchman, The March of Folly 387 (1984).

3. Quoted in S. Terkel, American Dreams Lost and Found 312 (1981) (quoting a community organizer).

4. Quoted in Holmstrom, '*Reperception*' may be key to world peace, Christian Science Monitor, Feb. 4, 1986, p. 27.

5. Kennan, *On Nuclear War*, New York Review of Books, Jan. 21, 1982, p. 8. See Miller, *The Constitutional Challenge of Nuclear Weapons: A Note on the Obligation to Ward Off Extinction*, 9 Brooklyn Journal of International Law 317 (1983).

6. See W. Brandt, Arms and Hunger (1986).

7. See A. Koestler, The Ghost in the Machine 327 (1967).

8. B. Tuchman, supra note 2, at c. 1.

9. J. Platt, The Step to Man 195 (1966). He continues: "We may now be in the time of the most rapid change in the whole evolution of the human race, either past or to come.... The world has now become too dangerous for anything less than Utopia."

10. G. Lodge, The American Disease 63–4 (1984). (emphasis added).

11. Ibid.

12. R. Heilbroner, An Inquiry into the Human Prospect 175 (1974).

13. D. Ehrenfeld, The Arrogance of Humanism (1978).

14. A. Koestler, supra note 7, at c. 18.

15. Ibid.

16. See I. Carmen, Cloning and the Constitution (1985).

17. See J. Rifkin, Algeny (1983).

18. A. Koestler, supra note 7.

19. J. Rifkin, supra note 17.

20. Ibid.

21. Diamond v. Chakrabarty, 447 U.S. 303 (1980). See I. Carmen, supra note 16, *passim.*

22. Quoted in H. Muller, The Uses of the Past (1952).

23. H. Margenau, Ethics and Science 7–8 (1964). See Miller, *On the Choice of Major Premises in Supreme Court Opinions*, 14 Journal of Public Law 251 (1965).

24. A. Schmookler, The Parable of the Tribes: The Problem of Power in Social Evolution 21 (1984).

25. W. Yeats, The Second Coming (1923).

26. A. Schmookler, supra note 24, at 330.

27. Ibid., at 331–32.

28. H. Simon, Reason in Human Affairs 109 (1983).

29. A. Miller, A "Capacity for Outrage": The Judicial Odyssey of J. Skelly Wright (1984). See D. Miller, Social Justice (1976).

30. Letter from Professor Alfange to Arthur S. Miller, April 26, 1984, used with permission of the writer. Quoted in Miller, *Taking Needs Seriously: Observations on the Necessity for Constitutional Change*, 41 Washington and Lee Law Review 1243, 1301 (1984).

31. J. Ellul, The Political Illusion 20 (1967); Nisbet, *The Decline of Academic Nationalism*, 6 Change 26 (1974). See J. Ogilvy, Many Dimensional Man c. 1 (1979).

32. The term is taken from Wright, *The Role of the Courts in Expanding Freedom: The Conscience of a Sovereign People*, The Reporter, Sept. 26, 1963.

33. Quoted in Levinson, *The Specious Morality of the Law*, Harper's Magazine, May 1977.

34. S. Huntington, American Politics: The Promise of Disharmony (1982).

35. H. Cleveland, The Management of Sustainable Growth 15 (1979).

36. H. McClosky and A. Brill, Dimensions of Tolerance: What Americans Believe About Civil Liberties *passim* (1983).

37. Friedenberg, *The Struggle for Human Rights*, The Nation, March 20, 1982.

38. Levinson, *Why Not Take Another Look at the Constitution?*, The Nation, May 29, 1982.

39. W. Brandt, Arms and Hunger (1986).

EPILOGUE: ALTERING THE CONSTITUTIONS
IS INEVITABLE

1. M. Kammen, A Machine That Would Go of Itself: The Constitution in American Culture 13 (1986).

2. In Abrams v. United States, 250 U.S. 630 (1919).

3. Quoted in M. Kammen, supra note 1, at 18.

4. J. Platt, The Step to Man 195 (1966).

5. A. Koestler, The Ghost in the Machine c. XVIII (1967).

6. J. Diggins, The Lost Soul of American Politics 4 (1984).

7. S. Buchanan, So Reason Can Rule: Reflections on Law and Politics c. 2 (1982).

8. There is an immense literature on the North-South division. A good start may be made in the Brandt Commission reports: Independent Commission on International Development Issues, North-South: A Program for Survival (1980) and Common Crisis North-South: Co-operation for World Recovery (1983). See also W. Brandt, Arms and Hunger (1986); D. Seers, The Political Economy of Nationalism (1983).

9. J. Sundquist, Constitutional Reform and Effective Government (1986); J. Burns, The Power to Lead: The Crisis of the American Presidency (1984). To my knowledge, no one today, other than this author, is advocating major substantive changes in the formal constitution.

10. W. Ophuls, Ecology and the Politics of Scarcity: Prologue to a Political Theory of the Steady State 161–62 (1977).

BIBLIOGRAPHIC ESSAY

There is an enormous literature on constitutionalism, even on American constitutionalism. Since, however, the United States views its constitution as law—the fundamental law—much of that literature tends to be written in lawyers' language; a plethora of doctrinal analyses exists about certain Supreme Court decisions. The reason is easy to find: lawyers (and most other commentators) think mainly about judicial interpretations of the fundamental law when they write about the American constitution. That this is too narrow a focus is one of the messages of this book. This bibliographic essay, accordingly, ignores most of the books and articles that deal with doctrinal analysis. The constitution is much more than a mere lawyers' document; it is a statement of principles of political theory and of social ethics. The essay, furthermore, is highly selective; no attempt was made to list all of the relevant scholarly works. No one, however, should approach this subject without at least a speaking acquaintance with the classics in the field. These include, but are not limited to, the books by Plato, Aristotle, Thucydides, Machiavelli, Edmund Burke, Adam Smith, Jean-Jacques Rousseau, Thomas Hobbes, Montesquieu, and *The Federalist Papers*.

The *locus classicus* for analyses of constitutional dualism is Walter Bagehot, *The English Constitution* (1867; reprint; London: Fontana, 1963). The 57-page introduction by R. H. S. Crossman to the Fontana edition is worth careful study by anyone interested in constitutionalism. For a modern study of the difference between the "myth system" and the "operational code," see W. Michael Reisman, *Folded Lies: Bribery, Crusades, and Reforms* (New York: The Free Press, 1979), drawn upon by Justice Richard Neely of the West Virginia Supreme Court in *How Courts Govern America* (New Haven: Yale University Press, 1981). See also W. M. Reisman and G. Simson, "Interstate Agreements in the American Federal System," 27 *Rutgers Law Review* 70 (1973); Alexander George, "The 'Operational Code': A Neglected Approach to the Study of Political Leaders and Decision-Making," 13 *International Studies Quarterly* 190 (1969). Woodrow Wilson, *Congressional Government* (Baltimore: Johns Hopkins University Press; first published in 1885; reprint; Meridian, 1956) notes the difference between the constitution "in action" and the constitution "of the books." Hans Vaihinger, *The Philosophy of "As If": A System of Theoretical, Practical and Religious Fictions of Mankind* (London: Routledge & Kegan Paul, 2d English ed., C. Ogden trans., 1935) is a classic philosophical study of the difference between appearance and reality in human affairs. Michael Kammen, *People of Paradox: An Inquiry Concerning the Origins of American Civilization* (New York: Random House, 1972) is a prize-winning study of the forces that have shaped the American character. And Michael Kammen, *A Machine That Would Go of Itself: The Constitution in American Culture* (New York: Knopf, 1986) is necessary reading for anyone who would wish to understand the role of the constitution in American history. Two books by Garry Wills add insight into the origins of the nation: *Inventing America: Jefferson's Declaration of Independence* (Garden City, New York: Doubleday, 1978) and *Explaining America: The Federalist* (Garden City, New York: Doubleday, 1981). Robert Michels, *Political Parties: A Sociological Study of the Oligarchical Tendencies of Modern Democracy* (1915 in Germany; reprints; New York: Crowell-Collier Publishing Co., trans. by E. & C. Paul, 1962 paperback ed.) is well described by its title. And see, for a modern albeit partial, account of constitutional dualism, Don K. Price, *America's Unwritten Constitution: Science, Religion, and Political Responsibility* (Baton Rouge: Louisiana State University Press, 1983). Gaetano Mosca, *The Ruling Class* (New York: McGraw-Hill, H. Kahn trans., A. Livingston ed., 1939) sets forth a theory of the ruling class. It is criticized in James H. Meisel, *The Myth of the Ruling Class: Gaetano Mosca and the Elite* (Ann Arbor: University of Michigan Press, 1958). Also of interest are Peter Bachrach, *A Theory of Democratic Elitism* (Boston: Little, Brown, 1967); Michael Parenti, *Democracy for the Few* (New York: St. Martin's Press, 3d ed., 1980); and G. William Domhoff, *Who Rules America Now?: A View for the '80s* (New York: Simon & Schuster, 1983). Finally, for an account of the British experience, see Brian Sedgemore, *The Secret Constitution: An Analysis of the Political Establishment* (London: Hodder and Stoughton, 1980).

On the need for constitutional change, see James MacGregor Burns, *The Power to Lead: The Crisis of the American Presidency* (New York: Simon & Schuster, 1984). Also of importance are James L. Sundquist, *Constitutional Reform and Effective Government* (Washington, D.C.: Brookings Institution, 1986); Charles M. Hardin, *Presidential Power and Accountability* (Chicago: University of Chicago Press, 1984); Donald L. Robinson, ed., *Reforming American Government: The Bicentennial Papers of the Committee on the Constitutional System* (Boulder, Colo.: Westview Press, 1985); Rexford G. Tugwell, *The Emerging Constitution* (New York: Harper's Magazine Press, 1974); Herbert Agar, *The Price of Union* (Boston: Houghton Mifflin, 1950); Derrick Bell, *The Civil Rights Chronicles* (forthcoming in 1987; New York: Basic Books). See also Arthur S. Miller, "Taking Needs Seriously: Observations on the Necessity for Constitutional Change," 41 *Washington and Lee Law Review* 1243 (1984); Arthur S. Miller, "Pretense and Our Two Constitutions," 54 *George Washington Law Review* 375 (1986); Michael Kammen's *A Machine That Would Go of Itself,* mentioned above, lists previous calls for constitutional change, particularly in the 1920–1945 period.

On the matter of a great turning point in history, consult especially Rufus E. Miles, Jr., *Awakening From the American Dream: The Social and Political Limits to Growth* (New York: Universe Books, 1976); William Ophuls, *Ecology and the Politics of Scarcity: Prologue to a Political Theory of the Steady State* (San Francisco: W. H. Freeman & Co., 1977); Richard Barnet, *The Lean Years: Politics in the Age of Scarcity* (New York: Simon & Schuster, 1980); Fritjof Capra, *The Turning Point: Science, Society and the Rising Culture* (New York: Simon & Schuster, 1982); Hazel Henderson, *The Politics of the Solar Age: Alternatives to Economics* (Garden City, N.Y.: Doubleday, 1981); Arthur S. Miller, *Democratic Dictatorship: The Emergent Constitution of Control* (Westport, Conn.: Greenwood Press, 1981); Robert Heilbroner, *An Inquiry into the Human Prospect* (New York: Norton, 1974); and Donella H. Meadows, and others, *The Limits to Growth: A Report for the Club of Rome's Project on the Predicament of Mankind* (New York: Universe Books, 1974). A contrary view may be found in Herman Kahn, *The Next 200 Years: A Scenario for America and the World* (New York: Morrow, 1976).

In addition, see Walter Prescott Webb, *The Great Frontier* (Boston: Houghton Mifflin, 1952); David M. Potter, *People of Plenty: Economic Abundance and the American Character* (Chicago: University of Chicago Press, 1954); and William H. McNeill, *The Great Frontier: Freedom and Hierarchy in Modern Times* (Princeton, N.J.: Princeton University Press, 1983) for analyses of the impact of the Great Discoveries on American institutions. Frederick Jackson Turner, *The Frontier in American History* (New York: Henry Holt & Co., 1920) is the seminal study of the meaning of the frontier in the development of the United States. And Richard Falk, *This Endangered Planet* (New York: Random House, 1972) is a well-written analysis of the *problematique* of humankind. In this same vein, see Dennis C. Pirages and Paul R. Ehrlich, *Ark II: Social Response to Environmental Imperatives* (New York: Viking, 1974); Lester R. Brown, and others, *State of the World 1986* (New York: Norton, 1986); Paul R. Ehrlich, *The Machinery of Nature: The Living World Around Us and How It Works* (New York: Simon & Schuster, 1986); and Harrison Brown, *The Human Future Revisited* (New York: Norton, 1978).

On institutional inadequacy, consult Robert A. Dahl, *Dilemmas of Pluralist Democracy: Autonomy vs. Control* (New Haven: Yale University Press, 1982); Lawrence Goodwyn, *Democratic Promise: The Populist Movement in America* (New York: Oxford University Press, 1976); Henry Kariel, *The Decline of American Pluralism* (Stanford: Stanford University Press, 1961); Charles E. Lindblom, *Politics and Markets: The World's Political-Economic Systems* (New York: Basic Books, 1977); Theodore Lowi, *The End of Liberalism: The Second Republic in the United States* (New York: Norton, 2d ed., 1979); Grant McConnell, *Private Power and American Democracy* (New York: Knopf, 1966); Mancur Olson, *The Logic of Collective Action* (Cambridge: Harvard University Press, 1965); J. R. Pole, *The Pursuit of Equality in American History* (Berkeley: University of California Press, 1978); E. F. Schumacher, *Small Is Beautiful* (New York: Harper and Row, 1973); and Karl Polanyi, *The Great Transformation* (New York: Rinehart and Co., 1944). See also Robert A. Dahl, "Procedural Democracy," in Peter Laslett and James Fishkin, *Philosophy, Politics, and Society 97* (5th series, New Haven: Yale University Press, 1979); Arthur S. Miller, *Politics, Democracy, and the Supreme Court* (Westport, Conn.: Greenwood Press, 1985). For a comprehensive discussion of how power is exercised in the United States, see Morton Mintz and Jerry S. Cohen, *Power, Inc.: Public and Private Rulers and How to Make Them Accountable* (New York: Viking, 1976). See also Lionel Rubinoff, *The Pornography of Power* (New York: Ballantine

Books, 1968); J. L. Talmon, *The Origins of Totalitarian Democracy* (London: Secker & Warburg, 1975); Alan Wolfe, *The Seamy Side of Democracy: Repression in America* (New York: David McKay, 1973); Howard Zinn, *A People's History of the United States* (New York: Harper & Row, 1979); Hannah Arendt, *On Revolution* (New York: Viking, 1965); and David Wise, *The American Police State* (New York: Random House, 1976).

On the nature of a sustainable society, see Lester R. Brown, *Building a Sustainable Society* (New York: Norton, 1981); Dennis Clark Pirages, *The Sustainable Society: Implications for Limited Growth* (New York: Praeger, 1977); Herman E. Daly ed., *Toward a Steady-State Society* (San Francisco: W. H. Freeman, 1973); Arthur S. Miller, "The End of a 400-Year Boom," 24 *Technological Forecasting & Social Change* 255 (1983); Symposium, "The Woodlands Conference on Sustainable Societies: Future Roles for the Private Sector," 22 *Technological Forecasting & Social Change* 93–210 (1982) (nine essays); Warren Johnson, *Muddling Toward Frugality* (San Francisco: Sierra Books, 1978). In addition, consult Willis W. Harman, *An Incomplete Guide to the Future* (Stanford: Stanford Alumni Association, 1976); Barry Commoner, *The Closing Circle* (New York: Knopf, 1971); Lester R. Brown, *World Without Borders* (New York: Random House, 1972); and Duane S. Elgin and Arnold Mitchell, "Voluntary Simplicity: Lifestyle of the Future?", *The Futurist*, August 1977.

The concept of human needs is discussed in the following books and articles. Abraham H. Maslow, *Motivation and Personality* (New York: Harper & Row, 2nd ed., 1970) is the seminal account. A valuable collection of essays is *Human Needs and Politics*, Ross Fitzgerald ed., Rushcutters Bay, Australia: Pergamon Press Limited, 1977). Another worthwhile volume is *Rethinking Liberalism*, W. Anderson ed., (New York: Avon, 1983). See also William A. Galston, *Justice and the Human Good* (Chicago: University of Chicago Press, 1980); C. B. Macpherson, *The Rise and Fall of Economic Justice* (Oxford: Oxford University Press, 1985); Michael Walzer, *Spheres of Justice: A Defense of Pluralism and Equality* (New York: Basic Books, 1983); Marvin Zetterbaum, "Equality and Human Need," 71 *American Political Science Review* 983 (1977); Herbert McCloskey, "Human Needs, Rights and Political Values," 13 *American Philosophical Quarterly* 1 (1976); Thomas C. Grey, "Property and Need: The Welfare State and Theories of Distributive Justice," 28 *Stanford Law Review* 877 (1976); D. D. Raphael, "Conservative and Prosthetic Justice," 12 *Political Studies* 149 (1964).

Also of importance are John Rawls, *A Theory of Justice* (Cambridge, Mass.: Harvard University Press, 1971); David Miller, *Social Justice* (Oxford: Oxford University Press, 1976); Christopher Lasch, *The Minimal Self: Psychic Survival in Troubled Times* (New York: Norton, 1984); *Social Justice*, Richard B. Brandt ed., (Englewood Cliffs, N.J.: Prentice-Hall, 1962); Scott Gordon, *Welfare, Justice, and Freedom* (New York: Columbia University Press, 1980); Robert Nozick, *Anarchy, State, and Utopia* (New York: Basic Books, 1974); and Friedrich A. Hayek, *Law, Legislation, and Liberty* (London: Routledge & Kegan Paul, 1976).

Human deserts have a lesser literature. The leading discussion is Joel Feinberg, *Doing & Deserving: Essays in the Theory of Responsibility* (Princeton, N.J.: Princeton University Press, 1970). See also Ronald Dworkin, *Taking Rights Seriously* (Cambridge, Mass.: Harvard University Press, 1977); John Hospers, *Human Conduct* (New York: Harcourt, Brace & World, 1961); Richard A. Posner, *The Eco-*

nomics of Justice (Cambridge, Mass.: Harvard University Press 1981); John Kleinig, *Punishment and Desert* (The Hague: Martinus A. Nijhoff, 1973); and Wojciech Sadurski, *Giving Desert Its Due: Social Justice and Legal Theory* (Dordrecht, Holland: Reidel, 1985).

On the question of specific constitutional alterations, see the books by Burns, Sundquist, and Robinson (all mentioned above). The following are also of importance: Walter Lippmann, *An Essay on the Public Philosophy* (New York: Mentor, 1955); James L. Sundquist, *The Decline and Resurgence of Congress* (Washington, D.C.: Brookings Institution, 1981); Louis Fisher, *The Politics of Shared Power: Congress and the Executive* (Washington, D.C.: Congressional Quarterly Press, 1981); Edward S. Corwin, *The President: Office and Powers* (New York: New York University Press, 4th ed., 1984); Charles Hardin, *Presidential Power and Accountability* (Chicago: University of Chicago Press, 1974); and *The New American Political System*, Anthony King ed., (Washington, D.C.: American Enterprise Institute, 1980). Rexford G. Tugwell, *The Emerging Constitution* (New York: Harper's Magazine Press, 1974) is worth special mention as a full-blown proposal for truly major constitutional change.

Older studies well worth consulting include William MacDonald, *A New Constitution for America* (New York: B. W. Huebsh, 1921); William Yandell Elliott, *The Need for Constitutional Reform* (New York: Whittlesey House, 1935); Henry Hazlitt, *A New Constitution Now* (New York: Whittlesey House, 1942); and Thomas K. Finletter, *Can Representative Government Do the Job?* (New York: Reynal and Hitchcock, 1945).

For specific studies of the constitution, the reader is referred to the *Index of Legal Periodicals* under the title of "Constitutional Law." Other scholarly periodicals carry relevant articles from time to time. For example, see Lloyd Cutler, "To Form a Government," 59 *Foreign Affairs* 126 (1980). Most of the books mentioned above contain extensive bibliographies. See also the books and articles, and works cited therein, listed in the endnotes to this volume.

Finally, consult John P. Diggins, *The Lost Soul of American Politics* (New York: Basic Books, 1984); Robert Kuttner, *The Economic Illusion* (Boston: Houghton Mifflin, 1984); R. Jeffrey Lustig, *Corporate Liberalism: The Origins of Modern American Political Theory, 1890–1920* (Berkeley: University of California Press, 1982); Joel I. Nelson, *Economic Inequality: Conflict Without Change* (New York: Columbia University Press 1982); the several essays in *Political and Legal Development* J. Roland Pennock and J. S. Chapman eds. (New York: Atherton Press 1970); Arthur S. Miller, *Social Change and Fundamental Law: America's Evolving Constitution* (Westport, Conn.: Greenwood Press, 1979); Samuel Huntington, *American Politics: The Promise of Disharmony* (Cambridge, Mass.: Harvard University Press, 1981); J. Roland Pennock, "Political Development, Political Systems, and Political Goods," 18 *World Politics* 415 (1966); *Nuclear Weapons and Law*, Arthur S. Miller and Martin Feinrider eds. (Westport, Conn: Greenwood Press, 1984); and Arthur S. Miller and H. Bart Cox, "Congress, the Constitution, and First Use of Nuclear Weapons," 48 *Review of Politics* 211, 423 (1986) (in two parts).

INDEX

About the Author

ARTHUR S. MILLER is Professor Emeritus of Constitutional Law, The George Washington University. He is the author of *Racial Discrimination and Private Education* (1957), *The Supreme Court and American Capitalism* (1968), *The Modern Corporate State: Private Governments and the American Constitution* (Greenwood Press, 1976), *Presidential Power* (1977), *The Supreme Court: Myth and Reality* (Greenwood Press, 1978), *Social Change and Fundamental Law: America's Evolving Constitution* (Greenwood Press 1979), *Democratic Dictatorship: The Emergent Constitution of Control* (Greenwood Press, 1981), *Toward Increased Judicial Activism: The Political Role of the Supreme Court* (Greenwood Press, 1982), *A "Capacity for Outrage": The Judicial Odyssey of J. Skelly Wright* (Greenwood Press, 1984), and *Politics, Democracy, and the Supreme Court* (Greenwood Press, 1985). He is the editor of *On Courts and Democracy: Selected Nonjudicial Writings of J. Skelly Wright* (Greenwood Press, 1984), and coeditor of *Nuclear Weapons and Law* (with Martin Feinrider, Greenwood Press, 1984) and *Corporations and Society: Power and Responsibility* (with Warren J. Samuels, Greenwood Press, 1987). He is a frequent contributor to legal and political science periodicals.